MARX AND ENGELS AND
THE ENGLISH WORKERS

Other Cass books by W.O. Henderson

Friedrich List: Economist and Visionary, 1789–1846 (1983)

Friedrich List: 'The Natural System of Political Economy'
(translated and edited) (1983)

The Genesis of the Common Market (1962)

Industrial Britain under the Regency (1968)

J.C. Fisher and his Diary of Industrial England 1814–1851 (1966)

Life of Friedrich Engels, 2 vols. (1976)

Studies in the Economic Policy of Frederick the Great (1963)

The Zollverein (1959, 2nd ed. 1968)

Other books by W.O. Henderson

Britain and Industrial Europe (1965)

The Industrialisation of Europe 1780–1914 (1969)

The Rise of German Industrial Power 1835–1914 (1975)

(editor) *Engels: Selected Writings* (1967)

Manufactories in Germany (Verlag Peter Lang, 1985)

MARX AND ENGELS
AND THE
ENGLISH WORKERS
And Other Essays

W.O. HENDERSON

FRANK CASS

First published 1989 in Great Britain by
FRANK CASS AND COMPANY LIMITED
Gainsborough House, 11 Gainsborough Road,
London, E11 1RS, England

and in the United States of America by
FRANK CASS AND COMPANY LIMITED
c/o Biblio Distribution Centre
81 Adams Drive, P.O. Box 327, Totowa, N.J. 07511

Copyright © 1989 W.O. Henderson

British Library Cataloguing in Publication Data

Henderson, W.O (William Otto), *1904–*
    Marx and Engels and the English workers :
    and other essays
    1. Economics
    I. Title
    330

    ISBN 0-7146-3334-8

Library of Congress Cataloging-in-Publication Data

Henderson, W.O. (William Otto), 1904–
    Marx and Engels and the English workers : and other essays / W.O. Henderson.
        P.   cm.
    Includes index.
    ISBN 0-7146-3334-8
    1. Marx, Karl, 1818–1883. 2. Engels, Friedrich, 1820–1895.
3. List, Friedrich, 1789–1846. 4. Falk, Herman Eugen. 5. Rathenau,
Walther, 1867–1922. 6. Labor and laboring classes—England—
History—19th century. I. Title.
HX39.5.H45 1988
335.4'092'2—dc19   88-18994
                                              CIP

Printed and bound in Great Britain by
A. Wheaton & Co. Ltd, Exeter

CONTENTS

LIST OF ILLUSTRATIONS

ACKNOWLEDGEMENTS

The author thanks the publishers of the following books and journals for permission to include articles in the present volume: Chapter 1, *Transactions of the Lancashire and Cheshire Antiquarian Society*, Vol. 83 (1985); Chapter 2, in *Friedrich Engels 1820–1970* (Forschungsreihe des Forschungsinstitut der Friedrich Ebert Stiftung, Vol. 85, 1971); Chapter 3, *Internationale Wissenschaftliche Korrespondenz*, April 1971; Chapter 6, *Encounter*, July 1975 (with W.H. Chaloner); Chapter 7, *Archiv für Sozialgeschichte*, Vol. 14 (1974); Chapter 8, *Zeitschrift für die gesamte Staatswissenschaft*, Vol. 138 (1982); Chapter 9, *Journal of European Economic History*, Vol. X (1981); Chapter 10, *Jahrbücher für Nationalökonomie und Statistik*, Vol. 203, 5–6 (1987); Chapter 11, in *Preussens Grosser König* (Ploetz Verlag, 1986).

Chapters 4, 5 and 12 are previously unpublished.

The picture of Friedrich Engels senior is reproduced by permission of Rheinland Verlag- und Betriebsgesellschaft.

PREFACE

The essays included in Parts I and II of this volume deal with aspects of the careers of Marx, Engels and List which were dealt with only briefly in my biographies of Engels and List. The chapter on "Marx and Engels and Racialism" was written in collaboration with the late Professor W.H. Chaloner. Part III brings together essays on the economic activities of Frederick the Great and Walther Rathenau as well as an account of the contribution of a German entrepreneur (H.E. Falk) to the development of the salt industry in England.

I wish to thank Dr Douglas Farnie for checking the proofs of these essays.

W.O.H.

PART I

Marx and Engels and the English Workers

1

MARX IN MANCHESTER

For twenty years between November 1850 and September 1870 Friedrich Engels was living in Manchester while Karl Marx was living in London. They corresponded regularly and they met from time to time either in London or in Manchester. The frequency of Marx's visits to Manchester has not always been appreciated.[1] He was in the city nearly every year[2] and there were six years in which he was there twice. Several visits were paid over the Whitsun holiday. Marx's expenses were generally paid by Engels. His main purpose in visiting Manchester was to see Engels and other friends such as Wilhelm Wolff, Carl Schorlemmer, Eduard Gumpert and Samuel Moore.

It was natural that such close friends as Marx, Engels and Wolff should wish to meet as often as possible to discuss their joint literary projects and the fortunes of their communist friends in Germany and elsewhere. Sometimes there were other reasons for Marx's visits. Once he came to Manchester for a rest after an illness and he always took the opportunity to consult Dr Gumpert on his numerous complaints. There were times when Marx came to Manchester to escape from his creditors in London who were clamouring for a settlement of their accounts. He came to Manchester in May 1864 to see Wolff who was on his death-bed. Marx generally came alone but he was accompanied by his wife in 1855 and 1880, by Hermann Meyer in May 1867, by Lafargue in September 1867, and by his daughter Eleanor on three occasions in 1868–70. He stayed either in Engels's "official lodgings" or at a house rented for Mary and Lizzie Burns. The "official lodgings" were in Great Ducie Street, Thorncliffe Grove and Dover Street while (after 1864) Lizzie Burns lived in Mornington Street.[3] However in April 1869 on the eve of his retirement, he gave up his lodgings in Dover Street and moved to 86 Mornington Street.[4]

Marx's first visit to England was in the summer of 1845.[5] He arrived in the middle of July and returned to Belgium on about August 24. He was accompanied by Engels who had recently joined him in Brussels. Engels had told his family that he was going to Manchester to collect the books that he had left behind when he returned to Barmen after working for twenty months in the office of Ermen and Engels. Presumably he also hoped to see Mary Burns again. The two friends spent most of their time in Manchester. All that is known of their visit is contained in a letter which Engels sent to Marx many years later. On May 15, 1870, when he had retired from business, he recalled that in 1845 they had worked together in Chetham's Library. "During the last few days I have again spent a good deal of time sitting at the four-sided desk in the alcove where we sat together twenty four years ago. I am very fond of the place. The stained glass window ensures that the weather is always fine there. Old Jones, the librarian, is still alive but he is very old and no longer active. I have not seen him on this occasion."[6] Hitherto Marx had studied philosophy and law. Now, stimulated by the appearance of Engels' recently published book on the English workers, he turned his attention to economics. In Chetham's Library he continued the work that he had begun in the previous year[7] and studied the works of the English classical economists and statisticians. From Manchester Marx and Engels went to London where they met leading members of the League of the Just, the forerunner of the Communist League.

After the failure of the revolutions of 1848/1849 Marx had come to London as a refugee in August and Engels had followed him in November. A year later Engels moved to Manchester to serve as a clerk in the office of Ermen and Engels at 7 Southgate (off Deansgate). He found lodgings at 70 Ducie Street, Strangeways.[8] In February 1851 Marx wrote to Engels: "You will appreciate how much I miss you and how I wish that I could discuss my problems with you."[9] Marx visited Engels for a week in April 1851[10] and for ten days in November.[11] The purpose of Marx's second visit was probably to discuss with Engels their collaboration as contributors to the *New York Daily Tribune*, a liberal Republican paper, which had begun in the previous August and was to last for over ten years.[12] To raise money for the fare to Manchester Marx borrowed £2 which he promised to repay before December. On his return to London he asked Engels to repay this debt. Engels, however, was short of money himself and the debt was paid by Georg Weerth.[13]

In 1852 Marx was in Manchester from May 26 to June 26. His visit was delayed because Engels's father was in Manchester to discuss with his partners the future of the firm.[14] On May 19 Engels informed Marx that, following discussions with his father, his salary would be raised in July. Two days later he wrote: "My old man has left. All is right. I enclose the first half of a £10 note and I hope to see you here next week." The second half of the note was sent to Wilhelm Wolff to pass on to Marx. On May 22 Marx acknowledged the receipt of the first half of the note and informed Engels that he would travel to Liverpool by sea and then to Manchester by rail. Engels replied that if he wanted to go by sea it would be quicker to sail to Hull. It is not known which route Marx took. At the time of his visit the local press was devoting much space to the general election in which Bright and Milner Gibson were defending their seats in Manchester. But Marx was probably more interested in the pamphlet that he was writing (with Engels' help) attacking German refugees whose views were different from his own. Marx and Engels may have visited the Golden Lion in Deansgate since a few months later Engels asked Marx to enclose letters to him in an envelope addressed to the publican, "our old James Belfield."[15] By June 30 Marx was in London again since on that day Engels wrote that he had found a wallet that Marx had left in his lodgings.

In April 1853 Engels wrote that "the bedroom in my house is ready" and invited Marx to visit him. Engels had recently moved with his landlady to 48 Great Ducie Street which was two doors away from his former lodgings. Since Engels mentioned that the library of Peter Ermen – one of his father's partners – was at their disposal it may be assumed that the purpose of Marx's visit was to work on their joint literary projects. Marx, as usual, was in financial difficulties and needed money for his fare. He told Engels that he was unable to raise money on an American bill of exchange for £32 – doubtless payments for articles contributed to the *New York Daily Tribune*. Engels offered to cash the bill in Manchester with an American firm. Meanwhile Marx borrowed £2 from Bamberger[16] and wrote to Engels that he would travel to Manchester on Saturday, April 30.[17] He stayed with Engels until May 16.[18]

Marx did not visit Manchester in 1854. He had an opportunity to do so when he was invited to attend a meeting of a "Labour Parliament" which met in Manchester between March 6 and March 10. This conference of trade union delegates was organised by Ernest Jones to support the power loom weavers of Preston who had been on strike for 29 weeks. The *Manchester Guardian* reported on March 8 that Marx was "expected to be present today." But he was not present. He had written to the organisers: "I regret deeply to be unable, for the moment at least, to leave London and thus to be prevented from expressing verbally my feelings of pride and gratitude on receiving the invitation to sit as honorary delegate at the Labour Parliament. The mere assembling of such a parliament marks a new epoch in the history of the world. The news of this great fact will arouse the hopes of the working classes throughout Europe and America."[19] In April Engels informed Marx that when he had found new lodgings he would invite him to come to Manchester.[20] In September Marx congratulated Engels on having become "altogether respectable" by being elected to the Royal Exchange[21] and in October he wrote that "if circumstances permit" he would be glad to visit Engels in Manchester.[22]

Two visits were paid by Marx to Manchester in 1855. On April 6 he informed Engels of the death of his eight-year-old son Edgar. He thought that a change of scene would do his wife good and he proposed that they should both pay Engels a short visit, staying at a hotel or in private lodgings. Engels sent Marx £5 and gave him information concerning trains to Manchester. On April 16 Marx replied that he and his wife would come to Manchester on the "Parliamentary Train". This was a stopping train which left London at 7 a.m. and did not reach Manchester until 6.30 p.m. The fare was a penny a mile. The visit did not help Jenny Marx to get over her bereavement for when she was back in London on May 16 Marx wrote to Engels that she was still "very poorly."[23]

Marx was in Manchester again in the autumn of 1855. On September 11 he wrote to Engels that, owing to "force supérieur" he had to leave London quickly for "a week or so" to avoid being harassed by his creditors – particularly the family doctor. He asked that his visit should be kept a secret, except from Wilhelm Wolff.[24] Far from returning to London within a week Marx was still in Manchester on November 8. On that day he wrote to Lassalle from 34 Butler Street, Greenheys, where he had taken lodgings. In his letter he mentioned that he had met Georg Weerth and added that he did not know how long he would stay in Manchester.[25] Marx was back in London early in December.[26]

Little is known concerning a visit to Manchester by Marx in the summer of 1856. The correspondence between the friends refers only to Marx's travel arrangements and to the stock of beer and wine laid in by Engels in preparation for Marx's visit. At first, on his doctor's advice Marx planned to go by sea to Dundee, where he would stay with his friend Peter Imandt before joining Engels in Manchester a week later. But on June 6, Marx changed his mind and decided on a sea voyage to Hull, accompanied by his secretary Wilhelm Pieper. While Pieper would return to London from Hull, Marx would take the train to Manchester.[27] Marx stayed with Engels until the middle of July. *fr. Jun 6*

Marx was not in Manchester in 1857 as Engels was seriously ill during the second half of that year. He had glandular fever and was away from Manchester – in Waterloo (near New Brighton), Ryde and St. Helier – throughout the summer. Early in October Marx and Engels met in St. Helier. It was not until the middle of November that Engels was back in Manchester and even then he was able to work only part time in the office.[28]

In 1858 Marx visited Engels in May. Early in April Jenny Marx wrote to Engels that her husband had been ill for a week. On April 29 Marx told Engels that he was suffering from a liver complaint and that lack of money prevented him from taking a rest away from London as his doctor had advised. Engels, who was now living at 6 Thorncliffe Grove (off Oxford Road), replied: "If you ought to travel then at least come to Manchester. That's easy enough." He offered to pay Marx's fare. On May 1 Marx wrote that he would come on a train leaving London at 2.30 p.m. and arriving in Manchester at 7 p.m. On this holiday in Manchester Marx became an enthusiastic horse rider. When he returned to London after an absence of four weeks he declared that he missed horse riding. His health had greatly improved and he was now "in working order". In the same letter he enquired about Dr. Gumpert's progress in "the noble art of riding". This is the first reference in the Marx–Engels correspondence to Gumpert, a German doctor practising in Manchester, in whom Marx had great confidence.[29]

In the summer of 1859 Marx was away from London for about three weeks visiting Engels and Wolff in Manchester and Imandt and Heise in Dundee. On June 7 he wrote to Engels that he would visit him for a few days as soon as he could afford to do so.[30] In Manchester Marx collected about £25 to help finance *Das Volk*, a German radical weekly recently founded in London.[31] In a letter which he wrote to Lassalle early in July, Marx stated that he had recently returned to London.[32]

In 1860 Marx was in Manchester between February 16 and March 23. On receiving £5 from Engels on February 15 he wrote that he would catch the 7.30 a.m. train from Euston station on the following day.[33] He stayed with Engels at 6, Thorncliffe Grove,[34] the purpose of the visit being to discuss with Engels and Wolff a pamphlet attacking Karl Vogt that he was writing. Marx returned to London on May 23, the day after Engels had left Manchester for Barmen on hearing of his father's death.

Early in 1861 Marx went to Germany and Holland where he secured a loan from his uncle Lion Philips. At the end of his visit he proposed to sail from Rotterdam to Hull early in May and then go to Manchester to see Engels before returning to London. But he had to change his plans as one of his cousins wished to accompany him to England and to be shown the London sights.[35] Soon after his return Engels came to London to see him for a few days.[36] Marx was in Manchester later in the year – from the end of August to the middle of September.[37] His visit coincided with a meeting of the British Association in Manchester. From Manchester Marx wrote to the editor of *Die Presse* agreeing to contribute to this Vienna newspaper.

In 1862 Marx was in Manchester for most of April. Engels gave him a bill of exchange for £50 which was discounted by Borkheim. While he was in Manchester Marx was visited by the socialist Wilhelm Eichhoff. On his return to London Marx wrote to Engels that in his absence his debts had accumulated in an alarming manner.[38]

Marx did not visit Manchester in 1863. In a letter to Engels of August 15 he wrote that they had not met for a long time. He wished that they could get together in London for a few days "to gossip and to have a drink together".[39]

Marx paid two visits to Manchester in 1864. On February 25 he wrote to Engels that he was just returning from visiting relations in Holland and hoped to visit Engels shortly. But illness prevented him from doing so until March 12. He informed Engels that he would leave Euston station on that day at 10 a.m. and would arrive in Manchester at 5 p.m.[40] He stayed until March 25.

On May 1, 1864 Engels urged Marx to come to Manchester at once as their friend Wilhelm Wolff was seriously ill. Marx arrived on May 3 and stayed until May 19[41] when Marx and Engels travelled to London together. Wolff died on May 9 and Marx and Engels attended the funeral at Ardwick cemetery. Marx wrote to his wife: "I do not think that anyone in Manchester was held in such universal esteem as our poor little fellow."[42] The residue of Wolff's estate (£818) was left to Marx[43] and – as Jenny Marx recalled – this "afforded us help and relief and a year free from worry".[44] Marx also inherited Wolff's library.[45]

Marx was twice in Manchester in 1865. On his first visit in January he stayed for a week at 58 Dover Street, Chorlton on Medlock, where Engels was now living. All that is known concerning this visit is that when he returned to London he found that he had left behind a pair of shoes, a pair of socks and two handkerchiefs.[46] In the autumn of 1865 Marx had influenza and (as he informed Lieb-knecht) he subsequently "had to leave London for family affairs".[47] On this occasion he was in Manchester from October 20[48] to November 3. On his return he wrote to Engels that his luggage had been mislaid on the train.[49]

In 1866 Marx was ill during the early part of the year. When he was on the road to recovery Engels wrote that Dr. Gumpert advised at least four weeks' convalescence. Engels suggested that Marx come to Manchester and then go on to the seaside at Blackpool or New Brighton.[50] But Marx decided to go to Margate.[51] In June Engels urged Marx to come to Manchester for a week to consult Dr. Gumpert.[52] But it appears that Marx did not visit Engels in 1866.

Marx was twice in Manchester in 1867. On his first visit between May 22 and June 2, he was accompanied by Hermann Meyer who had come to England from St. Louis to see Marx and Engels. Marx had just returned from Germany where he had left the manuscript of the first volume of *Das Kapital* with the publisher. On May 22 Marx wrote from 86 Mornington Street to Engels to let him know that he had just arrived in Manchester.[53] This was the address at which Engels was living with Lizzie Burns. It is not known where Engels was when the letter was written. Possibly he was in his lodgings in Dover Street, but this is unlikely, since in that case Marx would have called upon him rather than write to him. The purpose of this visit was to show Engels some of the proofs of his book.[54]

The second visit of 1867 was from September 13 to September 23. On September 12 Marx received £5 from Engels and so he was able to travel to Manchester on the following day with his future son-in-law Paul Lafargue.[55] On this occasion Marx and Engels discussed how best to make *Das Kapital* known in Germany and elsewhere.[56]

In the summer of 1868 Marx spent a fortnight in Manchester with his youngest daughter Eleanor (Tussy) who was then 13 years old. On May 23 he wrote to Engels that they would travel to Manchester in the following week. "But you must send me the fare and some shillings for my wife."[57] Engels sent him £25 and advised him to travel from Kings Cross by the new Midland line which ran through some beautiful scenery in Derbyshire.[58] Marx replied that he and Eleanor would arrive on May 30 in time for Whit week.[59] Both enjoyed Engels' hospitality and they returned to London on June 20. In his letter of thanks Marx added that — as usual — his creditors

were waiting for him when he got back to London.[60] Engels promptly sent him £20.[61]

In May 1869 (shortly after giving up his lodging in Dover Street)
Engels sent Marx £15 so that he and Eleanor could come to
Manchester.[62] They stayed at 86 Mornington Street with Engels and
Lizzie Burns. Marx left on June 14 but Eleanor stayed behind and
she did not return to London until October 14. On June 2 Marx
wrote to his wife that he was taking Eleanor to see the fireworks at
Belle Vue and was planning to spend a week-end in Yorkshire with
several friends – Engels, Schorlemmer and Samuel Moore.[63] On
July 21 Engels wrote to Marx that the whole family, including
Eleanor, had seen the Prince and Princess of Wales who were
visiting Manchester to attend the Royal Agricultural Show at Old
Trafford.[64] While Eleanor was in Manchester Engels retired from
business on June 30.[65] In September he took Lizzie Burns and
Eleanor to Ireland for a week, visiting Dublin, Killarney and Cork.[66]
Marx and his daughter Eleanor again stayed with Engels for a week
in Manchester in the summer of 1870.[67]

After Engels moved to London in September 1870 Marx's visits to
Manchester were less frequent. He was in Manchester twice in 1873,
his expenses on both occasions being defrayed by Engels. The
purpose of the first visit was to consult Dr Gumpert. But when he
arrived in Manchester on May 22 – he stayed at Samuel Moore's
lodgings (25 Dover Street) – he found that Dr Gumpert was not at
home and was not expected to return to Manchester until the end of
the month. So Marx stayed in Manchester longer than he had
originally intended. He met several friends including Schorlemmer,
Dronke and Borchardt. From Manchester he made trips to Southport with Dronke and to Buxton with Samuel Moore. He saw Dr
Gumpert on June 2 and was advised to reduce his working day to
four hours.[68]

Towards the end of November 1873 Marx went with Eleanor to
Harrogate to take the waters. From Harrogate he twice went to
Manchester to see Dr. Gumpert who advised him to continue his
cure in Karlsbad.[69] Marx's last visit to Manchester was at the end of
July 1880 when he took his wife to consult Dr Gumpert.[70]

Many changes occurred in Manchester in the years when Marx was a
regular visitor.[71] On his first visit Engels could have shown him the
slums that he had recently so vividly described in his book on the
English workers. In the 1850s and 1860s Marx would have seen the
transformation of Manchester from what has been called "the

barracks of an industry" to a major centre of business, banking, communications, and culture of which its citizens could be proud. Many improvements were made and many amenities were provided – some by the municipal authorities and some by private enterprise. The city became healthier when the streets were swept, nuisances removed, sewers laid, and privies and ashpits cleaned – though it proved to be difficult to check the pollution of the Irk, the Irwell, the Medlock, and the Bridgewater canal. The construction of the Longdendale reservoirs in 1848, despite initial engineering set-backs, greatly improved Manchester's supply of water. The expansion of the municipal gas undertaking enabled an increasing number of streets to be lit at night. The coming of the railways not only made Manchester the main centre of communications in the north-west of England but also resulted in the removal of some undesirable properties when stations were built. On Marx's first visit the city was already linked by rail with Liverpool, Leeds, Sheffield and Crewe and by 1852 it had direct railway communication with nearly every part of the country.

At the same time the amenities of the city were being expanded. Manchester was an important centre of education. It had two ancient grammar schools – Manchester Grammar School and Chetham's Hospital (Blue Coat School). The former established a modern side in the 1860s so that modern languages, science and mathematics could be studied as an alternative to the classics. Owens College was founded in 1851 and was amalgamated with the Royal Medical College in 1872. Manchester also had a mechanics' institute, a museum, and an art gallery as well as several libraries including Chetham's Library, the Portico, the Athenæum and the Public Library. Its learned societies included the Literary and Philosophical Society and the Statistical Society. Three public parks were laid out in 1846 with money raised by public subscription. Two were maintained by Manchester Corporation and the third (Peel Park) by Salford Corporation. Other aspects of Manchester's cultural life included the inauguration of the Hallé concerts and the holding of an exhibition of the Art Treasures of the United Kingdom in 1857.[72]

Since Marx was in Manchester on many occasions he must have known the city well and he saw something of the surrounding districts on excursions to Liverpool, Southport, and Buxton. Information concerning the activities of Marx and Engels when they were together in Manchester is very limited. One can only speculate on how they spent their time. They may have seen something of the

German colony whose members formed the largest element in the community of foreign merchants in the city in the middle of the nineteenth century. Besides Wolff, Schorlemmer and Dr Gumpert, who were his close friends, Marx may have met other friends of Engels in the Schiller Anstalt and at the Albert Club in both of which Engels was a leading member. The Albert Club in Oxford Road was very close to Dover Street where Engels had lodgings between 1865 and 1869. And there were English acquaintances, such as Dr Watts, James Leach and Ernest Jones, who were sometimes in Manchester when Marx was there. Marx may have had a drink at the Golden Lion (where "old James Belfield" was the publican) or the Chatsworth Inn (where Wolff presided over social gatherings of German clerks) or the Thatched House Tavern (where some German scientists met on Saturday). He was certainly in Chetham's Library in 1845 and he may also have visited the Public Library which was opened in 1852 when he was in Manchester.[73] He may even have visited the Victoria Mill of Ermen and Engels in Weaste. Marx could hardly have failed to appreciate the "unprecedented prosperity" of the city in the early 1850s[74] and the temporary setbacks to its fortunes during the commercial crisis of 1857 and the cotton famine of the early 1860s. In the period covered by Marx's visits the output of the Lancashire cotton industry almost trebled though — owing to increased productivity — its gross value rose by only 127 per cent. Exports of piece goods increased fourfold in volume. The real wages of the cotton operatives probably rose by at least 60 per cent. Since Manchester was the centre of the cotton industry in the nineteenth century a knowledge of the city could not have come amiss to the author of *Das Kapital*.

APPENDIX

Marx's visits to Manchester

1845 July 12–August 21	Marx and Engels in England, spending most of the time in Manchester.
1851 April 20–26	Marx in Manchester
1852 May 26–June 26	Marx in Manchester. He collaborated with Engels in writing the pamphlet *Grosse Männer des Exils*.

1853 April 30–May 16	Marx in Manchester
1855 (i) April 18–early May (ii) September 12– December 4	Karl and Jenny Marx in Manchester Marx in Manchester escaping from creditors in London (particularly Dr Freund).
1856 June 7–mid-July	Marx in Manchester. (Sailed to Hull with Pieper.)
1858 May 3–24	Marx in Manchester recovering from illness.
1859 June 12–July 2	Marx in Manchester (excursion to Dundee).
1860 February 16–March 23	Marx in Manchester. Discussed with Engels and Wolff a pamphlet attacking Vogt.
1861 End of August– mid-September	Marx in Manchester
1862 April 1–25	Marx in Manchester. Visited by Wilhelm Eichhof.
1864 (i) March 12–25 (ii) May 3–19	Marx in Manchester Marx in Manchester: death of Wilhelm Wolff on May 9.
1865 (i) January 7–15 (ii) October 10– November 3	Marx in Manchester to discuss First International with Engels. Marx in Manchester. He "had to leave London for family affairs".
1867 (i) May 22–June 2 (ii) September 12–23	Marx (and Hermann Meyer of St Louis) visited Engels in Manchester. Marx and Lafargue visited Engels in Manchester.

1868
May 30–June 15   Marx and Eleanor Marx in Manchester.

1869   Marx and Eleanor Marx in Manchester.
May 25–June 14   Marx met the geologist John R. Dakyns. Eleanor stayed in Manchester until October 14.

1870
May 22–June 22   Marx and Eleanor Marx in Manchester.

1873
(i) May 22–June 3   Marx in Manchester to consult Dr Gumpert.

(ii) November 24–December 15   Marx in Harrogate. To Manchester on November 28 to consult Dr Gumpert.

1880
End of July   Karl and Jenny Marx to Manchester to consult Dr Gumpert.

NOTES

1. The author thanks Dr Douglas Farnie for his helpful comments on the first draft of this paper.
2. Marx's visits to Manchester are listed in *Karl Marx. Chronik seines Lebens in Einzeldaten* (1971). Jenny Marx mentioned her husband's "regular annual visits" to Manchester in her memoirs: see *Reminiscences of Marx and Engels* (1961), p.232.
3. Information kindly supplied by Mr Roy Whitfield. When renting houses for the Burns sisters Engels sometimes assumed the name "Boardman" (Marx to Engels, May 27, 1862: "My greetings to Mrs Bortman (sic) and sister").
4. Engels to Marx, April 4, 1869.
5. Georg Weerth to his mother, August 23, 1845 (G. Weerth, *Sämtliche Werke* (1957), Vol. V, pp.175–7) and Georg Weerth to Marx, August 19, 1845.
6. Engels to Marx, May 15, 1870. Thomas Jones (1809–75) was Chetham's Librarian from 1845 to 1875. Chetham's Library, founded in 1653, was the first public library in Europe to be open to all comers.
7. Karl Marx, *Economic and Philosophical Manuscripts of 1844* (1961).
8. For 70 Ducie Street see Jenny Marx to Engels, December 2 and 19, 1850; Engels to Marx, December 17, 1850 and the census return of April 12, 1851. Engels' landlady was Mrs Isabella Tatham. On April 1, 1852 the number of the house changed from 70 to 44.
9. Marx to Engels, February 11, 1851.
10. April 20 to 26, 1851; see Engels to Marx, May 1, 1851.
11. November 5 to 15, 1851: see Marx to Engels, November 24, 1851 and Engels to Marx, November 27, 1851. See also Georg Weerth (in Bradford) to Marx (in Manchester), November 11, 1851 in G. Weerth, *op. cit.*, Vol. V, pp.423–4.
12. Marx to Engels, August 8, 1851.
13. Georg Weerth to Engels, November 26, 1851 in G. Weerth, *op. cit.*, p.433.
14. See letters exchanged between Marx and Engels from May 4 to June 30, 1852 and Marx's letter to his wife, June 18, 1852.
15. Engels to Marx, October 27, 1852.

16. Simon and Louis Bamberger (father and son) were London financiers with whom Marx had many dealings.
17. Engels to Marx, April 26 and 27, 1853 and Marx to Engels, April 27 and 28, 1853.
18. Engels to Marx, *circa* May 18, 1853.
19. *People's Paper,* March 18, 1854; Marx and Engels, *On Britain* (1953), pp.402–3. The "Parliament" met between Monday, March 6 and Friday, March 10, 1854 (*Manchester Guardian*, March 8 and 11, 1854).
20. Engels to Marx, April 21, 1854.
21. Marx to Engels, September 2, 1854.
22. Marx to Engels, October 17, 1854.
23. Marx to Engels, March 30, April 6, 12 and 16, 1855 and Engels to Marx, April 10, 1855.
24. Marx to Engels, September 11, 1855.
25. Marx to Lassalle in G. Mayer (ed.), *Ferdinand Lassalle, Nachgelassene Briefe und Schriften*, Vol. III (1922 and 1967), pp.103–4.
26. Marx to Engels, December 7, 1855.
27. Engels to Marx, May 26, 1856 and Marx to Engels, May 29, June 5 and 6, 1856.
28. Engels to Marx, November 15, 1857.
29. Jenny Marx to Engels, April 9, 1858; Marx to Engels, April 29, May 1 and 31; Engels to Marx, April 30, 1858; and Engels to Jenny Marx, May 11, 1858. See also Marx to Lassalle, May 31, 1858 in G. Mayer (ed.), *op. cit.,* p.122.
30. Marx to Engels, June 7, 1859.
31. The contributors to the fund included Engels, Wolff, Dr Gumpert, Dr Borchardt and Dr Heckscher.
32. Marx to Lassalle, early July 1859 in G. Mayer (ed.), *op. cit.,* p.223. In a letter to Engels of July 14, 1859 Marx referred to his recent absence from London.
33. Engels to Marx, February 9 and 12, 1860 and Marx to Engels, February 15, 1860.
34. Marx to Lassalle, February 23 and March 3, 1860 in G. Mayer (ed.), *op. cit.,* p.253 and p.279 and Marx to Liebknecht, February 27, 1860 in G. Eckert (ed.), Wilhelm Liebknecht. *Briefwechsel mit Karl Marx und Friedrich Engels* (1963), p.31.
35. Marx to Lassalle, May 8, 1861 in G. Mayer, *op. cit.,* p.361, and Marx to Engels, May 7, 1861.
36. Marx to Lassalle, May 29, 1861 in G. Mayer, *op. cit.,* p.364.
37. Marx to Engels, September 28 and October 30, 1861.
38. Marx to Engels, April 28, 1862.
39. Marx to Engels, August 15, 1863.
40. Marx to Engels, February 25 and March 11, 1864.
41. Engels to Marx, May 1 and 2, 1864.
42. Marx to Jenny Marx, May 13, 1864 in *Marx–Engels Werke*, Vol. 30, pp.659–60.
43. Engels to Marx, March 6 and 11, 1865.
44. Jenny Marx, "Short Sketch of an eventful Life" in *Reminiscences of Marx and Engels, op. cit.,* p.233.
45. Marx to Engels, June 3, 1864.
46. Marx to Engels, January 25, 1865.
47. Marx to Liebknecht, November 21, 1865 in G. Mayer (ed.), *op. cit.,* p.66.
48. Marx to Engels, October 19, 1865.
49. Marx to Engels, November 8, 1865.
50. Engels to Marx, March 5, 1866.
51. Marx to Engels, March 15, 1866.
52. Engels to Marx, June 11, 1866.
53. Marx to Engels *circa* May 22, 1867.
54. Marx to Dr Kugelmann, June 10, 1867, in Karl Marx, *Letters to Dr Kugelmann* (1934), pp.46–7.
55. Marx to Engels, September 11 and 13, 1867 and Engels to Marx, September 12, 1867.
56. Marx to Engels, October 4, 1867 (Marx stated that he had caught a cold on the

journey from Manchester to London).
57. Marx to Engels, May 23, 1868.
58. Engels to Marx, May 25, 1868.
59. Marx to Engels, May 27, 1868. A letter from Marx to Engels of June 27, 1868 suggests that one reason for his recent visit to Manchester had been the desire to avoid taking the oath as a vestryman of St. Pancras.
60. Marx to Engels, June 20, 1868.
61. Engels to Marx, June 22 and 24, 1868 and Marx to Engels, June 23, 1868.
62. Engels to Marx, May 23, 1869.
63. Eleanor and Karl Marx to Jenny Marx, June 2, 1869 in Olga Meier and Faith Evans, *The Daughters of Marx* (1979), pp.49–50.
64. Engels to Marx, July 21, 1869 and Eleanor Marx to her sister Jenny, July 20, 1869. In a postscript Eleanor wrote: "What fun if a lot of children sing – The Prince of Wales in Belle Vue jail/For robbing a man of a pint of ale". See Olga Meier and Faith Evans, *op. cit.*, pp.51–2. For the visit of the Prince and Princess of Wales to Manchester on July 20, 1869 see the *Manchester Guardian*, July 20 and 21, 1869. The royal couple travelled to Manchester from Ellesmere Hall by barge on the Bridgewater Canal.
65. Engels to Marx, July 1, 1869 and *Reminiscences of Marx and Engels, op. cit.*, pp.185–6.
66. Engels to Marx, September 27, 1869.
67. Marx to Engels, May 18 and Engels to Marx, May 19, 1870. See also Karl Marx, *Letters to Dr Kugelmann, op. cit.*, p.111.
68. Marx to Engels, May 23, 25 and 31, 1873; Engels to Marx, May 24, 25, 26, 30, 1873.
69. Engels to Marx, November 29, December 5 and 10, 1873; Marx to Engels, November 30, December 7 and 11, 1873; and Marx to Kugelmann, May 18, 1874 in Karl Marx, *Letters to Dr Kugelmann, op. cit.*, p.135.
70. Julian Harney to Marx, August 10, 1880 in F.G. and R.M. Black (eds.), *The Harney Papers* (1969), pp.292–3. As early as 1851 Harney had referred to Marx and Engels as "friends of long standing" (*The Friend of the People*, March 15, 1851).
71. The Manchester that Marx knew covered a much smaller area than the modern city. When Manchester became a municipal borough in 1838 it included only the townships of Manchester, Hulme, Chorlton upon Medlock, Ardwick, Beswick and Cheetham: see map in Arthur Redford, *The History of Local Government in Manchester*, (1940), Vol. II, p.26.
72. For Manchester between 1844 and 1860 see Arthur Redford, *op. cit.*, Vol. II, pp.205–41.
73. *Manchester Guardian*, May 26, 1852: Arthur Redford, *op. cit.*, Vol. II, p.224.
74. Arthur Redford, *op. cit.*, Vol. II, p.207.

ENGELS IN MANCHESTER[1]

Friedrich Engels lived in Manchester between December 1842 and August 1844 and between November 1850 and September 1870. On both occasions he was employed by the cotton firm of which his father was a partner. Ermen and Engels operated the Victoria Mill at Weaste near Pendleton and had an office in Manchester.[2] In 1845 the local directory described the firm as "cotton spinners and manufacturers of knitting and sewing cotton".[3] Engels was 22 years of age when he first came to Manchester to complete his business training which had begun in Elberfeld and Bremen.

On his first visit some of Engels' spare time was devoted to journalism,[4] his most important article being his "Outlines of a Critique of Political Economy"[5] published in 1844 in the *Deutsch–Französische Jahrbücher*. Highly praised by Marx, it has been described as "a first brilliant gifted sketch of a socialist criticism of bourgeois economics".[6] In England Engels met some leading Chartists (Julian Harney[7] and James Leach[8]), Owenite socialists (Dr John Watts),[9] and a group of German revolutionary agitators in London. Engels described these workers – Karl Schapper, Heinrich Bauer, and Josef Moll – as "the first working class revolutionaries whom I met"[10] but he was not prepared to join their secret society.[11] Engels' main object in coming to England was to study at first hand the homes and the factories of the industrial workers. The fruit of his labours was his book on *The Condition of the Working Class in England*, published in 1845.

This book, written when Engels was only 24 years of age, has proved to be the most lasting of his numerous works.[12] It is in print in Germany, France, England and the United States and is widely read well over a century after it was written. Karl Marx thought highly of it. In 1863, for example, he wrote to his friend:

I have read your book again and I have realised that I am not getting any younger. What power, what incisiveness and what passion drove you to work in those days. That was a time when you were never worried by academic scholarly reservations! Those were the days when you made the reader feel that your theories would become hard facts if not tomorrow then at any rate on the day after. Yet that very illusion gave the whole work a human warmth and a touch of humour that makes our later writings – where 'black and white' have become 'grey and grey' – seem positively distasteful.[13]

Engels' book has had a curious fate since its purpose has been misunderstood and it has been praised for the wrong reasons. Socialists have argued that Engels' historical studies showed that the condition of the English workers in the 1840s was the inevitable result of the class struggle between the capitalist bourgeoisie and the industrial proletariat. They also suggested that Engels' sociological approach to the problem revealed that industrial capitalism carried within it the seeds of its own decay and was doomed to collapse. In fact Engels was not particularly successful in 1845 either as a historian or as a prophet. His historical introduction has little claim to originality since it is little more than a summary of a book by Peter Gaskell,[14] whose notion that yeomen, peasants and artisans led an idyllic existence in England in the eighteenth century would not be accepted by any modern historian. Nor did Engels prove to be a very successful forecaster of developments in England. He did foresee the commercial crisis of 1847 but his confident prophecy that a revolution of the proletariat would soon overthrow the capitalist system in England was quite wrong. In his old age Engels asked for the indulgence of his readers for his mistakes, explaining that they were due to his "youthful ardour".[15]

It has also been claimed that Engels gave a well balanced and accurate account of social conditions in England in the 1840s. There is undoubtedly much information of considerable value in the book – his descriptions of the slums in Manchester and other Lancashire cotton towns are particularly vivid – but Engels himself clearly stated that he was no impartial observer of the English scene. His object was not merely to reveal the social evils of an industrial society but to pillory those whom he considered to be responsible for these evils. While he was writing his book Engels wrote to Marx:

I shall present the English with a fine bill of indictment. At the bar of world opinion I charge the English middle classes with mass murder, wholesale robbery and all the other crimes in the calendar. I am writing a preface in English which I shall have printed separately for distribution to the leaders of the English political parties, to men of letters and to Members of Parliament. These chaps will have good cause to remember me.

He added that he was attacking the German as well as the English middle classes. He would tell the German bourgeoisie that "they are just as bad as the English middle classes – only more cowardly, more flabby and more stupid in their cruel oppression of the workers".[16]

So long as he was in such a mood Engels could hardly be expected to write in an impartial manner. Numerous examples could be given of his inaccuracies and his failure to be fair – faults that were due to his determination to prove at all costs that the English capitalists had been guilty of every conceivable crime in their dealings with their workers. He sometimes exercised little judgment in evaluating evidence. Cautious statements of informed observers – such as Alison's guess concerning the number of prostitutes in London – were given as facts which had been proved. Engels' interpretation of the motives of factory owners was also unsatisfactory. Thus Engels claimed that the Plug Plot riots (1844) in the north of England had been deliberately fomented by certain factory owners who cut wages in the expectation that their workers would go on strike. And the ensuing crisis, it was hoped, would force the government to repeal the Corn Laws. This version of events in Lancashire and Cheshire in 1842 had been hotly denied by the leaders of the Anti-Corn Law League but Engels simply gave one side of the story without even suggesting that any other explanation was possible.[17]

The merits of Engels' work were different from those sometimes claimed for it. It was a hard hitting political tract rather than a sober sociological survey and it was probably the most brilliant attack on the capitalist system to appear in Germany between the rising of the Silesian weavers and the publication of the Communist Manifesto in 1848. Engels went to the heart of various economic and social problems which were still being treated superficially by his contemporaries. While the orthodox economists of his day were discussing problems of rent, prices and the rational use of scarce resources Engels drew attention to the fundamental problems of economic growth. He was one of the first to discuss the trade cycle and to offer an explanation for this phenomenon. He saw the significance of the growth of big businesses at the expense of small undertakings. These topics were later discussed more thoroughly by

Karl Marx, but to deal with them at all in 1845 was no mean achievement. And Engels' chapter on the great towns discussed problems of urban planning in a way that was far ahead of his time.

2. BUSINESSMAN AND REVOLUTIONARY

Towards the end of 1850 Engels returned to his office stool in Manchester. In the previous year he had taken up arms against the Prussians, first in Elberfeld and then in Baden, and he might have faced a firing squad if he had gone home.[18] Marx and Engels were now without funds. Marx and his family were evicted from their Camberwell lodgings and moved into a couple of dingy rooms in Soho where Marx's young son Guido (Föxchen) died in November 1850. Nevertheless Marx was determined to devote his time to his economic studies and political activities and he refused – as he put it later – to give the bourgeoisie the satisfaction of turning him into "a money making machine".[19] Engels, too, had no taste for regular employment and – despite the strained relations between himself and his family – he tried to persuade his father to make him an allowance. It is hardly surprising that the elder Engels should have considered that a man of 30 should be capable of earning his own living and should not be dependent upon his parents. Engels' mother put the position clearly when she wrote to him: "I must agree with your father when he says that you cannot expect us to support you so long as you pursue a way of life which, to put it mildly, does not meet with our approval".[20] And again: "It might be convenient to send you money to live on ... but I find quite extraordinary your demand that I should give financial support to a son who is attempting to spread ideas and principles which I regard as sinful."[21]

So Engels decided that, however distasteful it might be, he would have to find work to support himself and to assist Marx financially so that Marx could devote himself to his major work on capitalism. One might have expected Engels to have secured a post in London so as to be near Marx. Other German exiles – such as the poet Freiligrath[22] – had been able to find work in London. There might well have been an opening for him in the business world or in journalism in which he could have made use of his exceptional knowledge of languages and his previous experience in the cotton trade. But instead of trying to find employment in London Engels not merely went to Manchester but actually accepted a junior position with Ermen and Engels. It was a surprising decision since at that time relations with his father could hardly have been worse. The elder Engels regarded Friedrich as the black sheep of the family whose conduct as an active revolutionary had disgraced the family name. Engels, for his part, heartily disliked his father whom he regarded as a typical example of a bourgeois capitalist – a domineering cotton lord who grew rich at the expense of his workers. Nevertheless there was a reconciliation of sorts. Engels was in urgent need of money and he was prepared to pocket his pride and to take a post with Ermen and Engels. For the elder Engels there was an advantage in having one of his sons working in Manchester to keep an eye on his interests in the firm. And Engels' father was anxious to remove his son from the influence of Karl Marx and other communist exiles in London.

Five years earlier Engels had written to Marx: "I suppose that it is possible for a communist to behave like a bourgeois and to engage in petty trade so long as he is not actually writing. But it is quite impossible to be actively engaged in communist propaganda and at the same time to be involved in the world of business."[23] Now that he had to keep regular office hours as a "corresponding clerk and general assistant" he had to mix every day with businessmen whom he detested. To retain his post he had to abstain from publicly advocating communism and he could publish his views only in anonymous articles. At first he did keep in touch with the rival Chartist leaders Julian Harney and Ernest Jones – contributing to Jones' *Notes of the People*[24] – and he was present when a new local Chartist committee was elected in Manchester, though he had the good sense to decline to be a member himself.[25] He also attempted – with what success is not known – to organise a group of Chartists in Manchester to study the Communist manifesto which had recently appeared in English translation in Harney's *Red Republican*.[26]

But when the Communist League finally collapsed Marx and Engels withdrew for a time from any active political agitation. Engels wrote to his friend:

> Now at last – for the first time for many years – we can show the world that we crave no popularity or support from any party anywhere. We are completely independent of any party disputes. We are now responsible to ourselves alone and when we are needed we shall be able to dictate our own terms. How can people like us, who flee from official positions as from the plague, belong to a "party"?

For twenty years Engels led a double life. In the daytime he was a respectable clerk in a Manchester cotton office. Here he sometimes had to work long hours. In February 1852, for example, he told Marx that "there is no question of my having any free time before seven or eight in the evening. For some time I will have to concentrate on dirty commerce. If I do not then everything will go wrong and my old man will stop my supplies."[28]

Only late in the evening and at weekends could Engels assume the mantle of a revolutionary conspirator. His letters to Marx and his meetings with communist friends – such as Wilhelm Wolff, Georg Weerth and later Carl Schorlemmer[29] and Samuel Moore – had to be kept secret from his colleagues in the cotton trade and from middle class acquaintances whom he met at the Albert Club,[30] the Schiller Anstalt[31] or on the hunting field.[32] Engels also tried to keep his association with Mary Burns a secret by maintaining two establishments. In 1862 he wrote to Marx: "I am now living practically all the time with Mary in order to save money. Unfortunately I cannot manage without my lodgings – otherwise I would be with her permanently."[33] But some of Engels' bourgeois friends did know about Mary Burns and when she died in 1863 they sent him letters of condolence.[34]

Engels achieved his main object in settling in Manchester as he was able to send Marx enough money to save him from destitution and to enable him to write *Zur Kritik der politischen Ökonomie* (1859) and the first volume of *Das Kapital* (1867). And he was also able to help Marx in another way by placing at his disposal information gained from his experience in the cotton trade. Marx's theoretical studies were buttressed by Engels' practical knowledge.

Although for twenty years his income depended upon the prosperity of Ermen & Engels and of the Lancashire cotton industry Engels never ceased to rejoice when the firm ran into difficulties or when the industry was depressed. So passionately did he detest the middle classes in general and the Manchester business community in particular that he derived the greatest pleasure from any misfortune that befell them. In the summer of 1851, for example, Engels wrote gleefully to Marx that there was likely to be a "crash in the market" and that "Peter Ermen is already shitting his pants when he thinks of it – and that little bullfrog is a good barometer of the state of trade".[35]

In his first years in Manchester Engels was able to send Marx only small sums of money – sometimes only postage stamps[36] – as he received no regular salary but was only allowed to draw living expenses from the firm. He would have liked to be recognised as his father's representative in the firm without filling any post that involved regular attendance at the office.[37] But the elder Engels naturally would not agree to this ingenious arrangement. When Engels' father visited Manchester in the summer of 1851 he agreed that his son should draw £200 a year living expenses from the firm[38] but in the following September he asked Engels to reduce his annual expenditure to £150. Since he had already drawn £230 from the firm in his first ten months in Manchester Engels would have had to reduce his expenditures very considerably to meet his father's wishes. Engels replied that he would leave the firm and go to London if his allowance was limited to £150 a year. But the quarrel was patched up and when the elder Engels visited Manchester again in the summer of 1852 Engels secured a welcome increase in his income.

Engels now received a salary of £100 a year and — what was worth much more — 5 per cent of the firm's profits. In 1859 this was raised to 7 per cent. By 1859 his income was over £1,000 a year, which was a substantial sum in those days.[39] When his father died in 1860 Engels agreed to waive his claim to a share of the capital of the German firm provided that £10,000 was placed to his credit in the Manchester firm. But it was not until 1864 that Engels at last became a partner in Ermen & Engels (Manchester), holding one fifth of the capital. He was now in charge of the office with a salary of £1,000 a year — and, of course, a share of the profits as well. Jenny Marx's prophecy of 1859 had come true and Engels had become a "cotton lord" — albeit a modest one![40]

As Engels' income grew so did his payments to Karl Marx, which rose from £240 a year in 1866 to £350 from 1867 onwards.[41] Gustav Mayer writes that "the correspondence of the two friends between 1868 and 1870 shows that Engels sent Marx more money than Marx himself estimated that he needed."[42] Engels helped Marx in other ways. He guaranteed loans which Marx had raised — for example £30 from Freiligrath[43] and £250 from Dronke[44] — and he contributed articles to the *New York Daily Tribune* which Marx sent to the editor as his own and for which Marx was paid. The heavy burden which Engels shouldered when he was in Manchester — his normal office work and his writing in the evening — took their toll and he was seriously ill from overwork in 1857 and 1858. Marx wrote to him early in 1858: "I suspected that you were not quite fit. Do take care of yourself. You have been overdoing things during your Manchester years of 'storm and stress'."[45]

Engels worked as a partner in Ermen & Engels for only five years. He had always disliked the Ermen family and he complained of overwork. He retired from business in 1869 – still under 50 years of age – and withdrew from the firm. On July 1, 1869 he wrote to Marx: "Hurrah! Today I have put an end to *doux commerce* and I am a free man."[46] The rest of his life was spent in London in comfort as a rich retired gentleman – a rentier living on the interest of the capital accumulated by his father and himself in the cotton business.

Engels' literary output in Manchester was considerable in view of his many other commitments. Though he wrote no major work which could be compared with *The Condition of the Working Class in England* or *Anti-Dühring* he did maintain a remarkably high output of articles on a variety of topics. In the 1850s he had no opportunity of placing articles in the German press but when Lassalle established the General German Workers' Union in 1863 he offered advice to its members on the attitude that they should adopt towards the constitutional conflict between Bismarck and the Prussian Landtag.[47]

Among Engels' more important essays written in Manchester were the articles on the revolution of 1848 in Germany which he contributed to the *New York Daily Tribune* in 1851–2. C. A. Dana, the editor of the paper, who had met Marx in Cologne in 1848, thought that Marx had written these articles. "The editor never knew that a great many of the articles which he received from his correspondent in London came from the pen of a Manchester businessman."[48] In these essays Engels showed that the doctrine of dialectical materialism could be applied with considerable success to the writing of contemporary history.[49] One of the articles discussed the technique of revolution in a brilliant passage which many years later had a strong influence upon Lenin's thinking on this subject.

Even more important were Engels' achievements in the field of military criticism which earned him the nickname of "the General".[50] Before 1850 he had written excellent accounts of the Hungarian campaign of 1848[51] and the Baden rising of 1849.[52] Now he embarked upon a serious study of military history and the art of warfare. In June 1851 he wrote to his friend Weydemeyer – a former lieutenant in the Prussian army – asking his advice on military literature.

> Since I arrived in Manchester I have begun to study military affairs, on which I have found fairly good material here – for a beginning at any rate. The enormous importance that the military aspect will have in the next movement, an old

inclination of mine, my articles on the Hungarian war in the *Neue Rheinische Zeitung*, and finally my glorious adventure in Baden, have all impelled me to this study, and I want to work in this field at least enough to be able to express a theoretical opinion without disgracing myself too much.[53]

It is curious that it was not until seven years later that Engels read Clausewitz's book on the art of warfare.[54]

Engels studied the art of war for two reasons. First, since – in his view – the workers would one day rise in revolt to overthrow their capitalist oppressors, it was important to discover how a popular rising could succeed against a trained professional army.[55] Consequently he was particularly interested in the volunteer movement in England,[56] the citizen armies that fought in the American civil war,[57] and the activities of the *francs tireurs* in the Franco-Prussian war.[58]

Secondly, Engels was encouraged in his military studies by Karl Marx, who recognised more clearly than many of his contemporaries the significance of armed forces in the development of national economies. Marx wrote to Engels in 1859:

> Nowhere is the relationship between factors of production and the structure of society more clearly illustrated than in the history of the army. Economic expansion is greatly influenced by the army. In recent times, for example, the payment of wages in money was first fully developed in the army. In Roman law the *peculium castrense* was the first legal recognition of the principle that property could be owned by anyone other than the head of the family. The same applies to the gild activities of blacksmiths (in Roman times). And after what Grimm calls the stone age the special value given to metals and their use as money appears to rest upon their importance in time of war. Moreover the division of labour within a single sphere of human activity was first seen in military forces. The whole history of the structure of middle class society is clearly summarised in the history of armies.[59]

Engels wrote articles for the press on most of the campaigns that took place between 1850 and 1870 and he was also a contributor – on military topics – to the *New American Cyclopaedia*. His essays were marked by a profound knowledge of geography, military history, armaments and the problems of the commissariat. His brochure on *Po und Rhein* (1859)[60] included a brilliant analysis of the Alpine passes dividing Austria from Italy. And in his examination of the routes by which German armies could invade France he correctly anticipated the Schlieffen plan and observed that Belgian neutrality was guaranteed only by a "scrap of paper" (*"ein Blatt Papier"*).[61] Engels' articles on the English volunteers in the *Volunteer Journal for Lancashire and Cheshire*[62] included practical proposals to increase the efficiency of this new militia. His articles on the Seven Weeks' War in the *Manchester Guardian* were among his less successful efforts at military criticism. On July 3, 1866 he confidently explained to his readers that the two Prussian armies invading Bohemia faced the "almost certain fate of being crushed in succession by superior numbers".[63] Three days later when the Prussians had inflicted a crushing defeat upon their enemies at Königgrätz, he had to eat his words.[64] In 1870, however, Engels was more fortunate since in the *Pall Mall Gazette* he forecast correctly the events leading to the battle of Sedan a week before the event.[65]

In 1867 Engels was at last rewarded for the long years that he had spent in the cotton business by news of the completion of the first volume of *Das Kapital*. In May Marx wrote to him that the printing of the book had begun. "Without you I could never have finished my book. I assure you that it has lain heavily on my conscience that your wonderful powers should have gone to rust in the world of business mainly on my account." "And you have had to share my *petites misères* into the bargain."[66] In August the correction of the proofs was completed and Marx wrote to Engels: "So this volume is ready. I have *you* and *you* alone to thank that this has been possible. Without your sacrifice on my behalf, I could not possibly have undertaken the immense researches required to write the three volumes. I embrace you full of thanks."[67]

Engels was determined that Marx's book should not be ignored by the "philistines". He wrote several reviews himself, each emphasising particular aspects of Marx's work which might be expected to interest the readers of various periodicals. They were written in such a way that no one would suspect that they actually came from the pen of the author's closest friend. This ingenious plan was not entirely successful. John Morley refused to print a review (written under Samuel Moore's name) and Dr. Kugelmann found difficulty in placing Engels' articles in German periodicals. Engels also desired that the first volume of *Das Kapital* should be translated into English and he arranged that his friend Samuel Moore (with whom he shared lodgings in Dover Street) should undertake this task. But 20 years elapsed before the translation was completed.

Engels' long period of residence in Manchester had a considerable influence upon his career. His business experience enabled him to give Marx valuable assistance in writing *Das Kapital* and his knowledge of the industrial towns of the north of England gave him a considerable insight into the lives of the factory workers. In Manchester he met Chartists such as James Leach and Ernest Jones – as well as John Watts, who was first a follower of Robert Owen but later became an orthodox liberal. In Manchester Engels found libraries – such as Chetham's and the Athenaeum – that enabled him to undertake his economic and military studies and some of his articles were published locally. In Manchester he met two men who became his close friends – Carl Schorlemmer who taught chemistry at Owens College and helped Engels with his scientific studies, and Samuel Moore who translated the first volume of *Das Kapital* into English.

Little is known of Engels' private life in Manchester. It is clear however that it was by knowing Mary and Lizzie Burns that he first became interested in Irish affairs. He visited Ireland in 1856 and later appears to have had some association – possibly a rather dangerous one – with Fenian conspirators. In view of his earlier revolutionary activities Engels found it necessary to live in obscurity in Manchester and only when he became a partner in the firm of Ermen and Engels did he play a modest part in the public life of the city as president of the Schiller Anstalt.

Much of the Manchester that Engels knew so well has disappeared in the century that has elapsed since his departure. The office in which he worked has been demolished and in recent years slum clearance operations around the University on both sides of Oxford Road have swept away many of the streets that he frequented. Ermen & Engels (later Ermen & Roby) became part of the English Sewing Cotton Company[68] and the Manchester Royal Exchange – once the most important in Europe – has closed its doors for ever. The Albert Club and the Schiller Anstalt have vanished. Only the words "Albert Club" on a pillar box in Oxford Road still remind us that the club was in existence on the other side of the street. Happily visitors to Manchester can still see in Chetham's library the desk in a pleasant alcove at which Marx and Engels once studied economics together.

POSTSCRIPT

In a pamphlet published in 1987 Michael Knieriem has thrown new light on Friedrich Engels' finances.[69] It is clear that the Manchester firm of Ermen & Engels was a prosperous undertaking. Engels' father made a profit of £35,518 in the 1840s and 1850s. Knieriem also lists the payments made to Friedrich Engels after 1850. It is now clear that the £10,000 which Engels received from his brothers in Germany which enabled him to become a partner in the English firm was actually paid by his mother. Engels regarded this as a loan and he had repaid it by the time that he retired. Knieriem indicates that while he was in Manchester Engels was earning commission on the side in dealings involving English firms and Friedrich Engels & Co in Barmen – a company independent of the undertakings run jointly by the Ermen and Engels families in Engelskirchen and Manchester. See also Thomas Schleper. *Ermen und Engels in Engelskirchen* (1987).

NOTES

1. A paper delivered to a conference held in Wuppertal in May 1970. See Hans Pelger (ed.), *Friedrich Engels 1820–1970* (Schriftenreihe des Forschungsinstitut der Friedrich Ebert Stiftung, Vol. 85, 1971), pp.27–38. References to Karl Marx – Friedrich Engels, *Historisch-Kritische Gesamtausgabe: Werke–Schriften–Briefe* (edited by D. Rjazanov) are given as *Gesamtausgabe*. The correspondence between Marx and Engels was published in four volumes in this series (Berlin, 1929–31).
2. Newmarket Buildings in the early 1830s and South Gate, St. Mary's off Deansgate in 1845.
3. Slater's *Directory of Manchester and Salford* (1845), p.112.
4. At this time Engels was a contributor to the *Rheinische Zeitung*, the *Schweizerische Republikaner, Vorwärts*, the *New Moral World* and the *Northern Star*.
5. First published in the *Deutsch–Französische Jahrbücher*, 1844: English translation in W.O. Henderson (ed.), *Engels. Selected Writings* (1967), pp.148–77.
6. Iring Fetscher's introduction to Marx–Engels, II *Politische Ökonomie* (1966), p.9. The *Deutsche–Französische Jahrbücher* was edited by Karl Marx and Arnold Ruge.
7. For G.J. Harney (editor of the *Northern Star*) see A.R. Schoyen, *The Chartist Challenge* (1958), John Saville's introduction to the reprint of *The Red Republican* and *The Friend of the People* (2 vols., 1966), F.G. and R.M. Black (eds.), *The Harney Papers* (Assen, 1969), and Peter Cadogen, "Harney and Engels" in the *International Review of Social History*, Vol. X, Part 1, 1965.
8. For James Leach, author of *Stubborn Facts from the Factories by a Manchester Operative* and a member of the committee of the National Charter Association, see several references in F. Engels, *The Condition of the Working Class in England* (1958), and F. Engels to Karl Marx, Jan. 8 and 29, 1851 in *Gesamtausgabe*, Part III, Vol. 1, p.128 and p.135.

9. For John Watts see the *Dictionary of National Biography*, Vol. LX, p.71.
10. F. Engels, "Zur Geschichte des Bundes der Kommunisten", introduction of 1885 to a new edition of Karl Marx, *Enthüllungen über der Kommunistenprozesses zu Köln* (1852).
11. *Das Bund der Gerechten* (League of the Just).
12. For more detailed assessments of Engels' book see the introduction by W.O. Henderson and W.H. Chaloner to their translation of Friedrich Engels, *The Condition of the Working Class in England* (1958 and 1970) and W.O. Henderson, *The Life of Friedrich Engels* (1976), Vol. I, pp.43–78.
13. Karl Marx to F. Engels, April 9, 1863 in *Gesamtausgabe*, Part III, Vol. 3, p.138. In 1867 Marx wrote as follows in *Capital* (Everyman edition, 1930), Vol. I, pp.240–1, note 3: "As far as concerns the period from the beginning of large-scale industry in England down to the year 1845 I shall only touch upon this here and there, referring the reader for fuller details to Friedrich Engels, *The Condition of the Working Class in England*. The fullness of Engels' insight into the nature of the capitalist method of production has been shown by the factory reports, the reports on mines etc. that have appeared since the publication of his book. When we compare what he says in that book with the official reports of the Children's Employment Commission published 18 or 20 years later (1863–67) we realise with what an admirable fidelity to detail he depicted the circumstances."
14. Peter Gaskell, *The Manufacturing Population of England ...* (1833). A new edition – entitled *Artisans and Machinery* – appeared in 1836 (reprinted Frank Cass, 1968).
15. Preface to English edition of 1892. Engels wrote: "I have taken care not to strike out of the text the many prophecies, amongst others that of an imminent social revolution in England, which my youthful ardour induced me to venture upon. The wonder is, not that a good many of them proved wrong, but that so many of them proved right, and that the critical state of English trade, to be brought on by Continental and especially American competition, which I then foresaw – though in too short a period – has now actually come to pass."
16. F. Engels to Karl Marx, Nov. 19, 1844 in *Gesamtausgabe*, Part III, Vol. 1, p.5.
17. For the Plug Plot riots see A.G. Rose, "The Plug Riots of 1842 in Lancashire and Cheshire" in the *Transactions of the Lancashire and Cheshire Antiquarian Society*, Vol. 67, 1957, pp.75–112.
18. Karl Marx to F. Engels, Aug. 23, 1849 in *Gesamtausgabe*, Part III, Vol. 1, p.113.
19. The phrase occurs in a letter from Marx to J. Weydemeyer, Feb. 1, 1859 in Karl Marx and F. Engels, *Letters to Americans 1848–95* (1963), p.60.
20. Elise Engels to F. Engels, Dec. 2, 1849 in K. Goebel and H. Hirsch, "Engels-Forschungsmaterialien im Bergischen Land" in *Archiv für Sozialgeschichte*, Vol. IX, 1969, p.124 (Letter 33).
21. *Ibid.*, April 11, 1850, pp.12–13 (Letter 34).
22. Freiligrath was earning £200 a year in 1852 as a clerk in a silk warehouse. Later he had a salary of £300 (rising to £350) as agent for the Banque Suisse in London.
23. F. Engels to Karl Marx, Jan. 20, 1845 in *Gesamtausgabe*, Part III, Vol. 1, p.13.
24. See for example F. Engels, "Real Causes why the French Proletariat remained comparatively inactive in December last" in *Notes of the People* (from the Continental Correspondent of the *Notes*), Feb. 21, 1852, pp.846–8.
25. F. Engels to Karl Marx, Feb. 12, 1851 in *Gesamtausgabe*, Part III, Vol. 1, pp.147–8.
26. F. Engels to Karl Marx, Jan. 8, 1851 in *Gesamtausgabe*, Part III, Vol. 1, p.129. The English translation of the Communist manifesto was by Helen Macfarlane.
27. F. Engels to Karl Marx, Feb. 13, 1851 in *Gesamtausgabe*, Part III, Vol. 1, p.148.
28. F. Engels to Karl Marx, Feb. 17, 1852 in *Gesamtausgabe*, Part III, Vol. 1, p.320. Sometimes life in the office was less hectic. On April 17, 1868 he wrote to Marx: "I think that I will have more time next week as business is slack. If I get home between 4pm and 5pm I shall have the whole evening free for work of a different kind" (*ibid.*, Part III, Vol. 1, p.39).
29. Engels met Schorlemmer at a regular gathering of young German scientists –

including Heinrich Caro and Ludwig Mond – who met on Saturday evenings at the Thatched Cottage tavern in Newmarket Place, Market Street, Manchester.

30. J.A. Petch, "Dover House (315 Oxford Road). A Link with Friedrich Engels" in the *Transactions of the Lancashire and Cheshire Antiquarian Society*, Vol. 72, 1962, pp.167–9.

31. Engels was president of the Schiller Anstalt in Manchester between 1864 and 1868. The centenary of Schiller's birth was in 1859. On November 10, 1859 a public meeting in the Free Trade Hall organised by Carl Siebel (a distant relation of Engels) decided to establish the Schiller Anstalt in Manchester. Dr L. Borchardt was chairman of the executive committee in 1860 and Charles Hallé was one of the vice-presidents. There is a copy of the statutes of the Schiller Anstalt in the Manchester Public Reference Library.

32. Engels mentioned his exploits on the hunting field with the Cheshire hunt in a letter to Marx on Dec. 31, 1857 (*Gesamtausgabe*, Part III, Vol. 2, p.286).

33. F. Engels to Karl Marx, Feb. 28, 1862 in *Gesamtausgabe*, Part III, Vol. 3, p.55. Engels' first lodgings in Manchester from 1850 to 1852 were at 70 (renumbered 44 in 1852) Great Ducie Street, Strangeways. Between 1852 and 1858 he lived at 6 Thorncliffe Grove, off Oxford Road, while from 1864 to 1870 he was in lodgings for a time with S. Moore. The original 25 Dover Street was near the site of the building now occupied by the Economics Faculty of Manchester University. Mary (and her sister Lizzie) lived at 252 Hyde Road, Gorton from 1856 to 1864. Mary died in 1863. Lizzie subsequently lived in Ardwick, first in Tennant Street and then at 86 Mornington Street (Stockport Road).

34. F. Engels to Karl Marx, Jan. 13, 1863 in *Gesamtausgabe*, Part III, Vol. 3, p.118.

35. F. Engels to Karl Marx, July 30, 1851 in *Gesamtausgabe*, Part III, Vol. 1, p.224.

36. For example £1 on January 8, 1851; £1 on February 5, 1851; £5 on May 8, 1851 and postage stamps on April 25, 1852 (*Gesamtausgabe*, Part III, Vol. 1, pp.128, 140, 195 and 341).

37. F. Engels to Karl Marx, Feb. 26, 1851 in *Gesamtausgabe*, Part III, Vol. 1, p.159.

38. F. Engels to Karl Marx, July 6, 1851 in *Gesamtausgabe*, Part III, Vol. 1, p.212.

39. For Engels' finances in 1850–70 see M. Knieriem, *"Gewinn unter Gottes Segen"* (1987) and Gustav Mayer, *Friedrich Engels* (2 vols., 1934), Vol. II, pp.12, 29, 61, 107, 172–5 and many references in the Marx–Engels correspondence. Four contracts between Engels and Godfrey Ermen are preserved in the Lancashire Record Office in Preston.

40. Karl Marx to F. Engels (postscript by Jenny Marx), Dec. 2, 1850 in *Gesamtausgabe*, Part III, Vol. 1, p.120. She wrote: "In my mind's eye I can already see you as Friedrich Engels junior, a partner of Friedrich Engels senior".

41. F. Engels to Karl Marx, March 28, 1869: "Enclosed draft on the Union Bank of London £87–10s for March to June" (i.e. £350 per annum) in *Gesamtausgabe*, Part III, Vol. 3, p.173.

42. Gustav Mayer, *Friedrich Engels* (2 vols., 1934), Vol. II, p.61.

43. F. Engels to Karl Marx, Feb. 6, 1861 in *Gesamtausgabe*, Part III, Vol. 3, pp.11–12.

44. F. Engels to Karl Marx, April 8, 1863 in *Gesamtausgabe*, Part III, Vol. 3, p.135.

45. Karl Marx to F. Engels, Feb. 10, 1858 in *Gesamtausgabe*, Part III, Vol. 2, p.285.

46. F. Engels to Karl Marx, July 1, 1869 in *Gesamtausgabe*, Part III, Vol. 4, p.196.

47. F. Engels, *Die Preußische Militärfrage und die Deutsche Arbeiterpartei* (1865).

48. Gustav Mayer, *Friedrich Engels* (2 vols., 1934), Vol. II, p.30.

49. The articles were collected by Marx's daughter Eleanor and published as a book in 1891. They were attributed to Marx. A German translation appeared in 1896. It was edited by Kautsky and he too attributed the articles to Marx.

50. F. Engels, *Ausgewählte militärische Schriften* (3 vols., 1958–64), G. Zirke, *Der General* (1957), and J.L. Wallach, *Die Kriegslehre von Friedrich Engels* (1968).

51. F. Engels, "Der magyarische Kampf" in the *Neue Rheinische Zeitung*, Jan. 13, 1849. Engels wrote to Marx on July 6, 1852: "At that time we discussed the Hungarian war in the *Neue Rheinische Zeitung* from information supplied by the

Austrian communiqués. The articles were brilliant and correct but also cautious. Our prophecies proved to be right." See also Wilhelm Liebknecht's comments on Engels' articles in *Reminiscences of Marx and Engels* (1961), p.138.

52. F. Engels, "Die Deutsche Reichsverfassungs-Campagne" in the *Neue Rheinische Zeitung. Politisch–ökonomische Revue* (reprint of 1955), pp.39–62, 94–104, and 149–74. See also Klaus Schreiner, *Die badisch-pfälzische Revolutionsarmee 1849* (1956).
53. F. Engels to J. Weydemeyer, June 19, 1851 in Karl Marx and F. Engels, *Letters to Americans 1848–95* (1963), p.21.
54. F. Engels to Karl Marx, Jan. 7, 1858 in *Gesamtausgabe*, Part III, Vol. 2, p.270.
55. W.O. Henderson and W.H. Chaloner, *Engels as Military Critic* (1959).
56. F. Engels, *Essays addressed to the Volunteers* (1861).
57. Karl Marx and F. Engels, *The Civil War in the United States* (1961).
58. F. Engels, *Notes on the War* (1923), pp.105–8.
59. Karl Marx to F. Engels, Sept. 25, 1857 in *Gesamtausgabe*, Part III, Vol. 2, pp.228–9. This point of view was later elaborated by W. Sombart in *Krieg und Kapitalismus* (1913).
60. Karl Marx to F. Engels, March 10, 1859 (*Gesamtausgabe*, Part III, Vol. 2, p.371). In this letter Marx praised *Po und Rhein* as being "exceedingly clever". When he was in Berlin in May 1861 he wrote to Engels that the Countess of Hatzfeld had told him that in the "highest military circles" the authorship of *Po und Rhein* was attributed to a senior Prussian general (*Gesamtausgabe*, Part III, Vol. 3, p.17).
61. In August 1914 Bethmann Hollweg told the British ambassador in Berlin that the treaty which guaranteed the neutrality of Belgium was only a "scrap of paper" ("*einen Fetzen Papier*").
62. Engels' articles have been reprinted in W.O. Henderson and W.H. Chaloner, *Engels as Military Critic* (1959). Marx wrote to Engels on October 2, 1860: "Your rifle-article has made the rounds of the entire London press. The *Observer*, a supporter of the ministry, has reviewed it. It was a sensation" (*Gesamtausgabe*, Part III, Vol. 2, p.514).
63. W.O. Henderson and W.H. Chaloner, *Engels as Military Critic* (1959), p.134.
64. *Ibid.*, pp.136–40.
65. F. Engels in the *Pall Mall Gazette*, Aug. 26, 1870, reprinted in F. Engels, *Notes on the War, op. cit.*, p.37.
66. Karl Marx to F. Engels, May 7, 1867 in *Gesamtausgabe*, Part III, Vol. 3, pp.388–9. In the same letter Marx wrote that he hoped to complete volumes 2 and 3 of *Das Kapital* by the next spring. But these volumes were not published in Marx's lifetime.
67. Karl Marx to F. Engels, Aug. 16, 1867 in *Gesamtausgabe*, Part III, Vol. 3, p.408.
68. H.E. Blyth, *Through the Eye of a Needle. The Story of the English Sewing Cotton Company* (1947).
69. Michael Knieriem, *"Gewinn unter Gottes Segen". Ein Beitrag zu Firmengeschichte und gesellschaftlicher Situation von Friedrich Engels* (Nachrichten aus dem Engels-Haus, V, 1987).

3

THE FIRM OF ERMEN & ENGELS[1]

In 1860 when the Lancashire cotton industry had attained the zenith of its prosperity it had over 2,000 factories, 300,000 power looms, and 21,500,000 spindles which consumed over 1,000 million lbs of raw cotton every year. It was the largest industry of its kind in the world and was responsible for nearly 40 per cent of Britain's exports. The cotton factories were of various kinds – spinning mills, weaving sheds, dyeworks, bleachworks, calico printworks and so forth – and they ranged from very small establishments to small weaving sheds which appeared and flourished in times of prosperity.

One of the medium sized cotton firms was Ermen & Engels which operated the Victoria and Bencliffe spinning mills at Weaste and had an office in Manchester. In the 1860s it had a capital of about £60,000 and employed some 800 operatives. Its fortunes would be of interest only to local historians but for the fact that Friedrich Engels worked in its office for many years, first as a clerk and then as a partner in charge of the office. The detailed knowledge of the manufacturing district which he gained in the service of Ermen & Engels was readily placed at Karl Marx's disposal and a number of passages on the English cotton industry in the first volume of *Das Kapital* bear witness to the help which Engels gave to his friend.

Ermen & Engels was one of a relatively small number of firms engaged in a highly specialised branch of the cotton industry – the spinning of cotton thread for sewing and for hosiery-knitting. At the end of the nineteenth century only 14 companies had to be brought together to establish a concern embracing the major manufacturers of cotton thread in England. (The powerful Scottish cotton thread industry was already dominated by the great J. & P. Coates and J. & J. Clark combine.[2]) As the sewing machine came into general use, the demand for thread greatly increased and it is not surprising that there was a boom in this branch of the cotton industry in the 1850s and 1860s.

There were significant differences between the major branches of the cotton industry – spinning, weaving and printing – and the production of cotton thread. The end product – a reel of cotton – cost only a few pence and was sold to a wide range of customers who would not necessarily be purchasers of yarn or cloth. Because a reel of cotton was very cheap and soon had to be replaced, the demand for it was not greatly affected by factors which influenced the demand for the products of other sections of the cotton industry. It was possible for manufacturers of thread to enjoy high sales while their colleagues in other branches of the cotton industry were facing hard times. And since thread had many outlets – cotton firms, tailoring and dressmaking establishments and millinery shops for example – the problems of marketing thread were rather different from the problem of selling yarn, cloth or printed calicos. The success of a firm like Ermen & Engels depended not only upon the smooth operation of its spinning mill but also upon the development of an efficient marketing organisation. When Engels became a partner of a firm producing cotton thread he carried a heavy responsibility for maintaining and expanding the outlets for the sale of the products manufactured by Ermen & Engels.

The firm had been founded by Peter Ermen and Friedrich Engels senior. Peter Ermen had been born in Holland in 1802 but had been brought up at Hachenberg in Nassau. In 1825, at the age of 23, he migrated to England. Like many other foreigners he sought his fortune in Manchester, the centre of the Lancashire cotton industry. After a brief period of service with a firm of shippers, he went into business on his own account in a small way as a doubler. His works were in the Blackfriars district of Salford. By 1834 the expansion of the firm made it possible for Peter Ermen to bring his younger brother Anthony over from Germany to assist him. In 1839 Anthony Ermen patented "machinery for spinning, doubling, or twisting cotton, flax, wool, silk, or other fibrous materials".[3] Peter and Anthony Ermen were then joined by a third brother named Godfrey who soon showed that he possessed great business acumen as well as a sound knowledge of the technical side of the cotton industry. He too was an inventor and eventually his "Diamond Thread" proved to be an invaluable asset to the firm.

The three Ermens traded under the name of "Ermen Brothers". They had a foothold in Manchester – an office off Deansgate – as well as their works in Blackfriars (Salford). Another sign of Peter

Ermen's success in business in the 1830s was that he could afford to move his private residence from the industrial quarter of Chorlton on Medlock to the more salubrious neighbourhood of Lower Broughton.[4] In his well known description of Manchester Engels mentioned that "the villas of the upper classes are surrounded by gardens and lie in the higher and remoter parts of Chorlton and Ardwick or on the breezy heights of Cheetham Hill, Broughton and Pendleton".[5]

The continued growth of the business made it desirable to expand output by securing a larger mill than the small works in Blackfriars. Peter Ermen therefore looked for a partner who would bring additional capital into the firm. He found one in Friedrich Engels senior of Barmen. Friedrich Engels senior had been born in 1796 and belonged to a family which for three generations had been engaged in the textile industry of the valley of the River Wupper. He was over 40 years of age and had had considerable business experience. Friedrich Engels junior gave the date of his father's partnership with Peter Ermen as 1837[6] but the following printed letter (circulated to Peter Ermen's customers) shows that the partnership began on August 1, 1838:

Manchester, 1st August, 1838

I beg to inform you that in consequence of a Partnership entered into with Mr Frederick Engels, the business of Spinning and Manufacturing, will from this day be carried on under the Firm of "Ermen and Engels". You will please to take notice of our Signatures at foot.

I have the honor [sic] to remain
Your most obedient Servant

PETER ERMEN[7]

This letter is of interest not merely because it gives the date on which the new firm was established. It is significant because it shows that at first the partnership was between only Peter Ermen and Friedrich Engels senior. Neither Anthony nor Godfrey Ermen were partners when the business was founded in 1838. The existing firm of Ermen Brothers (in which Peter, Anthony, and Godfrey Ermen were partners) was not absorbed by the new venture but maintained an independent existence. The co-existence of the two firms – sharing an office in Manchester – proved to be a source of friction between

Friedrich Engels (senior) and Godfrey Ermen

the Ermen and Engels families in the future. It is also significant that
Peter Ermen's letter of August 1, 1838 described the business of the
firm in very general terms as "spinning and manufacturing" and that
there was no specific mention of the production of cotton sewing
thread. It seems very likely that the development of Ermen &
Engels as a firm specialising in cotton thread occurred rather later.

The newly established firm operated the Victoria Mill, which was
erected in about 1838. The factory was built at Weaste Lane on what
was then open country. The spinning mill lay on the River Irwell
near a station on the Manchester–Liverpool railway. There has
been some confusion concerning the address of the mill which has
been given as Eccles, Pendlebury, Pendleton and Salford. This
is because when it was built the factory lay in Eccles parish
and belonged to the manor of Pendlebury for purposes of local
administration. To complicate matters the land upon which it was
built was an enclave in the township of Pendleton. Today the factory
– now rebuilt – lies in the borough of Salford. The thread produced
at the Victoria Mill bore a trade mark of three red towers, the arms
granted to a remote ancestor of the Ermens in the sixteenth century.
When the Victoria Mill was opened Ermen & Engels moved their
office in Manchester first to 3 New Market Buildings (off Market
Street), and later to 2 South Gate, St. Mary's (off Deansgate). Peter
Ermen moved his private residence from Lower Broughton to Gore
Crescent, Pendleton, so as to be near the mill. Godfrey Ermen also
moved to the vicinity of the new factory.[8]

In about 1840 Ermen & Engels set up a cotton mill at Engelskirchen, near Cologne. The office of the firm was in Barmen.[9]
According to Gustav Mayer the German branch of the firm was not
successful at first, being subsidised for some time from the profits of
the English branch.[10] It was presumably in connection with these
developments that Anthony and Godfrey Ermen became partners
of the firm of Ermen & Engels. Friedrich Engels senior ran the
German side of the enterprise with the assistance of Anthony
Ermen while the English mill was run by Peter and Godfrey Ermen.
This arrangement was advantageous to the Ermens since they were
represented in both the English and the German branches of
the firm while Friedrich Engels senior had no representative in
England and had to trust the Ermens to operate the Manchester
business efficiently. Friedrich Engels senior proposed to remedy
the situation by sending his eldest son Friedrich to Manchester to
complete his commercial training with the firm of Ermen & Engels.
Although Friedrich Engels was at that time a young man of 22 with

little experience of the business world – except for a period of service in Bremen in the office of the merchant Heinrich Leupold – he would be on the spot and could report to his father on the way in which the Ermens were running the business in Manchester. Friedrich Engels senior hoped that his son would eventually be appointed to a post in the office of Ermen & Engels and would then be in a position to safeguard the interests of the Engels family in the English firm. But Friedrich Engels had political ambitions, which did not include earning his living in the cotton trade, and some years elapsed before it was possible for Friedrich Engels senior to put into operation his plan to have a member of his family working in the office of Ermen & Engels.

Engels arrived in Manchester in the middle of November 1842 and left towards the end of August 1844.[11] He came to Lancashire when the industrial districts of the north of England were just recovering from the effects of the Plug Plot riots. Shortly before he came to Manchester, Ermen & Engels had inserted an advertisement in the *Manchester Guardian* thanking the police for the protection given to their property during the disturbances.[12] As Engels' correspondence for the period when he was in Manchester in 1842–44 has not survived, little is known of his impressions of the firm of Ermen & Engels at this time, though his various activities outside the office can be pieced together from scattered statements which appear in his later writings. He made a close study of the social question in London and in the industrial North by visiting working class districts and by studying the literature on the subject. The fruits of his labours appeared in 1845 in his book on *The Condition of the Working Class in England*. He made contact with Owenite socialists like John Watts, Chartists like Julian Harney and James Leach, and exiled German revolutionaries like Karl Schapper, Heinrich Bauer, and Josef Moll. And from the correspondence of the young German revolutionary poet Georg Weerth – then employed by a Bradford woollen firm – it is known that Weerth and Engels (who shared the same political views) spent the Whitsuntide holiday of 1844 together in Manchester.[13]

There is, however, no contemporary evidence concerning Engels's work in the office of Ermen & Engels or any contacts that he may have had with the spinning mills at Weaste. It is reasonable to assume that he did not find life pleasant during office hours. He disliked the two partners under whom he worked and in later years he referred to Peter Ermen as a "little bullfrog" and to Godfrey Ermen as a "pig", a "dog", and "shitpants".[14] In Bremen Engels had enjoyed working in an easy going office in which no objection was raised to the clerks keeping bottles of beer under their desks.[15] But this sort of thing was not allowed in Ermen & Engels's office in Manchester. There is evidence to suggest that Peter Ermen, the senior partner, was a hard taskmaster. When his brother Anthony first came to England he complained – in a letter to his fiancée Julie Sartorius of Cologne – that he had to get up at six in the morning and was expected to study at night school when the day's work was over.[16]

Again, little is known of Engels's private life during his first visit to Manchester. In his address "to the working classes of Great Britain" which appeared as a preface to the first edition of his book on the English workers Engels declared: "I forsook the company and the dinner parties, the port wine and champagne of the middle classes, and devoted my leisure hours almost exclusively to the intercourse with plain working men."[17] Certainly some of his leisure time was devoted to enjoying the company of a working girl. This was Mary Burns, an Irish millhand, who lived in Ancoats at 18 Cotton Street, off George Leigh Street. Engels wrote that Ancoats contained "the majority and the largest Manchester factories" as well as many workers' cottages.[18] Mary Burns's father (Michael Burns) was a dyer. Eventually Engels and Mary Burns lived together as man and wife though they were never married. It is not clear whether they started to live together when Engels was in Manchester in 1842–44. They certainly did so in Brussels in 1846.[19] Many years later Marx's daughter Eleanor stated that – according to family tradition – Mary Burns in her twenties had been "pretty", "witty" and "charming". "Of course she was a Manchester (Irish) factory girl, quite uneducated, though she could read and write a little". But in later years she "drank to excess".[20]

Engels left Manchester in August 1844 to the relief of Peter and Godfrey Ermen. In the following year, in July and August, he was back again – with Karl Marx – for a brief visit. They pursued their studies on economics together in Chetham's Library. When Engels returned to the Continent he took Mary Burns with him. Five years elapsed before Engels returned to Manchester to work again in the office of Ermen & Engels. He rejected his parents' plea that at the age of 25 he should cease to be dependent upon his father and should start to earn his own living. He had been trained for a career in commerce and there were openings for him with Ermen & Engels in Manchester or in Barmen. But after his meeting with Karl Marx in Paris in the autumn of 1844 Engels was determined to lead the life of a communist writer and agitator. As soon as his book on the English workers was completed he left home to join Karl Marx in Brussels. There — and also in Paris — he was engaged in various revolutionary activities which culminated in the publication of the Communist Manifesto in 1848. When revolutions broke out in Germany in that year he moved to Cologne where he acted as Marx's right hand man on the editorial staff of the *Neue Rheinische Zeitung*, while in the following year he took up arms against the Prussians first in Elberfeld and then in Baden. When the reaction triumphed Engels fled to England to join Marx in exile in London.

While Engels was leading the life of a communist agitator on the Continent the firm of Ermen & Engels in Manchester appears to have been in a flourishing condition. The invention (in the United States) of the sewing machine by Elias Howe — patented in 1846 — led to the establishment of clothing factories in Manchester, Leeds and other towns. At first the sewing machines were operated by hand but before long they were driven by steam power. Clothes of superior quality, however, continued to be made by tailors and dressmakers. These developments increased the demand for sewing thread and there was no lack of orders for the Victoria Mill. That the firm was making satisfactory profits may be seen from the fact that the capital invested by Friedrich Engels senior in the Manchester firm doubled between 1838 and 1851.[21] In the 1850s "the business continued to expand without cessation, being greatly increased by the effect of Mr Godfrey Ermen's patent for polishing cotton thread".[22] This invention — described as a "method or apparatus for finishing yarns or threads" — was patented in 1851. The improved thread was marketed as "Godfrey Ermen's Diamond Thread".[23] It appears that Godfrey Ermen succeeded in retaining the right to earn royalties on his invention wherever he pleased — "becoming thereby a moderately wealthy man apart from his interest in the firm".[24]

After living for about a year in London in 1850 Engels decided to accept his father's offer of a post with Ermen & Engels in Manchester. He did so with great reluctance for he detested Manchester and had a strong aversion to being tied to the regular hours of office routine. Moreover he had no wish to leave Marx. But he was short of money and could not help Marx who was in dire financial straits. Engels could find no suitable employment in London — where many refugees from the Continent were looking for work — and he decided to sacrifice his own ambitions as a writer to go to Manchester to earn enough money for himself and for Marx to live on. This arrangement would enable Marx to devote his time to writing his book on economics. And so Friedrich Engels senior got his way. His eldest son returned to his office stool and there was now a representative of the Engels family working for the Manchester firm. Friedrich Engels senior suspected that the Ermens were running the business to further their own interests. Now he expected his son to let him know if anything of the kind occurred. At first Engels thought that his stay in Manchester would be a short one. Within a few weeks of arriving there he told Marx that his father did not seem inclined to let him stay any longer than was absolutely necessary.[25] In any case Engels was confident that a revolution would soon break out on the Continent again and then he would leave Ermen & Engels and again draw the sword that he had sheathed when the Baden insurrection collapsed. But no revolution took place and Friedrich Engels senior found that his son was paying assiduous attention to his duties in the office. In the end Engels stayed with the firm for nearly twenty years.

When Engels arrived in Manchester he was soon involved in a crisis in the affairs of Ermen & Engels. Peter and Godfrey Ermen were at loggerheads and it became clear that the situation could be resolved only if the brothers parted company. The cause of the quarrel is not known. There may have been a clash between two strong personalities, each trying to control the firm. And Godfrey Ermen's determination to secure for himself the lion's share of the profits derived from his "Diamond Thread" may have aggravated the situation. Friedrich Engels senior at first held aloof from the quarrel but he had to make up his mind what to do when the partnership expired at the end of 1853. Eventually he threw in his lot with Godfrey Ermen and told his son that he would not renew his contract with Peter Ermen.[26] He hoped that Godfrey Ermen would agree to the amalgamation of Ermen & Engels with Ermen Brothers since the continued existence of the two firms was leading to difficulties, especially as both used the same office.[27] Ermen Brothers ran a small spinning mill (producing coarse yarn) and a bleachworks. At one time the annual profits had amounted to only about £600 but there had been recent signs of improvement.[28]

Engels tried to secure the maximum advantage for himself from the situation. He followed Jenny Marx's advice and tried to entrench himself firmly between the hostile Ermens and so make himself indispensable to his father. But his status in the office was an equivocal one. At first he was not on the staff of the firm but received an allowance from his father. The other clerks – Charles Roesgen and Hill for example – were more likely to support one of the

Ermens rather than the son of an absentee partner. Eventually, however, Engels secured Charles Roesgen as an ally against the Ermens. The crisis ended with Godfrey's triumph and Peter's defeat. Peter Ermen retired – ostensibly on grounds of ill health. Godfrey Ermen and Friedrich Engels senior renewed their partnership. The firms of Ermen & Engels and Ermen Brothers were united.[29] Engels's position in the firm was regularised. He became a member of the clerical staff and drew a salary of £100 per annum to which was added 5 – later $7\frac{1}{2}$ – per cent of the firm's profits. On the whole Ermen & Engels flourished in the 1850s, though trade fluctuated from year to year. According to Engels there was "a positive loss" in 1851,[30] though business was "very good indeed" in 1858.[31] The prosperity of the firm can be seen from the increase in Engels's income which reflected the profits earned each year.[32]

Engels's father died in 1860. Godfrey Ermen was confident that his hour had struck and he could now drive Engels out and gain complete control of the Manchester firm. He had ambitious plans to exploit his invention and to expand the business by establishing a new cotton mill.[33] He proposed to pay Engels's mother the capital which her husband had invested in the Manchester firm. But he would offer Engels nothing except to continue to employ him as a clerk under his existing contract.[34] Engels – who had reluctantly waived his claim to a share of the German business in favour of his three brothers[35] – insisted that he had a moral (though of course not a legal) claim to succeed his father as a partner in the Manchester firm. If he did not get his way he threatened to leave Ermen & Engels and set up a rival sewing thread business of his own. The strain of the negotiations with Godfrey Ermen – a hard bargainer – led to a breakdown of Engels's health and his brother Emil came to Manchester from Barmen to deal with Godfrey Ermen. Emil Engels proved to be a tough negotiator and the matter was brought to a successful conclusion.[36] Although Engels did not secure a partnership immediately he was given a definite promise of a partnership in 1864 if he invested £10,000 in the Manchester firm.[37] After some delay, articles of agreement were signed by Engels and Godfrey Ermen on September 25, 1862 "with provisions for an eventual partnership between them".[38]

In the early 1860s, when Godfrey Ermen was in sole control of the Manchester firm, he expanded his business interests in two ways. First, he revived Ermen Brothers as an independent firm separate from Ermen & Engels.[39] Ermen Brothers purchased the Bridgewater Mill at Pendlebury where fine spinning and doubling was carried out under the direction of Godfrey's nephew Henry Ermen. Some of the yarn was sold through Ermen & Engels. A brief description of this mill was given by H. E. Blyth in 1947.[40] Secondly, the firm of Ermen & Engels − while continuing to operate the Victoria Mill − leased Bencliffe Mill at Little Bolton (Eccles) to manufacture cotton sewing thread. A description of this mill appeared in a local newspaper in 1871 when the premises were extensively damaged by fire. The writer of the article stated that the factory was four storeys high and employed about 800 operatives.[41] Despite the grave shortage of raw cotton when the North blockaded the southern ports during the American civil war[42] Godfrey Ermen's enterprises flourished in the early 1860s.

In 1864 Godfrey Ermen could no longer deny Engels his partnership. Engels had now invested £10,000 in the firm − his share of his father's estate. But before accepting the inevitable Godfrey Ermen brought his brother Anthony into the firm as a partner and as manager of Bencliffe Mill.[43] Since Anthony invested a mere £500 in the business it was obvious that he was being made a partner simply to ensure that there would be two Ermens and only one Engels in the firm. The Ermen−Engels partnership deed was signed in the following September.[45] Jenny Marx had once expressed the hope that Engels would one day become a "cotton lord". Now, although he could hardly claim to be a "cotton lord", Engels had become a partner in a successful firm and he enjoyed a good income which enabled him to make Marx a regular allowance.

The Lancashire cotton industry was slow to recover from the effects of the cotton famine and in 1868 Engels told Marx that in recent years "the balance has been very bad".[46] But Ermen & Engels survived and continued to produce sewing thread of high quality. The firm was awarded medals for its thread at industrial exhibitions held at Coventry (1867) and at Amsterdam (1869).[47] Godfrey Ermen and Friedrich Engels had never got on well together and their partnership was marred by many disputes.[48] In October 1865, for example, Engels wrote to Marx that his office was like a pigsty because Godfrey Ermen had engaged three inexperienced clerks and had insisted that Engels should train them.[49] In April 1867 Engels declared that his dearest wish was to be free from his office duties.[50]

Engels made up his mind to retire when his contract with Godfrey Ermen expired in June 1869. Godfrey Ermen took advantage of the situation to drive a hard bargain. He knew that Engels had definitely decided to give up his business career and that there was no danger that Engels would start up a rival business of his own. In the circumstances Godfrey Ermen was able to reach an agreement with Engels for the dissolution of the partnership on terms very favourable to himself. Engels naturally was able to withdraw the capital that he had invested in the firm, but he secured only £1,750 as his share of the goodwill. And Engels agreed that the firm might continue to trade under the name of "Ermen & Engels" for another five years.[51] On July 1, 1869 Engels went to the office for the last time. When he returned home he wrote to Marx: "Hurray! Today sweet commerce is at an end."[52] And in December he told Marx that Godfrey Ermen had paid him the last instalment of the money due to him — "and from now onwards we shall presumably turn our backsides on each other if we meet again".[53]

Engels left Manchester in 1870 and retired to London where he lived for the rest of his life. In February 1871 he received a letter from Charles Roesgen — a former colleague in the office of Ermen & Engels — describing the great fire which had burned down part of Bencliffe Mill. Roesgen wrote that the reeling and making-up sheds were a total loss but that the dye shed had escaped damage.[54] Losses, estimated at £25,000, were fortunately covered by insurance. The firm repaired Bencliffe Mill, sold the old Victoria Mill, and erected a new factory (Nassau Mill) at Patricroft.[55] An illustration of Nassau Mill appears in the abridged English translation of Gustav Mayer's biography of Friedrich Engels[56] though Engels never had anything to do with this factory.

In April 1874 Godfrey Ermen asked his former partner if he might continue to trade under the name "Ermen & Engels". Engels refused to agree to this. He wrote to Godfrey Ermen as follows:[57]

London, 1st June, 1874

Dear Sir,

A fortnight's absence from London and subsequently a slight cut on my hand which however disabled me for some time from writing, have caused some delay in my replying to your letter of the 16th of April.

When, in 1869, we discussed the conditions on which ultimately I left the business, I certainly gave you reason to hope that, even after the lapse of the five years stipulated, I might consent to allow you to retain my name in the firm. But this was always made dependent upon certain circumstances.

Had these contingencies been realised, I should have been quite willing, on application, to allow you to continue the use of my name in the firm.

But certainly, no word ever uttered by me could have induced you to consider yourself entitled to continue using my name after the 30th instant as a matter of course, without my express permission.

The principal amongst these contingencies were

1. that there should occur no collisions between the Manchester House, and that of my brothers in Barmen. I am glad to say that none such have occurred, and that moreover from what I heard from my brothers last autumn, none are likely to occur, the two houses scarcely ever coming into competition.

2. that Mr Aston's views as to my not incurring any liability should prove correct.

Now I have consulted upon this point ever so many lawyers and they are one and all unanimous as to my responsibility for all the debts of the firm so long as I allow my name to remain in the firm.

If you would be good enough to send me Mr Aston's opinion on the point written by himself, I believe I could make short work of this misunderstanding.

The point is so notorious, that it is laid down in plain terms in all handbooks on the law of partnership. I quote from one by a barrister of high reputation: "If any retiring partner consent to be held out to the public as connected with the firm, as for instance by allowing his name to be written over the shop, or used in the advertisements or invoices of the firm, he will continue to be liable." So that, if there be anything positive in English law (which I should not risk to assert) it must be this point.

But even supposing Mr Aston to be right on the point, and all the other lawyers wrong; the contrary opinion of the others would merely prove the point to be such a knotty one that, if the very improbable cases now under consideration should ever occur, and if my money should not go to the creditors, it would surely go to the Chancery lawyers.

However I shall be quite willing to give my consent to the old firm being continued for a period not extending beyond the 30th June 1875, on the condition of your giving me a distinct promise, that after the 30th of September 1875 my name shall not any longer appear as that of a partner of any goods sent out by the firm.

You see I am quite willing to do everything to facilitate the change of firm, giving you the use of my name there, where it is of most value to you, on the tickets and wrappers, for three months longer than you ask for.

Hoping that this letter will find you in good health and spirits, I remain

Yours very truly

F. Engels

G. Ermen Esq.

In the circumstances the name of the firm was changed from "Ermen & Engels" to "Ermen & Roby" – H.J. Roby being Peter Ermen's son in law.[58] Godfrey Ermen had achieved his ambition and the firm was now owned and controlled by the Ermen family. Godfrey Ermen had made a fortune by the time that he retired from business and went to live in Devon in 1877. Twenty years later a writer in a trade journal described him as "the grand old man" of the sewing cotton trade.[59] In 1896 the firm of Ermen & Roby ceased to be a private partnership and was incorporated with a capital of £134,000. Godfrey Ermen held 8,000 of the 13,400 shares.[60] In the following year Ermen & Roby was one of 14 firms which amalgamated to form the English Sewing Cotton Company.[61] Godfrey Ermen died in 1899 leaving about £400,000. After legacies had been paid, the residue of the estate – amounting to about £200,000 – was administered by a charitable trust which built the Godfrey Ermen memorial (Church of England) schools in Eccles in 1904.[62] It may be added that there is an Ermen Road in Eccles and an "Engels House" on the Cawdor Street Development. It is appropriate that Engels, who had once so vividly described the horrors of the Manchester slums in the 1840s, should have his name associated with a modern workers' estate.

NOTES

1. For the firm of Ermen & Engels see articles in the *Eccles Advertiser*, Feb. 11, 1871, the *Warehousemen and Drapers' Trade Journal*, 1894, and the *Drapers' Record*, Sept. 18, 1897; H.E. Blyth, *Through the Eye of a Needle. The Story of the English Sewing Cotton Company* (1947); A.C.G. Ermen, R.N., "Cotton and Communism" (1964, typescript in possession of English Calico Ltd) and "The Three Red Towers" (1965, typescript in Eccles Public Library); J.B. Smethurst,

"Ermen and Engels" in the *Marx Memorial Library Quarterly Bulletin*, January–March, 1967, pp.5–11, and "Ermen & Engels in Eccles" (typescript) and several references in the Marx–Engels correspondence. The location of the spinning mills operated by Ermen & Engels (Victoria Mill and Bencliffe Mill) or by Ermen Brothers (Bridgewater Mill) and the offices jointly occupied by the two firms and the private addresses of various partners are taken from local directories. There are references to Ermen & Engels in J. Scholes, *List of Foreign Merchants and Firms in Manchester 1784–1870* (manuscript in Manchester Reference Library).

2. A.J. Robertson, "The Decline of the Scottish Cotton Industry 1860–1914" in *Business History*, Vol. XII, No. 2, July 1970, p.121 and p.123 (note 2).

3. Bennett Woodcroft, *Alphabetical Index of Patentees of Inventions* (1854, new edition of 1969), patent 8,290 of Dec. 2, 1839. In 1848 Anthony Ermen patented "machinery for twisting cotton or other fibrous substances". It is stated that in 1875 Anthony Ermen patented a breech-loading mechanism for rifles: see A.C.G. Ermen, "Cotton and Communism" (typescript: English Calico Ltd).

4. *The Drapers' Record*, Sept. 18, 1897; Pigot and Son's *Directory of Manchester and Salford*, 1832–33, p.96 and p.382; 1834, p.398 and p.447; 1836, p.118 and p.391; 1838, p.118; and Pigot and Slater's *Directory of Manchester and Salford*, 1840, p.91; 1843, p.102; and 1845, p.112.

5. F. Engels, *The Condition of the Working Class in England* (trans. and ed. W.O. Henderson and W.H. Chaloner, 1958), p.55.

6. F. Engels to Karl Marx, July 6, 1851 in *Gesamtausgabe*, Part III, Vol. 1, p.212. The date 1837 was accepted by Gustav Mayer in *Friedrich Engels* (second edition, 1934), Vol. 1, p.6 and by many other writers. The date 1837 was also given by J. Scholes in his *List of Foreign Merchants and Firms in Manchester 1784–1870* (manuscript in Manchester Reference Library).

7. A copy of the circular letter is in the possession of English Calico Ltd, Industrial Division.

8. It may be added that in 1844 the firm of Ermen & Engels was a member of the Manchester Chamber of Commerce: see the *24th Annual Report ... of the Chamber of Commerce and Manufacturers at Manchester for the Year 1844* (1845), p.19.

9. Paul Steller, *Führende Männer des Rheinisch–Westphälischen Wirtschaftslebens* (1930), p.88 and p.142.

10. Gustav Mayer, *Friedrich Engels, op. cit.*, Vol. 1, p.6.

11. For Engels in Manchester in 1842–44 and 1850–70 see W.O. Henderson, chapter 2, above; W.O. Henderson and W.H. Chaloner, "Friedrich Engels in Manchester" in *Memoirs and Proceedings of the Manchester Literary and Philosophical Society*, Vol. 98, 1956–57; and M. Jenkins, *Frederick Engels in Manchester* (1951).

12. *Manchester Guardian*, Aug. 27, 1842.

13. Georg Weerth to his mother, July 6, 1844 in Georg Weerth, *Sämtliche Werke*, (1957), Vol. V, p.128.

14. Peter Ermen – "der kleine Laubfrosch" (F. Engels to Karl Marx, July 30, 1851 in *Gesamtausgabe*, Part III, Vol. 2, p.224). Godfrey Ermen – "Hosenscheißer" (F. Engels to Karl Marx, Sept. 9, 1862 in *Gesamtausgabe*, Part III, Vol. 3, p.100); "Sau – Gottfried" (F. Engels to Karl Marx, April 27, 1867, *ibid.*, p.386).

15. F. Engels to Marie Engels, August 4, 1840 in *Marx–Engels Werke*, supplementary volume (1967), Part II, p.452.

16. A.C. G. Ermen, "Cotton and Communism" (typescript: English Calico Ltd).

17. F. Engels, *The Condition of the Working Class in England, op. cit.*, p.7.

18. F. Engels, *op. cit.*, p.68.

19. George Weerth to his mother, June 13, 1846 in Georg Weerth, *Sämtliche Werke*, Vol. V, p.215. He wrote: "Moreover Friedrich Engels is here. You have read his book about England. He has an English girl friend so our conversation is partly in English and partly in German." See also Stephan Born, *Erinnerungen eines Achtundvierzigers* (1898), pp.73–4 and Eleanor Marx to Karl Kautsky, March 15, 1898 in the Kautsky papers (DVVI. 489) in the International Institute of Social

History, Amsterdam.

20. Eleanor Marx to Karl Kautsky, March 15, 1898, *op. cit.*
21. F. Engels to Karl Marx, July 6, 1851 in *Gesamtausgabe*, Part III, Vol. 1, pp.212–13.
22. *The Drapers' Record*, Sept. 18, 1897.
23. Bennett Woodcroft, *Alphabetical Index of Patentees of Inventions, op. cit.*, patent 13,670 of June 17, 1851. The trade name "Diamond Thread" is now registered in the name of English Sewing Cotton Ltd and is still in force.
24. A.C.G. Ermen, "Cotton and Communism" (typescript: English Calico Ltd).
25. F. Engels to Karl Marx, Dec. 17, 1850 in *Gesamtausgabe*, Part III, Vol. 1, pp.122–23.
26. F. Engels to his brother-in-law Emil Blank, Dec. 3, 1850 in *Marx–Engels Werke*, Vol. 27 (1965), pp.541–2.
27. In a letter to Karl Marx of April 3, 1851, Engels mentioned that there was a clerk in the office "who is more in the service of Ermen Brothers than of Ermen & Engels" (*Gesamtausgabe*, Part III, Vol. 1, p.171).
28. F. Engels to Emil Blank, Dec. 3, 1850 in *Marx–Engels Werke*, Vol. 27, pp.541–2.
29. Friedrich Engels senior to F. Engels, June 30, 1852 and Dec. 20, 1853 in the Marx–Engels papers (L. 1609) in Amsterdam.
30. F. Engels to Karl Marx, Feb. 17 and March 2, 1852 in *Gesamtausgabe*, Part III, Vol. 1, pp.319–20 and p.328.
31. F. Engels to Karl Marx, Oct. 7, 1858 in *Gesamtausgabe*, Part III, Vol. 2, p.339.
32. Engels's share of the profits (5 per cent in 1854–55, $7\frac{1}{2}$ per cent in 1856) was £168 in 1854, £163 in 1855, £408 in 1856, £837 in 1857, £840 in 1858 and £987 in 1859. See Gustav Mayer, *Friedrich Engels, op. cit.*, Vol. 2, pp.12, 29, 61, 107 and 172–5.
33. "Monsieur Gottfried has considerable plans for changes and reorganisation as soon as he is absolutely the one and only master in the firm" (F. Engels to Karl Marx, May 7, 1860 in *Gesamtausgabe*, Part III, Vol. 2, p.484).
34. F. Engels to his brother Emil Engels, April 11, 1860 in *Marx–Engels Werke*, Vol. 30, p.528.
35. Engels withdrew his claim in the German firm since he did not wish his mother to be distressed by an unseemly family quarrel. He wrote to her: "I would not for the world act in the slightest way to throw a cloud over the evening of your life by becoming involved in a family dispute over the inheritance" (F. Engels to Elise Engels, Feb. 13, 1861 in *Marx–Engels Werke*, Vol. 30, p.582).
36. "When father died I went through the most difficult time imaginable and I was so ill that I was incapable of taking a single necessary decision. It was Emil who brought the negotiations to a successful conclusion. He had a clear vision, a decisive attitude and a complete mastery of the whole affair. I have Emil to thank for the fact that today I am living in London as an independent man" (F. Engels to Charlotte Engels, Dec. 1, 1884 in *Marx–Engels Werke*, Vol. 37, p.248).
37. F. Engels to Karl Marx, April 8, May 7 and 8, and Dec. 3, 1860 in *Gesamtausgabe*, Part III, Vol. 2, pp.477, 484, 485 and 524.
38. The agreement of Sept. 25, 1862 is preserved in the Lancashire Record Office in Preston. Although Engels was not a partner in 1863 he was a member of the Manchester Royal Exchange: see *Slater's ... Directory ... of Manchester and Salford* (1863), p.163. In 1862 the firm of Ermen & Engels was listed as a member of the Manchester Chamber of Commerce: see *42nd Annual Report ... of the Manchester Chamber of Commerce for the Year 1862* (1863), p.43.
39. Engels told Marx in a letter of May 10, 1868 that the younger Ermens (Godfrey's nephews) were forbidden to discuss the affairs of the Bridgewater Mill with him (*Gesamtausgabe*, Part III, Vol. 4, pp.53–4).
40. H.E. Blyth, *Through the Eye of a Needle, op. cit.*, p.63 and illustration on p.67.
41. *Eccles Advertiser*, Feb. 11, 1871.
42. See W.O. Henderson, *The Lancashire Cotton Famine 1861–65* (1934, second edition 1969). In a letter of September 9, 1862 Engels wrote to Karl Marx that he was

very busy since he continually had to write to customers to tell them about successive increases in the price of cotton thread. "A certain number of fellows have made a pile of money by this increase in the price of cotton. But we will not share in these profits, partly because the worthy Godfrey is a shit-pants and partly because the spinning firms have earned nothing in this period. The commission agents have swallowed the lot" (*Gesamtausgabe*, Part III, Vol. 3, p.100). On Jan. 26, 1863 Engels informed Karl Marx that business was very slack (*ibid.*, p.122).

43. Anthony Ermen retired in 1873.
44. The agreement of June 30, 1864 is in the Lancashire Record Office at Preston.
45. F. Engels to Karl Marx, Sept. 2, 1864 in *Gesamtausgabe*, Part III, Vol. 3, p.186.
46. F. Engels to Karl Marx, Nov. 29, 1868 in *Gesamtausgabe*, Part III, Vol. 4, p.130.
47. In the 1870s the firm of Ermen & Engels (later Ermen & Roby) gained awards at industrial exhibitions held in Vienna (1873) and Paris (1878). The medals are now in Eccles Public Library.
48. There are several references in the Marx–Engels correspondence to Engels' quarrels with Godfrey and Anthony Ermen – for example "many quarrels with Monsieur Godfrey" (F. Engels to Karl Marx, June 16, 1867 in *Gesamtausgabe*, Part III, Vol. 3, p.393). On November 28, 1867 Engels wrote to his brother Hermann: "Here things go on as before. From time to time I have a squabble either with Anton or with Godfrey ..." (in *Marx–Engels Werke*, Vol. 31, p.572).
49. F. Engels to Karl Marx, Oct. 4, 1865 in *Gesamtausgabe*, Part III, Vol. 3, pp.292–3. In October 1867 Engels explained to Marx why he could not guarantee a loan which Marx proposed to raise. He wrote: "... My contract prohibits me from acting as a surety and my relations with Monsieur Godfrey are such that he would seize any opportunity to put me in the wrong before a court of arbitration" (F. Engels to Karl Marx, April 27, 1867 in *Gesamtausgabe*, Part III, Vol. 3, p.386).
50. "I long for nothing more than to be free of this hellish business which is such a waste of time as to demoralise me completely". (F. Engels to Karl Marx, April 27, 1867 in *Gesamtausgabe*, Part III, Vol. 3, p.386).
51. The agreements of June 24 and Aug. 10, 1869 dissolving the Ermen–Engels partnership are in the Lancashire Record Office at Preston.
52. F. Engels to Karl Marx, July 1, 1869 in *Gesamtausgabe*, Part III, Vol. 4, p.198.
53. F. Engels to Karl Marx, Dec. 9, 1869 in *Gesamtausgabe*, Part III, Vol. 4, p.256.
54. Charles Roesgen to F. Engels, Feb. 12, 1871 in the Marx–Engels papers (L. 5434) in Amsterdam. For an account of the fire see also the *Eccles Advertiser*, Feb. 11, 1871.
55. Nassau Mill (Patricroft) was closed in about 1945.
56. Gustav Mayer, *F. Engels: a Biography* (English translation, 1936), p.132.
57. F. Engels to Godfrey Ermen, June 1, 1874 in M. Jenkins, *Frederick Engels in Manchester* (1951). The letter is in the Lancashire Record Office at Preston.
58. For John Henry Roby see the *Concise Dictionary of National Biography* (1961), p.371.
59. *The Drapers' Record*, Sept. 18, 1897.
60. Information kindly supplied by my colleague Dr. D.A. Farnie.
61. For a brief account of the English Sewing Cotton Company see H.E. Blyth, *Through the Eye of a Needle, op. cit.*
62. K. Joyce, *Godfrey Ermen Memorial Church of England Schools Development Appeal* (1970). For the German firm see Thomas Schleper, *Ermen und Engels in Engelskirchen* (1987).

4

MARX AND ENGELS AND THE FREEDOM OF THE PRESS

The rulers of communist societies habitually deny to their subjects the right to express their opinions freely. Newspapers, journals and books are censored as a matter of course and those who express views contrary to those held by the authorities soon find themselves in serious trouble. Solzhenitsyn could consider himself fortunate to be banished from Soviet Russia rather than to be packed off to a labour camp or to a mental hospital. Yet Marx and Engels were lifelong champions of freedom of speech and freedom of the press. They never tired of denouncing attempts by autocratic governments to suppress views with which they disagreed either by the imposition of a censorship or by hauling before the courts those who made speeches or wrote articles which were critical of the régime or of its officials. Marx was a professional journalist. He edited the *Rheinische Zeitung* (October 1842–March 1843) and the *Neue Rheinische Zeitung* (May 31, 1848–May 18, 1849) in Cologne and when he lived in exile in London he endeavoured, with no great success, to support himself and his family by writing regularly for the *New York Daily Tribune* and for *Die Presse* (Vienna). Engels, too, was a contributor to several newspapers. Among his more important articles were those on reform movements on the Continent in the *Northern Star* (September 1845–December 1849), on foreign affairs in the *Neue Rheinische Zeitung* (1848–9), on the Volunteer movement in the *Volunteer Journal for Lancashire and Cheshire* (September 1860–March 1862),[1] on the Franco-Prussian war in the *Pall Mall Gazette* (July 29, 1870–March 16, 1871),[2] and on trade union policy in the *Labour Standard* (May 7–August 6, 1881).[3] And in his later years he was a regular contributor to various socialist journals published in Germany (*Der Sozialdemokrat*, 1881–90 and *Vorwärts*, 1892–4) and elsewhere.

The German Federal Act of 1815 had provided that the Diet of the

Confederation should, at its first meeting, consider recommending laws on copyright and freedom of the press which should be the same in all the federal states. The promise was not kept. Instead of enjoying freedom of the press journalists in many German states were subjected to severe censorship regulations, particularly between 1819 and 1830. Even when Marx and Engels began to write for the press in the early 1840s the censorship was still being widely enforced. In Prussia the edict of October 18, 1819 made it very difficult for critics of the government to express their views in the press. Every town in Prussia had its censor who was generally a police official.

Marx and Engels, like other radical journalists, strongly objected to the censorship. In July 1842 Engels denounced the way in which the press was restricted in Prussia. In an article in the *Rheinische Zeitung* he observed that all manuscripts intended for publication had to be submitted to a censor before going to the printer.[4] Attempts to evade the censorship by publishing in another German state or in a foreign country were met by confiscating the offending periodical and prosecuting the author. Charges were made under various sections of the penal code (*Landrecht*) concerning treason, lèse-majesté, and offensive criticisms of the country's laws and courts. Engels argued that the penal code was so vaguely worded that the attitude of the courts could be discovered only by analysing judgments delivered in particular cases. He therefore examined the reasons given by the court for its decision in the case of Johann Jacoby, who was charged with criticising the Prussian system of government and Prussian bureaucracy in a pamphlet published in Mannheim (Baden) in 1841.[5] Jacoby was found not guilty of high treason but guilty of lèse-majesté and of an offensive attack on the legal system.

Engels criticised the penal code for failing to define precisely what constituted an attack upon the legal system. The prosecutor had to satisfy the court that such an attack was both impudent and disrespectful, and that it held the law up to ridicule. Engels argued that, in practice, the decision to prosecute a writer for criticising the legal system − and the attitude of the court if the case came to trial − depended far more upon political considerations than upon legal principles. Soon after his accession Frederick William IV had relaxed the censorship in Prussia. In December 1841 new instructions were issued to the censors telling them to interpret the regulations in a more liberal spirit than had been customary in the past. Engels pointed out that, as a result, articles in radical papers, such as the *Rheinische Zeitung* and the *Königsberger Zeitung*, which would have been banned in 1840, "now received the imprimatur of the Prussian censor".[6] And writers of articles and pamphlets critical of the government published abroad, were not prosecuted with the same vigour as in the past. But the king's brief honeymoon with the press was soon over. A Cabinet Order of November 15, 1842 once more tightened up the censorship in Prussia.[87]

Engels' cautious approval of the royal instructions to the Prussian censor of December 1841 was not shared by Marx, whose first criticism of the censorship, entitled "Comments upon the most recent Instructions to Prussian Censors", had been written before Engels' article but was not published until February 1843.[8] Marx observed that if the censors had been carrying out their duties properly during the past 20 years there would be no need to issue new instructions. He observed that the censors were now told not to suppress any "serious and discreet search after the truth", not to place "unreasonable restraints" upon writers, and not to hamper the normal activities of publishers. Marx argued that freedom of expression was an inalienable human right and that there was no moral justification for placing restrictions upon the search for the truth. It was quite wrong to try to limit that search to those who expressed their views in a "serious and discreet" manner. What an author considered to be "serious and discreet" might well be regarded in a somewhat different light by the censor. Each writer should decide for himself how best to present what he believed to be the truth. It was not for a censor to make an arbitrary decision as to whether a writer's views had been presented in an acceptable manner or not.

Marx condemned what he regarded as contradictions in the royal instructions. Censors were told to act in the spirit of the edict of 1819. But since the spirit of that edict had been extremely reactionary the new advice to the censors could hardly be regarded as a step in the direction of a liberal interpretation of the edict. The edict of 1819, for example, included a sweeping condemnation of writers who "attempted to place in a favourable light the views of those who aimed at the overthrow of constitutional authority in any country". Marx went on to point out that sometimes there was little to choose between the edict of 1819 and the new instructions to censors. The edict had condemned attacks against "all general principles of religion" while the instructions condemned "frivolous and hostile" criticisms not merely of the Christian religion but of "particular beliefs" – whatever that might include.

The advice given to censors in the instructions of 1841 concerning criticisms of the country's constitution or laws was condemned by Marx. Such criticisms were to be allowed only if their "tendency were well-meaning" and their views were presented in a "respectful manner". Marx declared that this subjected writers to an intolerable "jurisdiction of suspicion". The instructions were "laws lacking objective standards – laws of a reign of terror, comparable to the legislation of the Roman emperors or Robespierre." "It is actually a positive sanction of lawlessness if the criterion of an offence is not the act itself but the alleged thought behind the act." Laws should deal with actions, not thoughts. The state, in Marx's view, was inviting censors to do what ordinary citizens were forbidden to do. Writers were forbidden to criticise the moral or religious beliefs of individuals. Yet the daily task of the censors was to exercise the criticism denied to the press for they were expected to be able to distinguish infallibly between well-meaning critics and evil-minded critics.

Marx observed that the regulations concerning the appointment of editors of newspapers and periodicals had actually been tightened in 1841. The censorship edict of 1819 had left the appointment of editors to the proprietor. If he chose to confirm an appointment to which the censor objected he had to deposit a sum of money as a guarantee of good behaviour on the part of the editor. The instructions of 1841, on the other hand, stated that only men of irreproachable character and high standards of scholarship might be approved for appointment as editors. The proprietor lost the right to confirm the appointment of an editor who was not acceptable to the authorities. Marx caustically remarked that the instructions of 1841 were silent concerning the appointment of censors with "high standards of scholarship", yet they had the power to decide whether an editor had the qualifications necessary for his job. Marx wrote: "If the government is aware of the existence of such a horde of universal geniuses – and every town has at least one censor – why do these monuments of encyclopaedic knowledge not come into the open as authors themselves?" "The government knows all about these men, but the world of scholarship knows them not."

Finally Marx declared that the government was expecting the impossible from its censors, who were supposed to be capable of making accurate judgments on the character and scholarship of editors and of the intentions of writers of articles and books. He complained that the instructions of 1841 invited the censors to waive all objective criteria and to rely upon their intuition and personal impression of the intentions of the writers of articles and books. Decisions on these matters were subject to the arbitrary judgment of censors whose qualifications for assuming such responsibilities were of a very questionable nature. Marx concluded by demanding the abolition of press censorship.

In articles in the *Rheinische Zeitung* in May 1842 Marx discussed the debates on the censorship of the press which had taken place at the sixth meeting of the Rhenish Provincial Assembly in the previous year.[9] He declared that the discussion in the Assembly showed that it was the upper classes − the nobles and the landed gentry − who were the most enthusiastic supporters of press censorship. It was their representatives who insisted that a censorship was necessary to curb criticisms of the authority of church and state and envious attacks upon the nobility. Marx argued that the only true "censorship" was the free criticism of a free press. Where that existed the truth would emerge from the conflicting views put forward by various writers in different newspapers. Marx claimed that the Prussian censorship was ineffective. Instead of suppressing views regarded as undesirable by the government it gave them publicity which they would not have had if the press were free. Insignificant authors, punished by the courts for their views, achieved the status of martyrs and their writings were eagerly sought after, because they had been banned.

In the middle of October 1842 Marx became the chief editor of the *Rheinische Zeitung* which was published in Cologne. Journalists enjoyed a little more freedom in the Rhineland than elsewhere in Prussia, since the Code Napoléon was in force in that province. It is true that Marx denounced the code as "Napoleonic press despotism" and declared that articles 367 and 368 of the Penal Code were in flat contradiction to the freedom of the press.[10] Engels, however, pointed out that under the code "if a writer were charged merely with a misdemeanour and not with a political offence, his case was heard before a jury".[11] And juries in Cologne were by no means unsympathetic to critics of the government in Berlin.

The first number of the *Rheinische Zeitung* had appeared on January 1, 1842 with the support of several liberal Rhenish business-men. Since it proposed to challenge the virtual monopoly long enjoyed in the Rhineland by the ultramontane *Kölnische Zeitung* (8,000 subscribers) the new paper secured the necessary concession from the Prussian censor. The authorities soon had cause to regret their decision. The two young men who ran the paper in its early days − Georg Jung and Dagobert Oppenheim − belonged to the

Young Hegelian group and their radical policies soon alarmed the authorities in Berlin. They had even more cause for alarm when Marx was placed in charge of the *Rheinische Zeitung* and quickly gained control over its editorial policy.

When the censor complained that the paper was disseminating radical French ideas Marx replied that he was trying to promote distinctively German liberal doctrines as opposed to a mere copying of foreign liberal ideas. He stated that several articles had appeared in the *Rheinische Zeitung* supporting Prussia's political aims – for example the inclusion of Hanover, Hamburg and Bremen in the Zollverein. He claimed that the policy of the paper was in complete accord with the spirit of the King's instructions to the censors of December 1841. He added that, in view of the deplorable state of the German press, a group of public-spirited citizens in Cologne had founded the *Rheinische Zeitung* so that the King could hear the true voice of his people.[12]

In January 1843 Marx again championed the cause of the freedom of the press when he denounced the banning of the *Leipziger Allgemeine Zeitung* in Prussia. This newspaper was subject to censorship in Saxony but the Prussian authorities considered that their colleagues in Saxony were not paying sufficient attention to Prussian susceptibilities. The banning of the *Leipziger Allgemeine Zeitung* in Prussia was justified because "it prints one rumour after another, at least half of which are later proved to be false".[13] "Moreover instead of sticking to facts the paper is always on the lookout for motives. Its judgments are frequently later proved to be erroneous, yet they are always presented not only with an authoritative air of infallibility but in a hateful passionate manner." In his first article on the subject Marx claimed that even if these criticisms were correct the attitude of the *Leipziger Allgemeine Zeitung* was perfectly understandable since the popular press was still in its infancy in Germany. In the circumstances it was natural that journalists should not pull their punches but should present their views in a brash and forceful manner. They might sometimes get their facts wrong but the spirit in which they wrote truly reflected the ideas and aspirations of their readers.

On January 19, 1843 the Prussian government decided to ban the *Rheinische Zeitung* and to place it under strict censorship control until it was closed. The government declared that, since its inception, the *Rheinische Zeitung* had pursued a reprehensible editorial policy. It had "attacked the very foundations of the consti-tution, propounded anti-monarchical doctrines, poisoned public opinion against government policy, aroused opposition to existing laws, and vigorously attacked foreign states with which Prussia enjoys good relations." At an extraordinary general meeting, held on February 12, the shareholders of the *Rheinische Zeitung* decided to give way and to moderate criticisms of the government in the hope that the government would have second thoughts on banning the paper.

Marx protested against this policy of appeasement to the authorities. Replying to the criticisms of the government, Marx denied attacking the Prussian constitution since there was no agreement concerning the philosophical basis of the constitution. At one time Hegel's philosophy of law had been officially accepted by the government but by the 1840s Hegel's ideas had been subject to considerable criticism. Marx also denied attacking the monarchical principle. He admitted criticising class privileges, biased civil servants, and press censorship but that had nothing to do with the principle of monarchy. Marx claimed that no newspaper in Germany had published such serious articles – based upon scholarly research – as the *Rheinische Zeitung*. To the charge that the paper had attacked the legal system Marx replied that in any state laws must be amended as society develops and conditions change. To criticise laws was to pave the way for their amendment. Marx denied that he had consistently opposed the Prussian government. He shrewdly observed that had he wished to do so he could have fanned the flames of religious controversy by supporting the militant Catholics of the Rhineland against the Lutherans in the older Prussian provinces. He could have advocated French radical and socialist doctrines instead of promoting specifically German liberal ideas. He could have supported attempts to strengthen the powers of the Prussian provinces as opposed to the authority of the central government in Berlin. But the *Rheinische Zeitung* had done none of these things. Marx concluded by mentioning various aims of Prussian policy which had been supported in the columns of the *Rheinische Zeitung*.[14] These included the extension of the Zollverein and the establishment of Prussia's political leadership in Germany. Marx did not wait until April before resigning. On March 18, 1843 the paper announced that "in view of the present censorship the undersigned has today resigned his post as editor of the *Rheinische Zeitung* (Karl Marx)".[15]

Five years later, during the revolution of 1848, Marx was back in Cologne as editor-in-chief of a new radical paper, the *Neue Rheinische Zeitung*. His sub-editors included his communist friends

Friedrich Engels, Wilhelm Wolff, and Georg Weerth. Throughout Germany at this time the freedom of the press was among the reforms most frequently demanded. The Federal Diet authorised the abolition of the censorship of the press. But the press could still not be regarded as free. In some states the censorship survived or was quickly reimposed during the reaction of 1849. In March 1849 Marx complained that in two districts in Prussia the censorship was working "in all its glory".[16] Moreover the Prussian government rarely hesitated to ban newspapers or to bring journalists before the courts. Publication of the *Neue Rheinische Zeitung* was suspended from September 26 to October 12, 1848 and when Marx was expelled from Prussia in May 1849 the paper was forced to cease publication. At that time it had about 6,000 regular subscribers. During the brief life of the paper writs were showered upon the editors alleging such offences as defaming the administration, incitement to revolt, and high treason. But juries refused to convict and Marx never saw the inside of a Prussian gaol. His colleague Georg Weerth was not so fortunate, for he served three months' imprisonment for writing a satirical novel – serialised in the *Neue Rheinische Zeitung* – which painted a highly unedifying picture of the morals of the landed gentry in Prussia.[17]

As editors of the *Neue Rheinische Zeitung* Marx and Engels championed the cause of revolution on the Continent. But in dealing with the great issues of that time they did not forget to denounce those who imposed censorship or took writers to court for criticising government policies. They attacked various draft censorship laws prepared by the Prussian government which were designed to prevent any criticism of civil servants in the press or on posters. In July 1848[18] and again in March 1849[19] Marx protested against these bills and declared that they would stop newspapers from trying to obtain redress for citizens who suffered from the arbitrary misuse of powers by the police. In March 1849 Marx protested against the silence of the German press concerning the reintroduction of the censorship in various parts of the country.[20] In the following month Engels criticised a bill before the Prussian national assembly which proposed to ban political posters from the streets. He declared that this was a typical piece of class legislation – an attempt to stifle the political activities of the urban proletariat. "The longing for the establishment of law and order", he wrote,

> means the stifling of the class struggle and the suppression of the oppressed classes. That is why the party of law and order

must abolish the free exchange of views in the newspapers and must monopolise the press by censorship laws, prohibitions and so forth. And it must, if possible, suppress the free literature of posters and pamphlets.[21]

When Marx and Engels faced charges in connection with articles which they had written in the *Neue Rheinische Zeitung* attacking the Prussian government and its officials, they used the court as a platform from which to denounce those who, in their view, were sabotaging the cause of revolution. In his speech of February 14, 1849 Marx claimed that it was the duty of the press to expose any arbitrary actions on the part of the police or civil servants. He declared that the future of the freedom of the press in the Rhineland lay in the hands of the jury.[22]

Between 1850 and 1870 Marx and Engels were both active as journalists, but as they wrote mainly for newspapers and periodicals published in Britain or in the United States, where there was no censorship of the press, they had no cause to complain of any interference with their freedom to express their views.

During the Franco-Prussian war the Prussian authorities tried to suppress any opposition to government policy. Although there was no fighting on Prussian soil – except for the bombardment of Saarbrücken – virtually the whole of north Germany was declared to be a war zone under military control. This meant that those who opposed the war, such as the five members of the socialist executive committee in Brunswick, could be arrested and packed off to exile in East Prussia without further ado.[23] Bebel and Liebknecht, the socialist leaders who sat in the Reichstag and opposed the granting of war credits and the annexation of Alsace and Lorraine, were sentenced to two years' imprisonment for high treason.

In 1871 in a letter to the *Daily News* Marx protested against the arbitrary denial of the right of free expression in Prussia. He denounced Bismarck's attempts to persuade foreign governments to curtail criticisms of the Prussian government by their subjects. Marx declared that Prussia had made diplomatic protests to Belgium, Sweden and Russia concerning newspaper articles in those countries which expressed sympathy for France in her defeat. He concluded by declaring that the French were now fighting not merely for their own freedom but for the freedom of Germany and all Europe.[24]

In October 1878 the Anti-Socialist Law was passed by the German Reichstag. It prohibited all organisations which aimed at overthrowing "the existing political or social order through social-democratic, socialist, or communist endeavours". By June in the following year 127 periodicals and 278 books and pamphlets had been banned. Marx and Engels protested against this prohibition of the expression of socialist views, which went far beyond the censorship exercised by the Prussian authorities when Marx and Engels were young journalists in the Rhineland in the 1840s. They took part with Bebel and Liebknecht and other leaders of the German Social Democrat Party in discussions concerning the establishment of a new socialist journal to be printed abroad and then smuggled into Germany. Such a paper (*Der Sozialdemokrat*) was established in 1879 and was published in Zürich until 1888 when it was transferred to London. Engels gave financial support to the paper and became a contributor. When Bernstein edited *Der Sozialdemokrat* in London "his ideas were firmly moulded by Engels, particularly as far as international affairs were concerned".[25]

When the Anti-Socialist Law expired in September 1890 and was not renewed *Der Sozialdemokrat* ceased publication. Engels contributed an article to the last number in which he declared that the paper had for many years been "the banner of the Social Democrat Party". In his view its success had been in no small measure due to the fact that, since it had been published in Switzerland and in England, it had "enjoyed the advantage of complete freedom of the press".[26]

The establishment of a socialist press in Germany posed new problems for Marx and Engels. Once they had demanded freedom to express their views without interference from autocratic governments. Now they asserted the right of the editors of socialist journals to determine the policy of their papers without interference from the party leadership. This may be illustrated by the controversy in which Engels was involved in 1885 when he denounced an attempt by the leaders of the German Social Democrat Party to exercise control over the editor of a party newspaper. The socialist deputies in the Reichstag claimed the right to determine the policy of *Der Sozialdemokrat* and Engels supported Bernstein, the editor, in rejecting their demands. *Der Sozialdemokrat* had criticised the attitude adopted by the socialist deputies in the Reichstag with regard to the Steamship Subsidy Bill and Bismarck's colonial policy. The deputies were incensed that Bernstein should presume to comment unfavourably upon their actions and they demanded the right to determine the policy of *Der Sozialdemokrat* in future. They claimed that normally the party executive should lay down the policy to be followed by the party newspaper. But since no executive committee could legally function at that time in Germany the socialist deputies argued that it was their duty to assume the functions of the executive. Bernstein resisted this attempt on the part of the socialist deputies to censor what appeared in the paper. Engels agreed with the stand taken by Bernstein. He wrote to Bebel that if the socialist deputies succeeded in gaining control over *Der Sozialdemokrat* it would be impossible for him in the future to defend the German Social Democrat Party "through thick and thin" as he had done in the past.[27] Bernstein refused to print a declaration of the socialist deputies putting forward their point of view. Liebknecht, one of the leaders of the Social Democrat Party, went to Zürich and persuaded Bernstein to print a modified version of the declaration. A few weeks later, however, the socialist deputies climbed down and gave up their claim to dictate the policy of *Der Sozialdemokrat*. In April 1885 Engels suggested that, to ensure independence of editorial policy, *Der Sozialdemokrat* should cease to be the official organ of the Social Democrat Party. His advice was taken in November 1886. It is clear from this incident that Engels believed that the party leadership had no right to try to exercise any control over the editorial policy of a socialist newspaper.

In 1891 Engels was even more directly involved in a controversy with German colleagues regarding the freedom of the socialist press. He wrote an article in *Die Neue Zeit* in which he printed a slightly shortened version of a memorandum by Marx, dated May 1875, criticising the Gotha programme of the recently united German Social Democrat Party.[28] The leaders of the party had long maintained silence concerning Marx's attack upon their programme, fearing that publication of his criticisms of the Lassallean wing of the party would endanger the somewhat fragile unity of the German Social Democrat Party.

But now that a new party programme was under discussion Engels considered that the time was ripe for socialists to be told what Marx had thought of the Gotha programme. The leaders of the Social Democrat Party – Bebel and Liebknecht in particular – were annoyed and alarmed that Engels should have made Marx's memorandum available for publication and that Kautsky should have printed it in *Die Neue Zeit*. Bebel attempted to prevent the publication of Engels' article and when it appeared he wrote "a furious letter" to Kautsky, the editor of *Die Neue Zeit*[29] and even threatened that, in the event of any similar indiscretion in the future, the journal might be taken over by the Party. Engels strongly resisted any claims by the leaders of the German Social Democrat Party to decide what should appear and what should not appear in a socialist journal. He wrote to Bebel: "If you introduce an Anti-Socialist Law in your own ranks are you any better than Puttkamer?"[30] Since Robert von Puttkamer, as Minister of the Interior in Prussia from 1881 to 1888, had been a leading supporter of the Anti-Socialist Law, Engels was administering a particularly sharp rebuke to a leader of the German socialists.

In the following year, in a letter to Bebel, Engels returned to the problem of who should determine the policy of a party newspaper. In his view the editor of an official party journal had a thankless task to perform. "Marx and I were always in agreement that we would *never* accept such a post. We would consider acting as editors only if a paper were financially independent even of the party." Engels warned Bebel that it would be unwise for the German Social Democrat Party to try to gain direct control over as many socialist newspapers as possible. He argued that

> there *must* be a Party press which is not *directly* responsible to the national party executive or even to the national conference. That means that socialist journals must be free – within the bounds of the Party programme and agreed Party strategy – to oppose particular party tactics. They should also be free – within decent limits – to criticise the programme itself and party strategy.[31]

As a lifelong freelance journalist Engels wanted to establish for socialist journalists the right to express their opinions freely, whether they were writing for independent papers or for journals financed and controlled by a socialist party.

NOTES

1. Fourteen of Engels' 29 articles were reprinted as a pamphlet entitled *Essays addressed to Volunteers* (1861). All the articles were reprinted in W.O. Henderson and W.H. Chaloner (eds.), *Engels as Military Critic* (1959).
2. F. Engels, *Notes on the War* (60 articles reprinted from the *Pall Mall Gazette*, 1870–1), edited by Friedrich Adler (1923).
3. *The Labour Standard* (London), May 7 to Aug. 6, 1881: reprinted in F. Engels, *The British Labour Movement* (1934).
4. F. Engels, "Zur Kritik der preußischen Pressgesetze" in the *Rheinische Zeitung*, July 14, 1842, reprinted in Marx–Engels, *Gesamtausgabe*, Part I, Vol. 2, pp.310–17 and *Marx–Engels Werke*, supplementary volume (1967), "Schriften bis 1844", Part 2, pp.271–8. The original manuscript is in the Cologne historical archives. The

article has been wrongly attributed to Marx: see Karl Marx–Friedrich Engels, *Pressefreiheit und Zensur* (1969), p.100.

5. Johann Jacoby, *Vier Fragen beantwortet von einem Ostpreußen* (1841).
6. This sentence appeared in Engels' manuscript but was deleted by the editor of the *Rheinische Zeitung*.
7. The royal Cabinet Order of Nov. 15, 1842 is printed in Marx–Engels, *Pressefreiheit und Zensur, op. cit.*, pp.109–10.
8. The article appeared in February 1843 in the first number of the Swiss periodical *Anekdota zur neuesten deutschen Philosophie und Publicistik* (ed. Arnold Ruge) and was reprinted by Hermann Becker in a collection of Marx's essays (1851).
9. Karl Marx, "Debatten über Pressefreiheit und Publikation der landständischen Verhandlungen" in the *Rheinische Zeitung*, May 6 and 19, 1842, reprinted in *Marx-Engels Werke*, Vol. 1, pp.33–77. The sixth Rhenish Provincial Assembly had met in Düsseldorf between May 23 and July 25, 1841.
10. Karl Marx, "Der preußische Pressegesetzentwurf" in the *Neue Rheinische Zeitung*, July 20, 1848, reprinted in Marx–Engels, *Pressefreiheit und Zensur, op. cit.*, p.160.
11. F. Engels, "Marx und die *Neue Rheinische Zeitung*" in *Der Sozialdemokrat*, March 13, 1884, reprinted in Karl Marx–Friedrich Engels, *Die Revolution von 1848: Auswahl aus der Neuen Rheinischen Zeitung* (1955), p.32.
12. Karl Marx, "An den Oberpräsidenten der Rheinprovinz von Schaper", Nov. 17, 1842 in Marx–Engels, *Pressefreiheit und Zensur, op. cit.*, p.111.
13. Karl Marx in the *Rheinische Zeitung*, Jan. 1, 1843. For Marx's controversy with the rival *Kölnische Zeitung* concerning the ban on the *Leipziger Allgemeine Zeitung* see his articles in the *Rheinische Zeitung*, Jan. 4, 10, and 13, 1843. For his attack on the *Rhein- und Mosel-Zeitung* see the *Rheinische Zeitung*, Jan. 16, 1843. These articles are reprinted in Marx–Engels, *Pressefreiheit und Zensur, op. cit.*, pp.126–36.
14. Karl Marx, "Randglossen zu den Anklagen des Ministerialreskripts" in Marx–Engels, *Pressefreiheit und Zensur, op. cit.*, pp.137–42.
15. *Marx–Engels Werke*, Vol. 1, p.200.
16. *Neue Rheinische Zeitung*, March 15, 1849 reprinted in Marx–Engels, *Pressefreiheit und Zensur, op. cit.*, pp.182–3.
17. Georg Weerth, *Leben und Taten des berühmten Ritters Schnapphahnski* (1849), reprinted in Georg Weerth, *Sämtliche Werke* (1957), Vol. IV, pp.285–489.
18. Karl Marx, "Der preußische Pressgesetzentwurf" in the *Neue Rheinische Zeitung*, July 20, 1848 reprinted in Marx–Engels, *Pressefreiheit und Zensur, op. cit.*, pp.160–2.
19. Karl Marx, "Der Hohenzollersche Pressegesetzentwurf" in the *Neue Rheinische Zeitung*, March 22, 1849 reprinted in Marx–Engels *Pressefreiheit und Zensur, op. cit.*, pp.184–91.
20. Karl Marx, "Zensur" in the *Neue Rheinische Zeitung*, March 15, 1849 and Marx–Engels, *Pressefreiheit und Zensur, op. cit.*, pp.182–3.
21. F. Engels, "Die Debatte über das Plakatgesetz" in the *Neue Rheinische Zeitung*, April 22, 1849 and Marx–Engels, *Pressefreiheit und Zensur, op. cit.*, pp.192–202.
22. *Neue Rheinische Zeitung*, Feb. 14, 1849 (speeches by Marx and Engels) reprinted in Marx–Engels, *Pressefreiheit und Zensur, op. cit.*, pp.163–81. See also Engels' introduction to *Karl Marx vor den Kölner Geschworenen* (1885), printed *ibid.*, pp.153–9.
23. F. Engels to Karl Marx, Sept. 13, 1870 in Marx–Engels, *Briefwechsel* (1950), IV, pp.462–3.
24. *Daily News*, Jan. 19, 1871.
25. Gustav Mayer, *Friedrich Engels* (1934), Vol. II, p.378.
26. *Der Sozialdemokrat*, Sept. 27, 1890.
27. F. Engels to A. Bebel, April 4, 1885 in W. Blumenberg (ed.), *August Bebels Briefwechsel mit Friedrich Engels* (1965), p.218.
28. Karl Marx, *Randglossen zum Programm der deutschen Arbeiterpartei* and Karl

Marx to Wilhelm Bracke, May 5, 1875 in Karl Marx and Friedrich Engels, *Briefwechsel mit Wilhelm Bracke, 1869–80* (1963), pp.45–70. Marx's memorandum was first published, with the omission of "a few sharp personal expressions and judgments" by Engels in an article entitled "Kritik des Gothaer Programmes" in *Die Neue Zeit*, Vol. IX, 1891, p.502: English translation – Karl Marx, *Critique of the Gotha Programme* (1971).

29. Karl Kautsky to F. Engels, Feb. 6, 1891 in B. Kautsky (ed.), *Friedrich Engels' Briefwechsel mit Karl Kautsky* (1955), p.273.
30. F. Engels to A. Bebel, May 1–2, 1891 in W. Blumenberg (ed.), *August Bebels Briefwechsel mit Friedrich Engels, op. cit.*, p.417.
31. F. Engels to A. Bebel, Nov. 19, 1892 in W. Blumenberg (ed.), *August Bebels Briefwechsel mit Friedrich Engels, op. cit.*, p.617. In the same letter Engels criticised party members who, at a recent national conference, had attacked Liebknecht for drawing too high a salary as editor of the official party newspaper *Vorwärts*.

5

MARX AND ENGELS ON
TRADE UNIONS

In view of the strength of modern trade unions in the western world and their relatively limited rôle in communist countries, an examination of the views of Marx and Engels on these organisations may not be without interest. Those who have discussed the attitude of Marx and Engels to labour movements in various countries have tended to examine workers' associations in general rather than trade unions in particular. But since organisations such as co-operative workshops and retail stores, friendly societies, and sports clubs have different aims and functions from trade unions it is desirable to examine the attitude of Marx and Engels towards trade unions alone.

Marx and Engels gave their full approval only to organisations such as the Communist League, which gave unqualified support to Marxist doctrines. They regarded other workers' political and industrial organisations with some suspicion. Their admiration for the Chartist movement – particularly its militant left wing – was tempered by disappointment at their failure to persuade any of its leaders to accept their doctrines. They praised those trade unions which were led by militant leaders who challenged the authority of employers by bringing their members out on strike. Such a policy was in accordance with Marx's views on the class struggle which would bring the capitalists to their knees and pave the way for the triumph of the proletariat. On the other hand Marx and Engels denounced trade unions which were led by men who believed that more could be achieved by negotiation than by industrial action. Marx and Engels condemned such unions for being content to try and secure the highest wages and the shortest hours that they could within the framework of the capitalist system.

Engels was quicker than Marx to appreciate the significance of the rôle of trade unions in the labour movement. On his first visit to

England as a young man in 1842–4 he realised that the unions were – with the Chartists – in the vanguard of the struggle to gain greater economic security and greater political power for the workers. At that time trade unionism in Britain was more fully developed than on the Continent. Trade unions were no longer illegal organisations, though some actions taken by unions to further their objectives did fall foul of the law. Although only a small proportion of the English workers were trade unionists, there were numerous small but active craft unions as well as regional associations of textile and other factory workers and a few large unions covering the whole country. The Miners' Association, established in 1841, was one of the most important of the national unions. It had about 100,000 members and it employed the able solicitor W.P. Roberts to safeguard the interests of miners involved in legal proceedings.[1]

In a discussion of working-class movements in his book on *The Condition of the Working Class in England* (1845) Engels gave a detailed description of the trade union movement in Britain and attacked contemporary economists, such as Andrew Ure, who denounced associations of workers. Engels considered that competition for markets between employers encouraged them to cut costs by paying very low wages. He thought that wage reductions could be successfully resisted only by the opposition of workers organised in trade unions. Engels admitted that, during a trade depression, the wages that manufacturers had been able to afford during a boom were bound to fall, but he declared that "the workers must protest both against a reduction in wages and also against the circumstances which make that reduction necessary". "They must assert that since they are human beings they do not propose to submit to the pressure of inexorable economic forces." "On the contrary they demand that economic forces should be adapted to suit *their* convenience."[2]

Engels considered that since workers were competing for a limited number of jobs, employers could maintain wages at a very low level. But if workers were united in trade unions they could reduce competition among themselves and secure higher wages. "Trade unions have proved to be so dangerous to the existing social order simply because they have – if only to a limited degree – firmly opposed that competition of workers among themselves, which is the very corner stone of modern society."[3] An assiduous reader of the *Northern Star*, Engels was both astonished and gratified at the number of strikes which were taking place when he lived in

Manchester in 1842–4. He regarded such industrial action as "a training ground for the industrial proletariat and a preparation for the great campaign which draws inevitably nearer".[4] He gave an account of a strike of the bricklayers employed by the Manchester building contractors Messrs Pauling and Henfrey in May 1843 – a strike which culminated in violence.[5] In another chapter of *The Condition of the Working Class in England* Engels described the grievances of the coalminers of Northumberland and Durham and their long but abortive strike in 1844.[6]

Two years later Marx commented on the rôle of trade unions in the labour movement. He agreed with "bourgeois economists" who had declared that if a trade union called out its members on strike the cost to the workers of the stoppage in lost wages might well be greater than any gains secured by an increase in wages, if the strike were successful. He agreed that industrial action by trade unionists encouraged manufacturers to instal new machines and labour-saving devices, which would lead to a reduction in wages. Marx also agreed with economists who had argued that if trade unions succeeded in raising wages so much that industrial profits in a particular country fell below the average profits elsewhere, there would be a slump, causing firms to go bankrupt and men to be laid off. If trade unions existed only to secure higher wages they were bound to fail because it was impossible to override "the laws of competition". But, in Marx's view, trade unions were not organisations which existed simply to bargain with employers on wages, hours and conditions of work. "They are the means by which the workers are able to unite to prepare the way for the overthrow of the present social order, which is based upon class conflicts." "From this point of view the workers are justified in laughing at clever bourgeois schoolmasters who tell them that workers must face casualties and financial losses in this social war."[7]

In the Communist Manifesto of 1848 Marx and Engels argued that the industrial revolution had created a new social class – the proletariat – which was oppressed by the middle classes.[8] The first reaction of the industrial workers had been to resort to violence, such as machine-breaking, but when considerable numbers of workers were brought together in large factories in new manu-facturing towns it was possible for them to become organised in trade unions and to bring pressure to bear upon their employers by going on strike. Marx and Engels believed that trade unions could gain only temporary successes in their attempts to secure higher wages or shorter hours. But the growth of trade unions was significant because by working together in these associations the workers could recognise that they formed a social group which could overthrow its oppressors only by engaging actively in the class struggle. There would be setbacks because workers competed among themselves for available jobs but in the end they would triumph. The achievement of the English workers in securing the passing of the Ten Hours Bill had shown that united action could secure substantial concessions from the middle classes.[9]

In the 1850s Marx and Engels showed little interest in the development of trade unions in England. They maintained some contact with the declining Chartist movement but they were disappointed that the English workers appeared to have lost the revolutionary fervour that they had shown in the 1840s. Marx was asked to go to Manchester in 1854 to attend a conference of trade unionists – a "Parliament of Labour" – as an honorary delegate. This conference had been called by the Chartist leader Ernest Jones to discuss means of aiding the power-loom weavers of Preston whose long and bitter strike had been supported by contributions from cotton operatives throughout Lancashire. Marx declined the invitation but sent his cordial greetings to the delegates in a letter in which he declared that their meeting would mark "a new epoch in the history of the world".[10] Yet Marx did not have a word to say either about the strike in Preston or about the wave of industrial disputes from which English industry suffered at that time.[11]

Important changes in the trade union movement occurred in England in the 1860s. First, trades councils were set up in a number of manufacturing towns between 1858 and 1867. Representatives of various trade unions in a particular district met regularly to discuss common problems and to support workers involved in industrial disputes. One of the most important was the London Trades Council, founded in 1860. Secondly, the establishment of the Amalgamated Society of Engineers in 1852 marked "a turning point in the history of the trade union movement."[12] This amalgamation of formerly independent regional unions levied a high subscription (a shilling a week) on its members and accumulated funds which enabled it to pay generous friendly society benefits as well as strike pay. But the engineers sought to avoid strikes and to settle disputes by negotiations with employers. They pursued a less militant policy than some of the smaller provincial unions. Thirdly, there was a shift in the centre of gravity of the trade union movement from the north of England to London. In the first half of the nineteenth century the largest and most influential unions had been

organised by the coalminers and various textile workers in the
northern industrial towns. But by the 1860s some of the newly
established amalgamated national societies, such as the engineers,
the ironfounders, and the carpenters and joiners had their head
offices in London. The officials of these unions (William Allen,
Daniel Guile, and Robert Applegarth) and the officials of some
of the London trade unions (such as George Odger and Edwin
Coulson) came to dominate the London Trades Council. The
"junta" – as the Webbs called it – could be regarded as "an informal
cabinet of the trade union world".[13]

Members of the Junta and the London Trades Council played a
leading part in setting up the International Working Men's Association in 1864. Soon after its establishment Marx became the most
influential member of its General Council. At that time he seems to
have known little of the trade union leaders with whom he was
to be closely associated. He thought that Odger was the president
instead of the secretary of the London Trades Council and that the
carpenter W.R. Cremer was the secretary of the masons' union.[14]
Although he recognised that those who had organised the meeting
that set up the International were "the actual labour kings of
London"[15] he did not fully appreciate the strength of the trade
unions in England. In the inaugural address of the International
Marx praised the workers' co-operative workshops that had been
set up in England and paid a tribute to the achievements of the
Chartists in the past, but he had nothing to say concerning the rôle of
the trade unions in the labour movement. It was only after he had sat
on the General Council of the International with some of the
leading English trade unionists that he began to understand the part
played by the unions in the labour movement. Marx's trade-union
colleagues on the General Council included Robert Applegarth,[16]
W.R. Cremer,[17] George Odger,[18] George Howell,[19] John Hales,[20]
Robert Hartwell,[21] Benjamin Lucraft,[22] and Robert Shaw.[23]

Marx was faced with the problem of holding together an international association which included members holding very different
views. It was no easy matter at one and the same time to satisfy
supporters of Proudhon in France, Mazzini in Italy, Becker in
Switzerland, Schweitzer in Germany and trade union leaders in
England. To secure the support of English trade union leaders Marx
was prepared to see the General Council of the International
involved in industrial disputes. In 1866 when the journeymen tailors
of London and Edinburgh went on strike for higher wages the
International intervened, with some success, to stop the masters

from recruiting blackleg labour on the Continent. Again in 1871 when there was a prolonged strike of engineers and construction workers in Newcastle-upon-Tyne to secure a shorter working day, the International was associated with the Amalgamated Society of Engineers in sending James Cohn to the Continent to persuade foreign workers not to take the jobs of strikers in Newcastle. The International also passed on to strikers on the Continent funds raised by English workers for their support.[24] It denounced the use of troops to suppress a strike at the Cockerill ironworks at Seraing in 1869 and held the Belgian government responsible for the bloodshed that followed.[25] And in the next year, when some 3,000 building workers in Geneva were locked out by their employers, the International called upon "all honest working men and women, throughout the civilised world, to assist both by moral and material means, the Geneva building trades in their just struggle against capitalist despotism".[26] In 1871 a conference of the International, held in London, urged trade unions in different countries to co-operate as closely as possible. A resolution was passed inviting the General Council

> to assist, as has been done hitherto, the growing tendency of the trades unions of the different countries to enter into relations with the unions of the same trade in all other countries. The efficiency of its action as the international agent of communication between the national trades societies will essentially depend upon the assistance given by these same societies to the General Labour Statistics pursued by the International.[27]

When the coalminers in the Ruhr went on strike in 1872 Marx encouraged them to hold out for higher wages and 8-hour shifts. He warned them not to be intimidated by the Ruhr industrialists who had threatened to import coal from England. Marx declared that this was an empty threat since at that time English coal was expensive and in short supply.[28]

In 1866 Marx drew up some instructions for the delegates of the General Council who were attending the first congress of the International in Geneva. He urged the delegates to demand a shorter working day and a reduction in the hours worked by children and young people. He claimed that the International had already been successful in opposing "the intrigues of capitalists [who are] always ready, in cases of strikes and lockouts, to misuse the foreign workman as a tool against the native workmen". He repeated the advice to trade unionists which he had given to the General Council in the previous year.[29] Marx declared that trade unionists had "not yet fully understood their power of acting against the system of wage slavery itself. They therefore kept too much aloof from general social and political movements." He hoped that in future trade unions would "learn to act deliberately as organising centres of the working class in the broad interest of its *complete emancipation*". "They must aid every social and political movement tending in that direction."[30] The delegates attending the Geneva conference of the International declared that "the furtherance and formation of trade unions is the chief task of the working class, both at the present time and in the immediate future."[31]

In 1870 Marx referred to the trade union movement in England as "this great lever of proletarian revolution"[32] and he declared that "to hasten the social revolution in England is the most important object of the International Working Men's Association."[33] In the following year Marx argued that

> the attempt in a particular factory or even in a particular trade, to force a shorter working day out of the individual capitalists by strikes etc. is a purely economic movement. The movement to force through an eight-hour-*law* etc, however, is a *political* movement. And in this way out of the separate economic movements of the workers there grows up everywhere a *political* movement, that is to say a movement of the *class*, with the object of achieving its interests in a general form, in a form possessing general, socially coercive force.[34]

Marx hoped that by encouraging the General Council to oppose the use of foreign blacklegs by English employers he could gain the confidence of trade-union leaders and secure their support for his plans for a workers' revolution to overthrow the capitalist system. In 1870 he declared that "England alone can serve as the *lever* for a serious *economic* revolution ... It is the only country where the class struggle and organisation by *trade unions* have *acquired* a certain degree of maturity and universality".[35] Engels probably agreed with Marx that the support of a militant trade-union movement would be necessary to ensure the success of a workers' rising in England. But he thought that in Germany the trade unions – then still in a very early stage of development – had no rôle to play in any future revolution. He declared that Johann Philipp Becker had taken leave of his senses when he suggested that in Germany the trade unions were the only really effective workers' organisations.[36]

There were, however, as Marx himself appreciated, definite limits to his influence over the trade union leaders in london. At one time, for example, he was hampered by the activities of George Potter, the editor and publisher of the weekly journal *The Beehive*, which was the organ both of the London trade unions and of the First International. Marx denounced Potter as "a rat of a man" and tried to gain control of *The Beehive* by persuading Engels and other friends to buy shares in the company which owned the paper.[37]

Although, for a time, Marx dominated the General Council of the First International his efforts to extend his influence over the leaders of the trade unions met with little success. The unions affiliated to the International were mainly small London societies of skilled craftsmen. The only large union to join the International was the Operative Society of Bricklayers, Carpenters and Joiners. The big battalions in the provinces – the coalminers, the textile workers, and the engineers – held aloof. In the 1860s there were approximately 1,500,000 trade unionists in the United Kingdom but only about 50,000 of them belonged to unions affiliated to the International. In 1872 Henry Bruce, the Home Secretary, estimated that the International had only 8,000 members in England. In his view "the revolutionary designs which form part of the Society's programme are believed to express the opinion of the foreign members rather than those of the British workmen whose attention is turned chiefly to questions affecting wages".[38] And the financial support which the International received from English trade unions was insignificant. Marx was also mistaken in supposing that he could make much progress in persuading the trade unionists on the General Council of the International to accept his brand of socialism. They gave him a courteous hearing when he gave them a lecture on "Wages, Price and Profit" in 1865 but they were not converted to his economic doctrines.[39]

Meanwhile Engels could give Marx little help in running the International since so long as he was a partner in the cotton firm of Ermen and Engels in Manchester he could not openly avow his socialist opinions and could take no active part in politics. In 1865 he sent Marx £5 to buy shares in *The Beehive*[40] and in 1869 he wrote a report on the miners' gilds in the coalfields of Saxony for submission to the General Council of the International. Engels explained that these gilds were different from English trade unions since they were financed jointly by the coalowners and the miners. He declared that these associations would have to rely solely upon the contributions of the workers if they were to develop into genuine trade unions.

"Only thus can they become trade unions which protect individual workers from the tyranny of individual masters."[41]

Engels retired from business in 1869 and settled in London in the following year. He was elected to the General Council of the International and became its corresponding secretary for Spain and Italy. But he undid much of Marx's work in establishing good relations with the leaders of the English trade unions on the General Council. Engels always found it difficult to establish a satisfactory personal relationship with workers and he was disappointed at the lack of militancy on the part of many English trade unions.

The breach between Marx and the English trade-union leaders came as a result of Marx's enthusiastic support for the Paris Commune. In 1871 he wrote an address in *The Civil War in France* which was approved by the General Council in May. But Odger and Lucraft repudiated Marx's views and resigned from the General Council. Shortly afterwards Engels criticised the English workers for their failure to help the refugees who had fled from France after the fall of the Commune. He told the General Council in August 1871 that "the working class in England had behaved in a disgraceful manner: though the men of Paris had risked their lives, the working men of England had made no effort either to sympathise with them or to assist them."[42] Then in November Engels complained that John Hales, the secretary of the General Council, had compiled inaccurate minutes of the Council's proceedings. Hales resigned in June 1872.[43] Shortly afterwards he complained that the General Council was now "filled with distrust, mistrust, and suspicion, and possessed nothing of an international spirit."[44]

In July 1872 a recently established council of the English branches of the International held its first meeting in Nottingham and decided to correspond with foreign federal councils directly and not through the General Council. The founding of an independent English Federal Council of the International still further weakened Marx's precarious influence over the labour movement in England. The period of collaboration between Marx and the English trade-union leaders in the General Council had come to an end. Engels recognised this. He admitted that things were "shockingly bad in the movement here – worse than they ever were, as is to be expected with such industrial prosperity."[45]

When the First International collapsed Marx retired from active politics. Engels explained that while Marx was now writing "his great basic work" he had assumed responsibility for "the fight against opposing views."[46] Both Marx and Engels had lost interest in the English trade unions. In 1879 Engels told Bernstein that it was not worth while appointing a correspondent to write about English trade union affairs in a new German socialist journal because "at the moment no genuine labour movement in the continental sense exists in England". "Industrial action has been the ultimate aim of the trade unions. Indeed since they specifically ban participation in politics by their rules, as a matter of principle, they cannot promote any activity in the interests of the workers as a social class."[47]

On the other hand Marx and Engels had high hopes of the early trade-union movement in Germany. Trade unions were developing in Germany in the 1870s in quite a different way from the old established English unions. While English unions at that time held aloof from politics, the three main types of German unions were each linked with a political party – the Free Unions with the Social Democrat Party, the Christian Unions with the Catholic Centre Party, and the Hirsch-Duncker unions with the Progressive Party. There were also a few "Yellow Unions", promoted and subsidised by employers. The socialist unions had by far the largest membership and it is not surprising that Marx and Engels should have realised that in future they might play an important part in the German labour movement.[48]

In 1875 when the two German socialist parties united to form the Social Democrat Party Engels complained that its programme ignored the very existence of trade unions. He declared that

> no mention has been made of the organisation of the workers as a class by the establishment of trade unions. And this is very important since trade unions are the true class associations of the proletariat. Trade unions are a training ground for the workers and it is as trade unionists that they are engaged in daily struggles with the capitalists. And even the worst reaction – as in Paris today – is simply not capable of crushing the unions. In view of the importance which trade unions have attained in Germany I think that it is absolutely necessary that they should be mentioned in the Programme and that a place should be found for them in the Party's organisation.[49]

That Marx showed some interest in the early trade unions in France can be seen from a questionnaire which he prepared for a French socialist journal in 1880. He hoped that the answers to the questionnaire would provide information concerning the condition of the French workers at that time. The questionnaire included questions on the existence of trade unions (which Marx called "resistance associations") and the frequency of strikes and sympathetic strikes in different industries.[50]

Only two years after he had declared that the labour movement in England was in a moribund state, Engels sensed that the workers were poised for a new campaign for better wages and greater political power. In 1881 he resumed contact with the trade unions by writing leading articles for the weekly *Labour Standard*, edited by George Shipton, secretary of the London Trades Council. Engels praised the work of the trade unions since the repeal of the Combination Laws, declaring that their ability to secure better pay and working conditions for their members could be seen by comparing the situation of trade unionists with that of workers without any organisation to protect their interests. He considered the English trade unions to be more powerful than any working-class organisation abroad. "A few large trade unions, comprising between one and two millions of working men, and backed by the smaller or local unions, represent a power which has to be taken into account by any government of the ruling class, be it Whig or Tory."

Engels repeated the advice given by Marx to trade unionists in the days of the First International, urging them not merely to bargain with employers on wages and hours but to become "the advance guard of the working class". As successors of the Chartists they should establish "a political organisation of the working class as a whole". Engels regretted that, although workers in the towns had been enfranchised, they had not sent any representatives of their own class to Parliament. "It is not in the nature of things that the working class of England should possess the power of sending 40 or 50 working men to Parliament and yet be satisfied for ever to be represented by capitalists or their clerks, such as lawyers, editors etc.".[1] Engels soon ceased to contribute to the *Labour Standard*. His leading articles urged trade unionists to establish a political party to look after their interests in Parliament but in the rest of the paper Shipton was advocating much more moderate policies. Once more Engels had found himself unable to collaborate with English trade-union leaders.

In the 1880s the labour movement made striking progress in England, the most significant developments being a "sudden emergence of a socialist movement in England"[52] – as Engels put it – and the founding of trade unions of unskilled workers. The establishment of the Social Democratic Federation, the Socialist League, and the Fabian Society were the first attempts since Robert Owen's day to preach the gospel of socialism in England. Engels did not join any of these organisations but he kept in touch with them through Marx's daughter Eleanor and her friend Dr. Aveling. Engels had a poor opinion of "the various socialist cliques" and the English socialists in turn held aloof from Engels and ignored his writings.[53] Engels denounced the supporters of the Social Democratic Federation as "a crew of literary fellows, political careerists, and adventurers"[54] and he regarded their leader H.M. Hyndman as a jingoist, a racialist, and a careerist. He dismissed the leaders of the Socialist League – who broke away from Hyndman's society in 1884 – as "faddists and emotional socialists"[55] while the Fabians were "a dilettante lot of egregiously conceited mutual admirers".[56] Engels considered that none of these groups could hope to become a genuine socialist party with a marxist programme.

On the other hand Engels considered that the labour movement had taken a great step forward when strikes in London of match girls, gas workers, and dockers paved the way for the establishment of militant unions of unskilled workers. Eleanor Marx helped to set up the National Union of Gas Workers and General Labourers and assisted at the offices of the strike committee during the great dock strike of 1889. In the following year Eleanor Marx and Dr. Aveling supported a successful strike of gas workers in Leeds. Engels himself took no part in these activities but he helped Eleanor and Aveling with money and good advice. He believed that the movement for the establishment of a legal eight-hour day would promote the workers' cause more effectively than the socialist parties. Aveling was elected chairman of the committee, which organised a May Day demonstration in Hyde Park in 1890 in favour of an eight-hour day. Engels attended the demonstration which he regarded as a great success. He hoped that the Legal Eight Hours and International Labour League would become the nucleus of a new English socialist party dedicated to the propagation of Marx's doctrines. But this was not to be. Aveling was hardly cut out to become the leader of a new socialist party. He was a good speaker and organiser of demonstrations but he had neither the personality nor the experience to rise to the top in politics. Above all his bad character – he was a swindler and a seducer – made him quite unacceptable as a party leader.

Engels was disappointed at both the slow progress of socialism in England and the failure of the workers to establish their own political party, but he rejoiced at the militancy of the new trade unions of unskilled and semi-skilled workers. In 1892 he wrote that the East End of London was no longer the stagnant pool it was six years ago. It has shaken off its torpid despair, has returned to life, and has become the home of what is called the "New Unionism", that is to say, the organisation of the great mass of "unskilled" workers ... We see now these new unions taking the lead of the working class movement generally, and more and more taking in tow the rich and proud "old" unions ... And for all the faults committed in the past, present, and future, the revival of the East End of London remains one of the greatest and most fruitful facts of this *fin du siècle*, and glad and proud I am to have lived to see it.[57]

Engels considered that there were significant similarities between the labour movements in England and in the United States in the 1880s. In both countries the socialists had failed to form a party which could challenge the two major established political parties. In both countries the workers established strong unions which neither employers nor governments could ignore. In 1887 Engels discussed the significance of the Knights of Labour for the working classes in the United States. He wrote that

the Knights of Labour are the first national organisation created by the American working class as a whole; whatever be their origin and history, whatever their shortcomings and little absurdities, whatever their platform and their constitution, here they are, the work of practically the whole class of American wage-workers, the only national bond that holds them together, that makes their strength felt to themselves not less than to their enemies, and that fills them with the proud hope of future victories.[58]

Three years later Engels declared that a mass movement of the proletariat in the United States must start with the expansion of trade unions.[59]

Marx and Engels recognised the significant part played by trade unions in the labour movement in industrialised countries, though they were only occasionally involved directly in trade union affairs. They criticised the old established English unions of skilled workers which, in their view, accepted the existing capitalist system and were content to secure the highest wages and the lowest hours that they could. These unions favoured negotiations with their employers or arbitration of disputes, rather than industrial action. They preferred to use their funds to pay friendly society benefits rather than to support strikes. Moreover many of these unions adopted restrictive practices and would accept as members only those who had served a recognised apprenticeship. On the other hand Engels welcomed the founding of new unions of unskilled workers in England, which were more militant than the old unions. Marx and Engels were particularly pleased with the "free unions" in Germany because they were closely linked with the Social Democrat Party. The true function of trade unions, according to Marx and Engels, was to become the nucleus of a political party which would eventually pave the way for the overthrow of capitalism and the establishment of a socialist party.

NOTES

1. S. and B. Webb, *The History of Trade Unionism* (edn. of 1919), p.182.
2. F. Engels, *The Condition of the Working Class in England* (trans. and ed. W.O. Henderson and W.H. Chaloner, 1958 and 1971), p.147.
3. F. Engels, *op. cit.*, p.248.
4. F. Engels, *op. cit.*, p.254.
5. F. Engels, *op. cit.*, pp.256–7. In an article published in *Das Westfälische Dampfboot*, January and February 1846 (reprinted in *Gesamtausgabe*, Part I, Vol. 4, 1932, pp.393–405) Engels described a strike in 1844 by carpenters and joiners employed by Pauling and Henfrey.
6. F. Engels, *op. cit.*, pp.287–93.
7. Karl Marx, "Arbeitslohn" (Dec. 1847), manuscript printed in *Gesamtausgabe*, Part I, Vol. 6, pp.470–1 and in *Karl Marx und Friedrich Engels über die Gewerkschaften* (1953), pp.73–4. See also Karl Marx, *Misère de la philosophie* (1847).
8. Karl Marx–Friedrich Engels, *Manifest der Kommunistischen Partei*, 1848 (1957), pp.16–17.
9. Engels discussed the Ten Hours Bill in an article in the *Neue Rheinische Zeitung. Politisch-ökonomische Revue*, 1850, No. 4 (reprinted, 1955), pp.180–6.
10. Karl Marx's letter to the Labour Parliament appeared in the *People's Paper*, March 18, 1854: reprinted in Karl Marx and F. Engels, *On Britain* (1953), pp.402–3.
11. The Lancashire millowners, commenting on the Preston strike of 1854, complained that "the pretensions of Trades' Unions have reached a point which demands the most peremptory and effectual resistance ... The disease of the industrial organisation becomes infectious and epidemic. Miners, shipwrights, sailors, carpenters, engineers, porters, railway servants, lightermen, dock labourers, cutlers, factory operatives have struck within the year" (*The Master Spinners and Manufacturers Defence Fund: Report* ... (1854), p.21).
12. S. and B. Webb, *The History of Trade Unionism, op. cit.*, p.217.
13. S. and B. Webb, *op. cit.*, p.245.
14. Karl Marx to F. Engels, Nov. 4, 1864 in *Gesamtausgabe*, Part III, Vol. 3, pp.194–9.
15. Karl Marx to J. Weydemeyer, Nov. 29, 1864 in Karl Marx and F. Engels, *Letters to Americans 1848–95* (1963), p.65.
16. Robert Applegarth was secretary of the Amalgamated Society of Carpenters and Joiners and a member of the London Trades Council. See A.W. Humphrey, *The Life of Robert Applegarth* (1915).
17. W.R. Cremer was one of the founders of the Amalgamated Society of Carpenters and Joiners and the first general secretary of the General Council of the Working

Men's International Association (1864–66).

18. George Odger was a leading member of a small union of makers of ladies' shoes and secretary of the London Trades Council.
19. George Howell was secretary of the London Trades Council, 1861–2.
20. John Hales was secretary of the First International, 1871–2.
21. Robert Hartwell was one of the editors of *The Beehive*.
22. Benjamin Lucraft, a furniture-maker, was a member of the General Council of the First International (1864–71).
23. Robert Shaw, house painter, was a member of the General Council of the First International from 1864 until his death in 1869.
24. For the intervention of the First International in industrial disputes see an article by E.S. Beesly in the *Fortnightly Review*, November, 1870.
25. Karl Marx, *The Belgian Massacres. To the Workmen of Europe and the United States* (leaflet published in London in 1869). The address was approved by the General Council of the First International on May 4, 1869. It has been reprinted in *The General Council of the First International: Minutes* (1868–70), Vol. 3, pp.312–18.
26. Karl Marx, *The Lock-out of the Building Trades at Geneva* (leaflet published in 1870): approved by the General Council of the First International July 5, 1870: reprinted in *The General Council of the First International: Minutes, op. cit.*, Vol. 3, pp.369–71. There had been an earlier strike of building workers in Geneva in March and April 1868. On this occasion Graglia, an envoy of the building workers, had not been able to secure any help from London trade unionists: see J. Guillaume, *L'Internationale: Documents et Souvenirs (1864–1878)* (1905: reprinted 1969), Vol. I, p.63.
27. *Resolutions of the Conference of Delegates of the International Working Men's Association* (assembled at London from 17th to 23rd Sept. 1871): reprinted in *The General Council of the First International: Minutes* (1870–1), Vol. 4, p.443.
28. Karl Marx in *Der Volksstaat*, July 27, 1872, reprinted in *Karl Marx und Friedrich Engels über die Gewerkschaften, op. cit.*, pp.177–80.
29. Karl Marx, *Wages, Price, and Profit*, 1865 (1970). Marx concluded this lecture by stating that trade unions "fail generally from limiting themselves to a guerilla war against the effects of the existing system, instead of simultaneously trying to change it, instead of using their organised forces as a level for the final emancipation of the working class, that is to say, the ultimate abolition of the wages system" (p.55).
30. *The General Council of the First International: Minutes*, Vol. 1 (1864–66), pp.348–9.
31. Helga Grebing, *The History of the German Labour Movement* (1969), p.68.
32. Karl Marx, "The General Council of the Working Men's International Association to the Federal Council of Romance Switzerland" (Jan. 1, 1870) in *The General Council of the First International: Minutes*, Vol. 3 (1868–70), pp.401–2.
33. Karl Marx to Siegfried Meyer and August Vogt, April 9, 1870 in *Marx–Engels Werke*, Vol. 32, p.665: English translation in Karl Marx and F. Engels, *On Britain* (1953), p.507.
34. Karl Marx to Friedrich Bolte, Nov. 23, 1871 in Karl Marx and F. Engels, *Letters to Americans, 1848–95* (1963), pp.93–4.
35. Karl Marx, "The General Council of the Working Men's International Association to the Federal Council of Romance Switzerland" (Jan. 1, 1870) in *The General Council of the First International: Minutes*, Vol. 3 (1868–70), pp.401–2.
36. F. Engels to Karl Marx, July 30, 1869. In the previous year Marx and Engels had opposed Schweitzer's proposal to set up trade unions in Germany: Karl Marx to F. Engels, Sept. 19, 1868 and F. Engels to Karl Marx, Sept. 21, 1868; and Marx to Schweitzer, Oct. 13, 1868 in *Karl Marx und Friedrich Engels über die Gewerkschaften* (1953), pp.140–3.
37. Karl Marx to F. Engels, Dec. 2, 1864 and May 9, 1865.
38. Lord Granville to Mr. Layard in *Correspondence with the Spanish Government*

    respecting the International Association of Workmen (Parliamentary Papers, 1872, LXX, p.720).

39. Karl Marx, *Wages, Price and Profit, op. cit.*, p.55.
40. F. Engels to Karl Marx, May 12, 1865.
41. F. Engels, "Report on the Miners' Gilds in the Coalfields of Saxony" in *The General Council of the First International: Minutes*, Vol. 3, 1868–70, pp.390–7. Engels' report was based upon information supplied by the Miners of Lugau, Nieder-Wurschnitz and Oelsnitz when they applied to join the International. Marx wrote to Engels on Feb. 13, 1869: "These brave miners from Lugau are the first in Germany to make direct contact with us, and we must publicly support them".
42. *The General Council of the First International: Minutes*, Vol. 4 (1870–1), Aug. 8, 1871, p.256.
43. *Ibid.*, Vol. 5 (1871–2), June 11, 1872, p.219.
44. *Ibid.*, Vol. 5 (1871–2), July 9, 1872, p.251.
45. F. Engels to A. Hepner, Dec. 20, 1872 in Karl Marx and F. Engels, *Letters to Americans, 1848–95, op. cit.*, p.112.
46. F. Engels (C.P. Dutt, ed.), *The Housing Question* (1872) p.10.
47. F. Engels to E. Bernstein, June 17, 1879 in Karl Marx and F. Engels, *On Britain, op. cit.*, p.510.
48. Under the Anti-Socialist Law of 1878 21 socialist trade unions were banned in Germany.
49. F. Engels to August Bebel, March 18, 1875 in Werner Blumenberg, ed., *August Bebels Briefwechsel mit Friedrich Engels* (1965), p.31.
50. *La Revue Socialiste*, April 20, 1880: German translation in *Karl Marx und Friedrich Engels über die Gewerkschaften, op. cit.*, p.206.
51. F. Engels, *The British Labour Movement* (articles in *The Labour Standard*, 1881: reprinted 1934), pp.12–21.
52. F. Engels to August Bebel, Jan. 18, 1884 in W. Blumenberg, *op. cit.*, p.172 and Karl Marx and F. Engels, *On Britain, op. cit.*, p.517.
53. F. Engels to Mrs Wischnewtzky, May 2, 1885 in Karl Marx and F. Engels, *Letters to Americans, 1848–95, op. cit.*, p.200.
54. F. Engels to August Bebel, Oct. 28, 1885 in W. Blumenberg, *op. cit.*, p.240.
55. F. Engels to F.A. Sorge, Sept. 16, 1886 in Karl Marx and F. Engels, *Letters to Americans, 1848–95, op. cit.*, p.162.
56. F. Engels to Laura Lafargue, Oct. 11, 1887 in *F. Engels–Paul and Laura Lafargue: Correspondence* (1960), Vol. 2, p.65.
57. F. Engels, *The Condition of the Working Class in England* (1845), *op. cit.*, Appendix III: preface to the English edition of 1892, pp.370–1.
58. F. Engels, *ibid.*, Appendix II: preface to the American edition of 1887, p.357.
59. F. Engels to F.A. Sorge, Feb. 8, 1890 in Karl Marx and F. Engels, *Letters to Americans, 1848–95, op. cit.*, p.225.

6

MARX AND ENGELS
AND RACIALISM

While scholars on the Continent have long been aware of the fact that Karl Marx held anti-semitic views, the same cannot generally be said of their colleagues in England and America. Marx was a Jew and when he was growing up in Trier the Jews, although not persecuted, were treated as second-class citizens and excluded from certain professions. No Jew could hold a commission in the Prussian army or practise at the bar. To continue as a member of the legal profession Marx's father became a Christian and was baptised by a Lutheran army chaplain. As boy Marx realised that he was different from his fellows. He had been baptised, but he was a Jew by race and suffered from the anti-semitism prevalent in Germany in his day. His reaction to the situation was an extraordinary one. He ranged himself with the anti-semites and denounced his own race in a most violent fashion.[1]

His attitude towards the Jews was made clear in two articles which he wrote in 1843 at the age of 25. They were reviews of a book and an article by Bruno Bauer on the Jewish question and they appeared in the *Deutsch–Französische Jahrbücher*, published in Paris in 1844.[2] Marx regarded capitalism, as operated by the middle classes, as inherently evil and he argued that Jewish money-making activities lay at the very heart of the obnoxious capitalist system. The following extracts from Marx's articles indicate his point of view on the Jewish question in his day.

What is the worldly raison d'être of Jewry (Judaism)? The practical necessary of Jewry is self-interest. What is the worldly religion of the Jews? It is the petty haggling of the hawker. What is his worldly God? It is money.

So in Jewry we recognise a contemporary universal anti-social phenomenon, which has reached its present pitch through a process of historical development in which the Jews have zealously co-operated. And this evil anti-social aspect of Jewry has grown to a stage at which it must necessarily collapse.

The Jews have emancipated themselves in a Jewish fashion. Not only have they mastered the power of money but — with or without the Jews — money has become a world power. The Jews have emancipated themselves by turning Christians into Jews.

Money is the most zealous God of Israel and no other God can compete with him. Money debases all human Gods and turns them into goods. Money is the universal value of everything.

The God of the Jews has become secularised and has become a World God. The bill of exchange is the real God of the Jews.

Jewry reaches its climax in the consummation of bourgeois society — and bourgeois society has reached its highest point in the Christian world.

In 1845 in *The Holy Family* Marx claimed that in his articles in the *Deutsch–Französische Jahrbücher* he had "proved that the task of abolishing the essence of Jewry is in truth the task of abolishing Jewry in civil society, abolishing the inhumanity of today's practice of life, the summit of which is the money system".[3] In 1849 an article in the *Neue Rheinische Zeitung*, of which Marx was the editor, criticised the notion that Jews living in Prussia's Polish provinces should be regarded as Germans. The article declared that these Jews were "the filthiest of all races". "Neither by speech nor by descent — but only by their greed for profit — can they be looked upon as relatives of the Germans in Frankfurt."[4] Robert Payne has remarked that "this solution of the Jewish question was not very different from Adolf Hitler's, for it involved the liquidation of Judaism".[5]

There are numerous uncomplimentary references to Jews in Karl Marx's letters to his close friend Friedrich Engels in the 1850s and 1860s. At that time Marx was living in London and his earnings as a free-lance journalist — a regular contributor to the *New York Daily Tribune* — were quite insufficient for his needs. Engels, then employed as a clerk by the firm of Ermen and Engels in Manchester, sent him small remittances whenever he could. Even so Marx failed to make ends meet and — when there was nothing more to pledge at the pawnbrokers — he borrowed money from anyone who would lend it. He had many dealings with Jewish financial agents in the City of London. The Bambergers (father and son),[6] Stiefel and Spielmann were German Jews whose names frequently crop up in the Marx–Engels correspondence. Marx made use of the Jews to raise small loans and to discount bills of exchange received from Dana (editor of the *New York Daily Tribune*) in advance payment for articles which Marx had agreed to write. Marx complained bitterly that the Jews would not discount his bills until confirmation from Dana had been received[7] and he was furious when they pressed him to honour debts due for repayment. Marx showed his contempt by always referring to them as "Jew (or little Jew) Bamberger" and "Jew Spielmann" or by imitating the nasal twang characteristic of the way in which some Jews from eastern Europe spoke German.[8] Yet Marx had cause to regret the day when the Bambergers were not in business in London any more and were no longer available to discount his bills of exchange. In 1859 he wrote to Engels: "it is the devil of a nuisance that I have no Bamberger in London any more."[9]

Marx's anti-semitism may be illustrated by examining his attitude towards Lassalle, who was a Jew from Breslau in Silesia. As a young man Lassalle had led the workers of Düsseldorf during the revolution of 1848. But he had never been a member of the Communist League, since his application to join the Cologne branch had been turned down, and he had taken no part in the risings in Germany in 1849 in support of the Frankfurt constitution, since he had been in gaol at that time. Consequently in the 1850s, while nearly all the former supporters of the revolution were either in prison or in exile, Lassalle was able to live in Düsseldorf, without being unduly molested by the authorities. It was to Marx's advantage to keep in touch with Lassalle, who gave him news of the underground workers' movement in the Rhineland. And through his aristocratic connections – he was a close friend of the Countess of Hatzfeld – he was sometimes able to provide Marx with useful political information which he could use in articles contributed to the *New York Daily Tribune* and *Die Presse*. But while Marx regarded himself as the head of a great political movement who should be obeyed by his followers, Lassalle declined to be a mere disciple and was determined to be a leader of the German workers in his own right.

The correspondence between Marx and Lassalle[10] suggests that the two men were colleagues who – despite certain differences of opinion – were collaborating to achieve a common aim. But the letters exchanged between Marx and Engels tell a very different story. Here Marx showed his contempt for the Jew who presumed to have opinions and ambitions of his own. When Lassalle was Marx's guest in London in 1862 Marx wrote to Engels:

> It is now perfectly clear to me that, as the shape of his head and the growth of his hair indicate, he is descended from the negroes who joined in the flight of Moses from Egypt (unless his mother or grandmother on the father's side was crossed with a nigger). Now this union of Jewishness to Germanness on a negro basis was bound to produce an extraordinary hybrid. The importunity of the fellow is also niggerlike.[11]

Marx referred to his guest as a "Jewish nigger" who was "completely deranged." He frequently used derogatory epithets when writing about Lassalle, such as "Itzig" (Ikey), "Ephraim Gescheit" and "Judel Braun." And Marx's wife, in a letter to Engels, called Lassalle "the little Berlin Jew."[12]

After Lassalle's death in 1864 there are fewer uncomplimentary remarks about Jews in the Marx–Engels correspondence than before. In that year Engels became a partner in the firm of Ermen and Engels and from 1867 onwards he paid Marx an annual allowance of £350. So, although Marx's financial problems were by no means solved, he had less need than formerly to try to borrow money from Jews – such as Ignaz Horn[13] and Leo Frankel.[14] He wrote to Engels in 1875 that while travelling to Carlsbad, "a sly-looking Yid" had been his travelling companion from London to Rotterdam. The Jewish businessman was foolish enough to confide in Marx, who reported details of his rather odd business deals in textiles to Engels.[15] In his old age, when on holiday in Ramsgate, he declared that there were "many Jews and fleas" at the resort.[16]

It was not only in private letters to his closest friend that Marx indulged in anti-semitic outbursts. In an article in the *New York Daily Tribune* (January 4, 1856), in which he discussed an international loan to be raised by the Russian government to finance the war in the Crimea, Marx savagely attacked the Jewish financiers who co-operated to place the loan.[17] Marx wrote:

> This loan is brought out under the auspices of the house of Stieglitz at St. Petersburg. Stieglitz is to Alexander what Rothschild is to Francis Joseph, what Fould is to Louis Napoleon. The late Czar Nicholas made Stieglitz a Russian baron, as the late Kaiser Franz made old Rothschild an Austrian baron, while Louis Napoleon has made a cabinet minister of Fould, with a free ticket to the Tuileries for the

females of his family. Thus we find every tyrant backed by a Jew, as is every Pope by a Jesuit. In truth, the cravings of oppressors would be hopeless, and the practicability of war out of the question, if there were not an army of Jesuits to smother thought and a handful of Jews to ransack pockets.

Hope and Co. of Amsterdam played an important role in placing the Russian loan. This was not a Jewish firm, but Marx declared that

the Hopes lend only the prestige of their name; the real work is done by Jews, and can only be done by them, as they monopolize the machinery of the loan-mongering mysteries by concentrating their energies upon the barter-trade in securities, and the changing of money and negotiating of bills in a great measure arising therefrom. Take Amsterdam, for instance, a city harbouring many of the worst descendants of the Jews whom Ferdinand and Isabella drove out of Spain, and who, after lingering a while in Portugal, were driven thence also, and eventually found a safe place of retreat in Holland. In Amsterdam alone they number not less than 35,000, many of whom are engaged in this gambling and jobbing of securities ... Their business is to watch the moneys available for investment and keenly observe where they lie. Here and there and everywhere that a little capital courts investment, there is ever one of these little Jews ready to make a little suggestion or place a little bit of a loan. The smartest highwayman in the Abruzzi is not better posted about the locale of the hard cash in a traveller's valise or pocket, than those Jews about any loose capital in the hands of a trader.

Marx went on to attack the Jewish finance houses of Königs-warter, Raphael, Stern, Bischoffsheim, Rothschild, Mendelssohn, Bleichröder, Fould and many others. He declared that many of these families were linked by marriage and he observed that "the loan-mongering Jews derive much of their strength from these family relations, as these, in addition to their lucre affinities, give a compactness and unity to their operations which insure their success".

Marx concluded his article as follows:

This Eastern war is destined at all events to throw some light upon this system of loan-mongering as well as other systems. Meanwhile the Czar will get his fifty millions, and let the

English journals say what they please, if he wants five fifties more, the Jews will dig them up. Let us not be thought too severe upon these loan-mongering gentry. The fact that 1855 years ago Christ drove the Jewish money-changers out of the temple, and that the money-changers of our age enlisted on the side of tyranny happen again chiefly to be Jews, is perhaps no more than a historical coincidence. The loan-mongering Jews of Europe do only on a larger and more obnoxious scale what many others do on one smaller and less significant. But it is only because the Jews are so strong that it is timely and expedient to expose and stigmatise their organisation.

There was poetic justice in the fact that Marx, who detested his own race, should have suffered from the anti-semitic views of others. There were those who attacked Marx because he was a Jew and who branded the political movement that he led as a Jewish conspiracy.

Engels' attitude towards the Jews was different from that of Marx.[18] He had never denounced the Jews as a race of petty traders and moneylenders as Marx had done in his youthful article in the *Deutsch–Französische Jahrbücher*.[19] Indeed he later declared that anti-semitism was the mark of a backward culture and was confined to Russia, Austria and Prussia.[20]

In 1881 Bernstein sent Engels some examples of anti-semitic propaganda in Germany. Engels replied that he had never seen anything so stupid or childish. He praised the *Sozial-Demokrat* – the leading socialist paper in Germany at the time of Bismarck's Anti-Socialist Law – for coming out firmly against anti-semitism. Engels quoted with approval a passage from a letter which he had recently received from a Jewish correspondent (Carl Hirsch), who had just been to Berlin. Hirsch had written that "the official press which prints anti-semitic articles has few readers." "Whilst it is true that the Germans have a natural antipathy towards the Jews, it is also a fact that the working class, the radical petty bourgeoisie, and the middle-class philistines hate the government far more than they hate the Jews."[21] Bernstein, however, disagreed with Hirsch and claimed that anti-semitic propaganda was falling upon fertile soil in Germany as far as civil servants, teachers, craftsmen and peasants were concerned.[22]

Ten years later Engels wrote to Bebel that he was glad to learn that new Jewish recruits were joining the German Social Democrat

Party. But he warned Bebel that socialists would have to keep a watchful eye on these Jewish colleagues because they were cleverer than the average bourgeois socialist and were – owing to centuries of oppression – in the habit of pushing themselves forward.[23]

Although Engels disapproved of anti-semitism and welcomed Jews like Kautsky and Adler as party colleagues, he did criticise particular Jews and groups of Jews. For example, in a comment on English politics in 1852 he contemptuously dismissed Disraeli as a "Jewish swindler".[24] A few years later when he wished to express his disapproval of Lassalle's conduct, he referred to him as "a real Jew from the Slav frontier" and as "a greasy Jew disguised under brilliantine and flashy jewels".[25] In 1862 in a letter to Carl Siebel, he attacked the Jewish members of a German club (the Schiller Anstalt) in Manchester. He declared that he seldom visited this veritable "Jerusalem Club" any more because the noisy behaviour of the Jews inconvenienced other members.

> What has happened is what always happens when Jews are about. At first they thanked God that they had a Schiller Anstalt, but hardly had they got inside than they declared that it was not good enough for them and that they wanted to build a bigger club house – a true temple of Moses – to which the Schiller Anstalt could be moved. This would indeed be the quickest road to bankruptcy ... Look out! In a year or two you will get a circular reading like this: "In view of the bankruptcy of the late Schiller Anstalt ..."[26]

A few years later, however, when he was President of the Schiller Anstalt, Engels played a leading part in securing the larger premises that the Jewish members desired.

In 1864, during the crisis in the Lancashire cotton industry at the time of the American civil war, Engels complained of the vexations that he had to endure in the office of Ermen and Engels because of "Jewish chicaneries".[27] In October 1867, and again in May 1868, Engels complained that his time was being wasted by visits from "that damned old Jew" Leibel Choras, who was a refugee from Moldavia where the Jews were being persecuted.[28] Engels obviously had little sympathy for Leibel Choras. And in 1870 Engels dismissed Leo Frankel as "a real little Yid".[29]

In 1892 in a letter to the French socialist leader Paul Lafargue – Marx's son-in-law – Engels expressed a certain sympathy for the anti-Jewish movement in France. He wrote:

I begin to understand French anti-semitism when I see how many Jews of Polish origin with German names intrude themselves everywhere to the point of arousing public opinion in the *ville lumière*, of which the Parisian philistine is so proud and which he believes to be the supreme power in the universe.[30]

Engels also expressed his contempt for the Polish Jews who were, in his view, "caricatures of Jews".[31] He wrote to Laura Lafargue:

Business principle of the Polish Jew to ask much so as to be able to rebate, as for instance:
"How much is a yard of this cloth?"
"15 groschen."
He says 15, he means $12\frac{1}{2}$, he would take 10, and the cloth is worth $7\frac{1}{2}$. I am prepared to pay 5 so I will offer him $2\frac{1}{2}$ groschen.[32]

Just as Engels rarely showed any antipathy towards the Jews, so he had no prejudices against coloured peoples. He rejected the view commonly expressed by explorers and missionaries in his day that native peoples were heathen savages who were obviously inferior to white races. Indeed he argued that primitive peoples were superior to modern Europeans because they did not recognise private property or capitalism or the state. In 1884 in his book on *The Origin of the Family* – based upon the researches of the American anthropologist Lewis Henry Morgan – Engels gave a lyrical account of the "wonderful childlike simplicity" of the way of life in the Iroquois Indian tribes. He wrote:

Everything runs smoothly without soldiers, gendarmes, or police; without nobles, kings, governors, prefects, or judges, without prisons, without trials. All quarrels and disputes are settled by the whole body of those concerned ... The household is run in common and communistically by a number of families, the land is tribal property, only the small gardens being temporarily assigned to the households ... Not a bit of our extensive and complicated machinery of administration is required ... There can be no poor or needy – the communistic household and the *gens* know their obligations towards the aged, the sick, and those disabled in war. All are free and equal – including the women. There is, as yet, no room for slaves nor, as a rule, for the subjugation of alien tribes ...[33]

As an admirer of primitive races Engels, like Marx, was strongly opposed to the exploitation of native peoples by white colonists. He denounced the expansion of the empires of European states in India, Java, Algiers and elsewhere. For Marx and Engels the rising in India in 1857 was no mere mutiny of Sepoy troops but a national revolt against the English oppressors. In a series of articles in the *New York Daily Tribune* they analysed the causes and events of the Mutiny, which they regarded as an illustration of the "general disaffection exhibited against English supremacy on the part of the great Asiatic nations …".[34]

In view of Engels' attitude towards the Jews, the Iroquois, and the natives in colonial territories, his attitude towards some of the Slavs is difficult to understand. When a Pan-Slav movement developed with Russian support in central and eastern Europe during the revolution of 1848 Engels rejected the demands of the Czechs, Serbs, Croats, and Ruthenians for independence from Habsburg or Turkish rule. Early in 1849 in two articles in the *Neue Rheinische Zeitung*[35] he argued that these peoples had no natural capacity for self-government and were for ever doomed to be ruled by more advanced nations. They were "peoples without any history". Engels asserted that these peoples would always be subject races and would "never achieve national independence". "They are peoples who were either already under foreign rule when they entered into the first primitive phase of civilisation or who were actually *forced* into the earliest phase of civilisation by their foreign master."

NOTES

1. Arnold Künzli has examined the psychological roots of Marx's anti-semitism in *Karl Marx: eine Psychographie* (1966), esp. pp.33–169, 195–226, 289–93.
2. Karl Marx, "Zur Judenfrage" in *Deutsch–Französische Jahrbücher* (Paris, 1844), reprinted in *Marx–Engels Werke*, Vol. 1 (1964), pp.347–77. English translation: Karl Marx, *A World without Jews* (ed. D.D. Runes, New York, 1959). The first article reviewed Bruno Bauer, *Die Judenfrage* (Brunswick, 1843), the second Bruno Bauer's article on "Die Fähigheit der heutigen Juden und Christen frei zu werden" in *Einundzwanzig Bogen aus der Schweiz* (ed. Georg Herwegh, Zürich and Winterthur, 1843, pp.56–71). More recently a reprint of the *Deutsch–Französische Jahrbücher* has been issued in Leipzig, Verlag Philipp Reclam, 1973.
3. Karl Marx & F. Engels, *The Holy Family*, 1845 (Foreign Languages Publishing House, Moscow, 1956), p.148.
4. *Neue Rheinische Zeitung*, No. 285, Sunday, April 29, 1849 (second edition), p.1, col. 1. Marx was probably the author of the article.
5. Robert Payne, *The Unknown Karl Marx: documents concerning Karl Marx* (1972), pp.14–15.
6. A small colony of Bambergers can be traced in the City of London during the mid-

1850s, based on King Street, Snowhill. Zacharias Bamberger, for example, of 19 King Street, ship and commission agent, was a partner in the firm of Prager & Bamberger, 84 Lower Thomas Street, while Louis Bamberger & Co., merchants, and Abraham Bamberger & Co., wholesale boot manufacturers, both operated from 20 King Street, Snowhill (Kelly & Co., *Post Office London Directory*, 1855, p.813). Of these Zacharias Bamberger seems most likely to have been Marx's moneylender.

7. See Karl Marx to F. Engels, July 31, 1851 in *Gesamtausgabe*, Part III, Vol. 1, p.224 and Jan. 21, 1852, *ibid.*, p.444.
8. For example "Spielmann always sends one away with the nasal Jewish remark 'Kaine Nootiz da'" (i.e. "Keine Notiz da"): Karl Marx to F. Engels, Aug. 18, 1853 in *Gesamtausgabe*, Part III, Vol. 1, p.492. The word Yiddish, used to describe this form of speech, is noted as first appearing in print in English in the mid-1880s (*Oxford English Dictionary*).
9. Karl Marx to F. Engels, Sept. 21, 1859 in *Gesamtausgabe*, Part III, Vol. 2, p.416.
10. Gustav Mayer, *Der Briefwechsel zwischen Lassalle und Marx* (Vol. 3 of *Ferdinand Lassalle: Nachgelassene Briefe und Schriften*, first edition 1922, new edition issued by the Historical Commission of the Bavarian Academy of Science, 1967).
11. Karl Marx to F. Engels, July 30, 1862 in *Gesamtausgabe*, Part III, Vol. 3, pp.82–4. On Marx as "at once a racialist himself and the cause of racialism in others" see G. Watson, *The English Ideology* (1973), p.211.
12. Jenny Marx to F. Engels, April 9, 1858, in *Gesamtausgabe*, Part III, Vol. 2, p.314. See also the malicious and anti-semitic gossip about Moses and Sybille Hess, in K. Marx to F. Engels, Sept. 22, 1856, Part III, Vol. 2, p.147.
13. Karl Marx to F. Engels, Feb. 10, 1865 ("Jüd Horn") and Nov. 14, 1868 (first letter) ("Rabbi A. Einhorn generally known by the name of A.E. Horn") in *Gesamtausgabe*, Part III, Vol. 3, p.232 and Vol. 4, p.124.
14. Karl Marx to F. Engels, April 14 and July 8, 1870 ("little Jew Leo Frankel!") in *Gesamtausgabe*, Part III, Vol. 4, pp.302, 338.
15. Karl Marx to F. Engels, Aug. 21, 1875, in *Gesamtausgabe*, Part III, Vol. 4, pp.428–9.
16. Karl Marx to F. Engels, Aug. 25, 1879 in *Gesamtausgabe*, Part III, Vol. 4, p.490.
17. Reprinted in Karl Marx, *The Eastern Question* (ed. by Eleanor Marx and Edward Aveling, 1897: new edition Frank Cass, 1970), pp.600–6.
18. For the attitude of socialists to the Jews see E. Silberner, *Sozialisten zur Judenfrage* (1962) and G. Lichtheim, "Socialism and the Jews" in *Dissent*, New York, July–August 1968.
19. Karl Marx, "Zur Judenfrage", *op. cit.*, pp.347–77. See also Karl Marx and Friedrich Engels, *The Holy Family, op. cit.*, pp.149–50.
20. F. Engels to a correspondent in Vienna, April 19, 1890 in Karl Marx–Friedrich Engels, *Werke*, Vol. 22, p.49. See, however, Engels' 1892 preface to the London edition of his *Condition of the Working Class in England*, where he refers to "the pettifogging business tricks of the Polish Jew, the representative in Europe of commerce at its lowest stage" (p.360 in 1971 edition by W.O. Henderson and W.H. Chaloner).
21. F. Engels to Eduard Bernstein, Aug. 17, 1881 in Helmut Hirsch (ed.), *Eduard Bernsteins Briefwechsel mit Friedrich Engels* (1970), pp.28–9.
22. E. Bernstein to F. Engels, Sept. 9, 1881: *ibid.*, p.37.
23. F. Engels to August Bebel, December 1, 1891 in Werner Blumenberg (ed.), *August Bebels Briefwechsel mit Friedrich Engels* (1965), p.487.
24. F. Engels to Karl Marx, Sept. 24, 1852 in *Gesamtausgabe*, Part III, Vol. 1, p.405.
25. F. Engels to Karl Marx, March 7, 1856 in *Gesamtausgabe*, Part III, Vol. 2, p.122. English translation: W.O. Henderson (ed.), *Engels: Selected Writings* (Penguin Books, 1967), pp.129–30.
26. F. Engels to Carl Siebel, June 4, 1862 in Helmut Hirsch (ed.), *Friedrich Engels*

M E–G

Profile (1970), p.250.
27. F. Engels to Karl Marx, Nov. 2, 1864 in *Gesamtausgabe*, Part III, Vol. 3, p.192.
28. F. Engels to Karl Marx, Oct. 11, 1867 and May 6, 1868 in *Gesamtausgabe*, Part III, Vol. 3, p.432 and Vol. 4, p.52. It has not proved possible to identify Choras further.
29. F. Engels to Karl Marx, April 15, 1870 in *Gesamtausgabe*, Part III, Vol. 4, p.305.
30. F. Engels to Paul Lafargue, July 22, 1892 in *F. Engels–Paul and Laura Lafargue: Correspondence* (1960), Vol. 3, p.184.
31. F. Engels to Paul Ernst, June 5, 1890 in Helmut Hirsch (ed.), *Friedrich Engels Profile, op. cit.*, p.190.
32. F. Engels to Laura Lafargue, October 27, 1893 in *F. Engels–Paul and Laura Lafargue: Correspondence, op. cit.*, Vol. III, 1891–95, p.307.
33. F. Engels, *Der Ursprung der Familie, des Privateigentums und des Staates* (Hottingen–Zürich, 1884: new edition, 1962), p.96. English translation F. Engels, *The Origin of the Family, Private Property, and the State* (Foreign Languages Publishing House, Moscow), p.159. Engels' book was based upon Lewis Henry Morgan, *Ancient Society, or Researches in the Line of Human Progress from Savagery through Barbarism to Civilisation* (New York and London, 1877). Engels also made use of the notes which Karl Marx had made (probably in the winter of 1880–1) on Morgan's book. See Lawrence Krader (ed.), *The Ethnological Notebooks of Karl Marx* (1972).
34. For selections of articles and letters written by Marx and Engels on colonisation see Karl Marx and F. Engels, *On Colonisation* (Foreign Languages Publishing House, Moscow) and *The First Indian War of Independence, 1857–1859* (Foreign Languages Publishing House, Moscow) (London, 1960).
35. F. Engels, "Der magyarische Kampf" and "Der demokratische Panslavismus" in the *Neue Rheinische Zeitung*, Jan. 13 and Feb. 15, 1849: reprinted in Karl Marx and F. Engels, *Werke*, Vol. 6, p.165 et seq. P.W. Blackstock and B.F. Hoselitz have translated and edited a useful anthology of these articles in K. Marx and F. Engels, *The Russian Menace to Europe* (Glencoe, Ill., 1952). Pages 56–90 and 247 are important for "peoples without a history"; in the true spirit of Pan-Germanism Marx and Engels considered the Czechs, Slovaks and Ruthenians, together with the South Slavs, to be "ethnic trash".

7

A MARXIST HISTORIAN AND THE ENGLISH WORKERS

(Review of Jürgen Kuczynski,
Die Geschichte der Lage der Arbeiter in England ...,
Part 2, Vols. 22 to 28)

Jürgen Kuczynski deals with the history of the working classes in Britain and in the British Empire in seven volumes, one of which is a double volume. Two volumes are rather different from the remainder. One of these is concerned with the history of economic thought and the other describes the condition of the workers in the cotton mills of Shanghai which were owned by English firms. Before discussing each volume in turn a brief reference may be made to some general characteristics of the whole survey of the English workers. Kuczynski writes on a generous scale and his chapters on the workers are usually preceded by accounts of the development of the British economy in particular periods. Whatever he discusses Kuczynski provides numerous tables of statistics. The author is an acknowledged expert in this field and the statistics which he has prepared himself and those which he has taken from other scholars illuminate many of the topics that he discusses.

Kuczynski is a devout marxist. He accepts the historical interpretations of Marx, Engels, and Lenin without question and a quotation from one of these writers – or from the Soviet encyclopaedia – is not infrequently presented to the readers as a complete proof of the correctness of a particular point of view. A readiness to accept Marx's assertions as virtually infallible leads to some curious results. For example Marx and Engels believed that the continued expansion of capitalism would inevitably lead on the one hand to the concentration of wealth in fewer and fewer hands, and on the other to the pauperisation of the masses. Kuczynski therefore boldly asserts that the condition of the workers in Britain has declined in the industrial age. He apparently believes that they were worse off in the 1960s than they had been in the 1860s. In fact there is overwhelming evidence to show that this is not so. Increased real wages, shorter hours, paid holidays, and vastly extended social services have improved the standard of living of the factory workers. Faced with this situation Kuczynski argues that all these changes for the better have been counterbalanced by the increased intensity of work in the factories and mines. It is difficult to measure the intensity of work. Increased output per hour or per week can be measured but this may be due to the introduction of improved machinery and may make the task of the worker lighter rather than heavier.

1640–1760

Kuczynski's first volume on the English workers deals with the period from 1640 to 1760 with an introductory chapter on the later middle ages and the Tudor period. Unlike the later volumes there is in this book no chapter devoted specifically to the workers. The condition of the artisans and workers on the land however is discussed in section E of the first chapter (pp. 82–113). Here the author emphasises the problem of poverty in the sixteenth century. The author gives a very clear account of the transition in England from a feudal economy to a pre-capitalist economy and discusses – more effectively than some English historians – the reasons why these changes occurred in a different way in Britain than on the Continent. In dealing with the first half of the eighteenth century – when large workshops developed without power-driven machinery – Kuczynski observes that "before a factory can be established a really large capital sum has to be made available whilst at the same time there must be a strong advance in science and technology." It is true that before the industrial revolution relatively large amounts of capital were needed to launch certain enterprises such as sinking a coalmine, building a large ship, or sending a vessel to India. But other enterprises – such as establishing a spinning workshop or a weaving shed – could be started with only a little initial capital since the early manually operated textile machines were not very expensive and, if successful in the early years, an enterprise could be expanded by ploughing some of the profits back into the business. In *A Cotton Enterprise 1795–1840: a History of M'Connel & Kennedy, fine Cotton Spinners* (1972), C.H. Lee observes that there were abundant "opportunities for the man of ambition and enterprise in cotton spinning during the boom period in the late eighteenth and early nineteenth centuries. It was quite possible to begin in the trade without much capital". When John Kennedy formed his first partnership with the Sandford brothers and James M'Connel to build textile machinery and to engage in mule spinning, the initial capital of the firm was only between £600 and £700. When Josiah Wedgwood started business on his own account as a potter he was able to rent premises for a mere £10 a year. And Robert Owen began his successful business career with the aid of a loan of £100.

1760–1832

In the volume dealing with the period 1760–1832 Kuczynski covers very familiar ground. Ample evidence is available concerning the fate of the workers in Britain during the industrial revolution and the author has little difficulty in showing that at this time conditions in the factories and mines – and on the land – were very bad indeed. It was not easy for craftsmen who had been accustomed to work in their own time at home to adapt themselves to the monotonous routine of long hours of repetitive work in the factories and the harsh discipline imposed by the overseer. Factories were often poorly ventilated, inadequately heated and badly lit and many of the workers suffered from industrial diseases or were injured by being caught in the machines. Wages were generally low and their purchasing power was reduced by the truck system. Some workers received their wages not in cash but in vouchers which could be exchanged only at a shop owned by their employer. Here prices were above those charged elsewhere. The houses in which the workers lived left much to be desired while sanitary conditions in the industrial towns were disgraceful. The excessive use of the labour of women and children was another highly undesirable feature of the new industrial age. It was not surprising that such conditions led to social unrest, particularly immediately after the end of the Napoleonic wars.

Kuczynski quite rightly draws attention to these – and to many other – deplorable aspects of the fate of the workers in Britain during the industrial revolution. But this is not the full story. Craftsmen may well have suffered just as much as factory workers. The nailmakers in the Black Country and the seamstresses in London did not work in factories but they were probably worse off than many who did. Not all factory owners were monsters of iniquity. There were enlightened employers, such as Robert Owen, who treated their workers like human beings and not like slaves to the machines. Not all factory towns were collections of slum dwellings. Friedrich Engels, for example, reported that in Ashton under Lyne "the new bright red cottages give every appearance of comfort". And by the early 1830s Parliament – particularly after the passing of the Reform Act – placed on the Statute book some important Acts which improved the condition of the workers. The truck system was abolished, the hours worked by women and children in most textile factories were reduced, a small annual grant was made to promote elementary education, and the administration of the municipalities was reorganised. In addition some of the large towns were improving the condition of the workers by using powers secured under local Acts of Parliament. It may be added that, in an appendix to this volume, Kuczynski prints an extremely interesting report of 1814 on English factories by the Prussian official Factory Commissioner May.

1832–1900

In Volume 24 Kuczynski covers the years between the passing of the first parliamentary Reform Act and the end of the nineteenth century. During much of this period Marx and Engels were writing in their books, articles, and correspondence about the condition of the workers and about the labour movement in Britain. And on various occasions – at the time of the First International for example – they played an active part in working class politics. Kuczynski appears to accept as correct their interpretations and judgments. But historians who have examined various aspects of the history of the English workers in the nineteenth century have shown that Marx and Engels were not infallible.

A few examples may be given to suggest how dangerous it is to accept, without further enquiry, the views of Marx and Engels on the English labour scene at this time. Kuczynski considers – as Marx and Engels considered – that the object of the industrialists who advocated the repeal of the Corn Laws was to reduce wages as soon as bread became cheaper. This allegation was made at the time by the opponents of repeal but was strenuously denied by the leaders of the Anti-Corn Law League. And if employers did hope that repeal would enable them to cut wages they were unsuccessful since the standard of life of the proletariat improved in the second half of the nineteenth century.

Kuczynski states that in 1842 some Lancashire manufacturers

deliberately provoked the Plug Plot riots to bring pressure to bear upon the government to repeal the Corn Laws. This explanation of the origin of unrest was given both by Tory and by Chartist writers in 1842 and it was repeated shortly afterwards by Engels in his book on the condition of the English workers. In fact, A.G. Rose has shown in his essay on the Plug Plot riots in the *Transactions of the Lancashire and Cheshire Antiquarian Society* (1958) that the strikes of 1842 were not fomented by the employers but were a spontaneous explosion of discontent in the factory districts.

Kuczynski argues – as Marx and Engels argued – that the increase in the national income which occurred in this period of industrial expansion was spirited away into the pockets of the capitalists as surplus value. The workers did not share in this new wealth but had to survive on low wages. In the inaugural address of the First International Marx declared that there had been no improvement in the standard of living of the proletariat between 1848 and 1864. Marx and Engels later qualified this point of view by asserting that an "aristocracy of labour" – a group of foremen and skilled workers – had developed in England and these men had been able to secure a share of the wealth generated by economic growth. But the contributors to *The Long Debate on Poverty* (edited by Arthur Seldon in 1972) have shown that the real wages of virtually all workers – and not just a privileged few – rose very considerably in Britain in the nineteenth century. Poverty of course had not been eliminated. But poverty was not confined to industrialised countries. It was to be found all over the world.

It may be added that Kuczynski also argues that the 1840s were a period of exceptional distress – a view expressed by Engels at the time. There has been some controversy among historians on this question but attention may be drawn to Dr. Chaloner's pamphlet on *The Hungry Forties* (1957) and to an article by J.E. Williams on "The British Standard of Living" in the *Economic History Review* (Vol. XIX, 1966) which suggest that the condition of the workers in this period was not quite so black as is sometimes thought. Real consumption per head rose from £18.3 in 1841 to £25.3 in 1851.

When discussing the attitude of the Lancashire operatives to the American civil war during the cotton famine Kuczynski praises their support of the North as "a miracle of heroic class solidarity". This view was expressed at the time by such strange bedfellows as Karl Marx, John Bright, Henry Adams, and Gladstone. But Mary Ellison in her scholarly volume on *Support for Secession. Lancashire and the American Civil War* (1972) has shown that the cotton workers in Lancashire were far from unanimous in their views of the American civil war. She points out that the greater the unemployment in a cotton town owing to the shortage of the raw material, the more vociferous was the support for the Southern Confederacy and the more emphatic were the demands for intervention to break the northern blockade. The Lancashire operatives were motivated by considerations of economic self-interest rather than by a lofty opposition to the institution of slavery.

Throughout this volume Kuczynski argues that Britain was unique among the industrial nations in the nineteenth century because, having had a head start of her competitors, she enjoyed for a time a commanding position in international trade. She also controlled vast colonial territories which were a source of raw materials and foodstuffs and a market for manufactured products. Kuczynski accepts the view expressed by Lenin in a famous pamphlet, pubished in 1916, that imperialism marks "the highest stage of capitalism" – the last phase before the collapse of the capitalist system. This point of view, however, has by no means found universal acceptance.

1900 TO THE PRESENT DAY

In this volume Kuczynski gives a gloomy account of the fortunes of the English proletariat in the twentieth century. In his view capitalism in Britain was already beginning to decay before the first world war and it has been declining ever since. On his deathbed Charles II is said to have apologised to his courtiers for taking an unconscionable time in dying. Perhaps a similar apology is due from English capitalists. Kuczynski sees as signs of the last stage of capitalism the exploitation of colonial peoples, the concentration of industrial production in the hands of a few great combines, a decline in economic growth, and the occurrence of wars and of periods of chronic unemployment. The workers in England have certainly had their share of misfortunes in this period – two great wars, a world economic depression, and a period of inflation from 1940 onwards. By concentrating upon the effects of these disasters and by emphasising the significance of excessive overtime, industrial unrest, unemployment, factory accidents and bad housing Kuczynski is able to give a grim account of the condition of the workers.

But this is by no means the whole story. Anyone who was born in England in Edward VII's reign and has lived there all his life knows from personal experience that the condition of the workers has improved in the last seventy years. The forests of television aerials in working class districts, the full car parks outside the factories, and the crowds in the supermarkets are signs of the times. Today English workers enjoy the benefits of the welfare state – medical attention, sickness and unemployment benefits, compensation for industrial injuries, redundancy payments, and retirement pensions. When Marx lived in London and had no money, his wife had to visit a pawnbroker. Today she could draw national assistance. The housing problem has been tackled by clearing away many slums and by building new houses and flats for which the workers pay lower rents than those charged by private landlords for similar accommodation. The educational opportunities of the workers' children have been greatly improved by raising the school leaving age to 16 and by providing many more places at universities and technical colleges. The environment has been improved by the introduction of smokeless zones and by many other measures. At one time if a worker could take a holiday, he spent it at an English seaside resort. Today as likely as not he and his family are to be found in Benidorm or Torremolinos. And the English worker is free to emigrate if he thinks that he can secure a better standard of life elsewhere. The standard of living enjoyed by the workers has attracted many coloured immigrants from the West Indies and Pakistan. Moreover wealth in Britain is now rather more equally distributed than before. Statistics issued by the Inland Revenue show that the total personal wealth of the bottom 90 per cent of the population rose from eight per cent in 1914 to 17 per cent in 1960 and to 37 per cent in 1974. High income tax, death duties, and the capital gains tax have helped to reduce the assets of the wealthy. Obviously much remains to be done to improve working and living conditions in Britain. No one can view with complacency the loss of lives in the mines – over 7,000 since nationalisation – or the survival of old houses, schools, and hospitals that should have been pulled down long ago. Nevertheless what has been achieved since 1900 to raise living standards makes it a little difficult to accept the picture drawn by Kuczynski as an impartial assessment of the situation.

ECONOMIC THOUGHT IN ENGLAND

This volume appears in between Kuczynski's account of the condition of the workers in Britain and his survey of white and non-white workers in the dominions and colonies. It is a collection of studies on two main topics – the development of economic thought in Britain from the bullionists to J.M. Keynes and the relationship between literature and changes in the economic structure of society from the age of Shakespeare to that of Wordsworth. Any essays from Kuczynski's pen merit serious attention but it is a little difficult to see the relevance of the questions raised in this volume to his main theme.

In his preface Kuczynski quotes the following passage from Karl Marx's *Kritik der politischen Ökonomie*:

> "A comparative study of the writings and character of Petty and Boisguillebert – apart from the brilliant light that it would throw on the social contrasts between England and France in the late seventeenth and early eighteenth centuries – would also be a study of the contrasts between the economic doctrines widely held in the two countries. And there is a similar contrast between the writings of Ricardo and Sismondi.

Kuczynski follows up this suggestion by examining in some detail the history of English economic thought in this volume and the history of French economic thought in Volume 34. In their writings Marx and Engels frequently discussed the views of English mercantilists and of the classical economists. The detailed nature of Marx's study of Ricardo's theory of rent, for example, can be seen from the notes reproduced as an appendix to the so-called *Rohentwurf* and from the Marx–Engels correspondence. Kuczynski follows faithfully in the footsteps of his masters, giving his readers many quotations from their writings.

The essays on the history of economic thought vigorously criticise – from a marxist point of view – the doctrines of the leading English economists from Thomas Mun to J.M. Keynes. Kuczynski argues that, at any particular time, the accepted popular theory of economics is the one that accords closely with the interests of the ruling class in society. He suggests that – until the middle of the nineteenth century – leading English economists were "mainly professional businessmen, that is to say profit makers". It is true that two of the early mercantilists (Sir Josiah Childe and Thomas Mun) were directors of the East India Company, but Charles Davenant was a civil servant. Of the classical economists one – David Ricardo – was a stockbroker, but Adam Smith and McCulloch were both first university professors and then civil servants, while Malthus was a clergyman and a professor and John Stuart Mill was an official in the India Office. So several of the English economists were academic people or public officials.

BRITISH COLONIES

The first part of Kuczynski's volume on the workers in the English colonies deals mainly with native workers on plantations, in mines, and in factories in tropical Africa and in India. The volume also includes an interesting section on the fortunes of the workers in various former colonial territories – not all British – which have now attained independence. The account of the native workers under British rule can hardly be described as either balanced or impartial. The author is concerned to show that these workers were grossly exploited by their English masters. He denounces what he regards as a system of indirect forced labour in tropical Africa by which the imposition of a head tax made it necessary for natives to seek employment in enterprises owned by white settlers so as to earn the money to pay their taxes. The author gives many examples of long hours, low wages, inadequate diet, and poor accommodation. No wonder that such workers were undernourished and in poor health. Another drawback of the system was that traditional village life declined because so many men were away from home for long periods. And on India Kuczynski writes:

> The economic exploitation of India by English capitalists is the classic example of the creation of huge extra profits at the expense of a colony. These profits were obtained by "classic methods" – by shameless theft from peasants and craftsmen, by the horrible exploitation of factory workers and by the suppression of every kind of agitation in favour of political and economic reform.

Yet a comparison between conditions in the various territories in Africa and Asia before they became part of the British Empire and after they gained their independence suggests that English rule was not entirely detrimental to the native inhabitants. In India in the eighteenth century the authority of the Mogul emperors had declined after Aurangzebe's death to such an extent that law and order had collapsed and the country was rent by civil wars, while its inhabitants were plagued by the licentious soldiery of rival princes. Similarly, before it was conquered by European Powers, Africa south of the Sahara was a happy hunting ground for slave traders and there were fierce conflicts between rival tribes which made life a misery for countless natives. In both India and Africa periodic famines and lack of medical knowledge meant that health standards were deplorably low.

Both in India and in Africa English domination brought with it not only the establishment of law and order and the construction of public works (harbours, roads, railways, irrigation schemes and so forth) but also the development of hitherto untapped economic resources, and the opening of missionary schools. The essays in *Tropical Development, 1880–1913* (edited by Arthur Lewis, 1970) show the extent of economic progress in some of the British colonies before the first world war. In Nigeria and the Gold Coast the success of the Akwapim farmers in planting cocoa in the low-lying forest lands which they had bought from the Aim peoples illustrates the way in which natives responded to new opportunities to raise their standard of living. And the essay on Ceylon shows that the experience of this colony "confutes the stereotype of the plantation economy as one which benefits only expatriate shareholders, while doing nothing to prepare the indigenous economy for growth". Events in the former colonial territories after they became independent show how important a role British forces played in maintaining law and order. The bitter fighting in Biafra and Bangladesh might never have occurred if the British army had still been stationed in those territories.

The second part of Kuczynski's history of the workers in the English colonies deals with Australia, New Zealand, Canada, and South Africa. Students of the economic and social development of the British Empire will welcome this compact survey in a single volume of the history of the workers and of the various labour movements in the dominions. In the Australian colonies, which developed from convict settlements, the workers were in a relatively strong position in the nineteenth century. The population was small and the colonies failed to attract as many British immigrants as the United States or Canada. Skilled artisans were scarce and could command relatively high wages. In the middle of the century, when gold was discovered, some workers moved to the diggings and those who remained behind could secure still higher wages. Trade unions of skilled workers began to develop in the 1820s and their power increased in the 1850s and 1860s. It was not until the early twentieth century that the sheep shearers, the dockers, and the transport workers were effectively organised. Although there were occasional acts of violence (such as the notorious affair of the Eureka stockade) and some bitter strikes (such as those of the

building workers in Victoria in 1858/1859 and the miners in Newcastle in 1873), the workers were for the most part able to secure a
number of their demands by agreement with their employers or
through the various state legislatures. The eight-hour day of skilled
workers, for example, was secured earlier in Australia than elsewhere. Kuczynski observes that in the twentieth century there were
fewer strikes in Australia than in many industrialised countries.
Lujo Brentano has observed that

> the Australian workers are better off than workers in other
> countries. They enjoy the highest wages, an advanced social
> security system, the eight hour day, and compulsory arbitra-
> tion boards to settle industrial disputes. The wage tribunals
> which protect women working at home have been a model for
> similar councils in Europe.

But Kuczynski, despite all evidence to the contrary, concludes his
survey of the Australian workers by declaring that

> The true account given by the Australian workers concerning
> their standard of living and working conditions is similar to
> accounts given by American, English and other industrial
> workers. The intensity of work is increasing in Australia
> just as it is increasing all over the capitalist world. The
> Australian worker is no more secure of his job than workers
> in other capitalist countries. Neither powerful trade unions
> nor a powerful Labour Party can give the workers much help
> unless these organisations are prepared to mount a vigorous
> challenge to the capitalist system.

As far as New Zealand is concerned, Kuczynski argues that in no
advanced capitalist country has the development of real wages been
so unfavourable to the workers. He believes that, while high wages
were earned by some skilled men in the early days of colonisation,
the general standard of living of the workers declined between 1873
and 1933. There has, however, been some improvement since 1939.
And it may be added that by the early twentieth century New
Zealand had established a system of social security which was one of
the most progressive in the world.

In Canada money wages have risen in the twentieth century,
except during the depression of 1929–33, but Kuczynski argues that
there has been no improvement in real wages although the intensity
of work has greatly increased. And he quotes with approval van der
Valk's assertion that the standard of living of the average Canadian

worker in the 1950s was from 20 per cent to 25 per cent lower than that of workers in the United States. Kuczynski observes that in Canada the forty-hour week has become nearly universal (except for farm workers) while at the same time output per hour in the factories and on the land has substantially increased. The welfare services provided by the provincial authorities are not so comprehensive as similar services in Britain.

In South Africa the workers were in a different position from those in other British dominions. Canada and Australia had almost entirely white populations and the original native inhabitants had dwindled to insignificant numbers. In the Union of South Africa, however, the white settlers were a small minority of the population. In 1921 there were only 1,500,000 whites (English and Boers) as compared with 7,000,000 non-whites (natives, Indians, and persons of mixed race). There were two groups of workers – whites and non-whites. The whites had a virtual monopoly of relatively well-paid skilled jobs, while the non-whites had to be content with poorly paid unskilled jobs. It was not only the white capitalists but also the white workers who exploited the cheap labour of the African workers. The coloured workers were farm labourers, domestic servants, and miners. The gold and diamond mines of the Transvaal and the Orange Free State employed many coloured immigrant workers from Basutoland, Bechuanaland, and Mozambique. Coloured workers were controlled by pass laws. An Act of 1922 endeavoured to perpetuate the restrictions on African workers that had developed on the Witwatersrand and subsequent amendments made it increasingly difficult for Africans to settle permanently in towns with their families.

Kuczynski considers that two groups of natives were engaged in forced labour. The first were those found guilty by the courts of infringements of the pass laws or the curfew and sentenced to terms of forced labour. The second were those who signed contracts to work in the mines and were accommodated in native compounds. It was hardly surprising that the wretched condition of the African workers should have led to strikes, such as the great miners' strike of 1946. Kuczynski closes his sombre review of the condition of the native workers in South Africa with an account of the massacre of 170 natives by the police at Sharpeville in March 1960.

BRITISH COTTON MILLS IN SHANGHAI

The last of Kuczynski's studies of the workers in Britain and the British Empire is, in certain respects, quite different from the previous volumes. It deals with the Chinese workers in the cotton mills of Shanghai – a territory that was never part of the British Empire. It includes a brief survey by Chung-Ping Yen of the cotton industry in China until 1937; an account by Kuczynski of the condition of the operatives in the Shanghai cotton mills run by English firms between the two world wars; and a report by Wolfgang Jonas on his interviews with Chinese operatives who had worked in Shanghai cotton mills formerly owned by foreigners. Kuczynski's chapters are particularly valuable as they are a piece of original research based upon an examination of business records.

Between 1919 and 1939 the textile industries of Shanghai employed over half of the labour force in the city. And over half of the textile workers were cotton operatives. The owners of the factories were English, Japanese, or Chinese firms. The Ewo Cotton Mills, Ltd., a subsidiary of Jardine, Matheson & Co., owned three large spinning and weaving enterprises. The mills were run by English managers and engineers, who had gained experience of the industry in Lancashire. Since language problems made it difficult for them to deal directly with Chinese workers a system of contract labour was evolved. A Chinese middleman would agree with the English millowners or their managers to supply, to supervise, and to pay the workers in return for a fee based upon the output of the factory. The day to day control of the operatives was entirely in the hands of the contractor who appointed overseers and their assistants to handle labour relations, leaving English engineers and mechanics to look after the running of the machinery.

Owing to the political instability of the country and periodic food shortages, large numbers of Chinese migrated to Shanghai in the hope of finding employment in the cotton mills. The fact that there were men and women at the factory gate ready to step into the shoes of any worker who was dismissed gave the contractors and their overseers the whip hand over the cotton operatives. The overseers expected a bribe before they would put a worker on to the pay roll. They diverted to their own pockets a percentage of the wages that they should have paid to children and to young workers. They swindled workers by paying them in small copper change instead of in silver dollars. The contract system was abolished by Ewo Cotton

Mills in 1937. Kuczynski publishes (in German translation) interesting letters exchanged between a Chinese engineer, trained in Lancashire, and the English company concerning this change of policy.

Kuczynski shows that in the 1920s and 1930s the pay of the weavers in the cotton factories in Shanghai was generally similar to the average industrial wages in the city but that the pay of the spinners was a good deal less than this. And the cotton operatives worked longer hours than those employed in other factories. Not only were children employed in the cotton mills but infants lay in the workshops while their mothers tended the machines. The exploitation of the Chinese workers in the Shanghai textile industry is undoubtedly an example of the "unacceptable face of capitalism". It is puzzling that cotton operatives could be found willing to work such long hours for so little money. A possible explanation is that their standard of life had been even lower in the villages that they had left before coming to Shanghai. Even today there appears to be no evidence to suggest that in Hong Kong – the only city in mainland China not under communist control – the factory workers are anxious to migrate to communist China.

Having completed his lengthy study of the condition of the workers in capitalist countries it is to be hoped that Kuczynski will now turn his attention to the workers in the communist world. It would certainly be interesting to have a really authoritative account of the condition of the workers in the Russian labour camps.

PART II

Studies on Friedrich List

8

FRIEDRICH LIST AND THE SOCIAL QUESTION[1]

I

At the opening of the List archives in Reutlingen in 1934 the Burgomaster complained that List had been unfairly accused of turning a blind eye to the harsh conditions of work in factories and to the wretched lot of domestic craftsmen displaced by new machines.[2] It has certainly been argued that List was so busy promoting the interests of the capitalists that he had little time to pay much attention to the social consequences of industrialisation. It is indeed surprising that one who was a leading publicist and journalist in Germany should have had so little to say about the widespread poverty and distress that existed in Europe between 1815 and 1848.

In 1834 Villeneuve-Bargemont estimated that there were over 13 million paupers and beggars in Europe. In England and Wales over a million paupers were relieved in 1840 and this figure rose to 1,700,000 in 1847. In France in 1833 it was officially estimated that over a million paupers either received outdoor relief or were admitted to almshouses or hospitals.[3] In any society provision must be made for those unable to support themselves – the aged and infirm, orphans, widows, and deserted wives – but what alarmed people in the first half of the nineteenth century was the large number of able-bodied adults who were either out of work or unable to earn enough to support themselves and their families.

After 1815 the dislocation caused by the Napoleonic wars was responsible for much distress since the labour market could not quickly absorb all the soldiers who were demobilised. Bad harvests, as in 1817, caused distress on the land, while trade depressions had the same effect upon craftsmen and shopkeepers in towns and villages. The industrial revolution, first in England and later in various regions on the Continent, led to unemployment and poverty among those whose skills were becoming obsolete owing to the introduction of new machines. The Luddites in England, the silk weavers in Lyons, and the linen weavers in Silesia were among those whose distress drove them to violence. List of course was well aware of these problems. But while he frequently discussed his doctrines concerning phases of economic growth and productive forces, it was only occasionally that he turned his attention to social questions that many of his contemporaries regarded as matters of vital importance. When List was concerned with running a coalmine in America and in constructing a colliery railway he had little to say in his writings or correspondence about the miners or the labourers who built the railway. And in the years preceding the revolutions of 1848 when governments throughout western Europe faced a rising tide of unrest, List seemed to be much more concerned with tariff policy and railway projects than with the grievances of peasants, artisans, and factory workers.

II

As a young man List was a civil servant in Württemberg for eleven years, starting as a probationer in 1806 and ending as a senior official with the title *Regierungsrat*. One of his last assignments was in Heilbronn where he was sent in 1817 to question a number of peasants and artisans who were on the point of leaving Württemberg for America.[4] He was instructed to find out why they were emigrating and, if possible, to dissuade them from doing so. The emigrants whom he interviewed left him in no doubt as to why they were going to America. They stated that a harvest failure, rising prices, and high taxes had left them virtually destitute. They complained of oppression by their feudal lords and by government officials. A peasant, who submitted his evidence in writing, declared:

> The most grievous poverty forces us to emigrate to America. As we have not received the seed that we were promised, our fields have not been sown and we can expect nothing but shortage of food. We cannot afford to pay taxes to two masters and no one listens to our complaints. If we take a little straw or brushwood from the woods we are punished by the forest court even though we have done no damage. The records of the forest court substantiate this. The present high prices and shortage of food is so serious that we cannot save our families

Friedrich List

from starvation. Death by famine is at the door. And so we must seek a new home in another country as no one will help us here.

List urged the government to remedy conditions which forced peasants to emigrate. And he suggested that the state should control emigration by curbing the activities of dishonest agents who gave emigrants a false picture of conditions in America and sometimes robbed them of their savings.

After his mission to Heilbronn List frequently argued that emigration could play an important rôle in solving the problems of unemployment and pauperism. He appreciated the risks run by those who left Europe to settle in America but suggested that these risks could be reduced if the state were to control emigration and protect emigrants. A few years after his visit to Heilbronn List was an emigrant himself. Having been imprisoned for his political activities he was released before completing his sentence on condition that he left Württemberg. He went to the United States in 1825 and remained there until 1832. In Heilbronn he had talked to emigrants when they were leaving for America. Now he saw how immigrants were faring in a new country. He learned by bitter experience that, without previous experience, it was a mistake to try to run a farm. But he was more successful as a journalist, an entrepreneur, and a politician. He played a leading part in establishing a colliery undertaking near Tamaqua and in constructing a railway from Tamaqua to Port Clinton. He edited the *Readinger Adler*, an influential German paper in Pennsylvania. In its columns he argued that more immigrants from Europe were needed to promote the economic expansion of the United States. In 1826 he printed a report which had appeared in the London *Courier* that unemployed English factory workers were being encouraged to migrate to Canada and he expressed the hope that some of them would find their way to Pennsylvania.[6]

During his stay in the United States List was involved in some abortive schemes to settle Germans in the United States. In 1828 he wrote to Dr. Rush (Secretary to the Treasury) that he proposed to establish a German settlement in Lycoming County in Pennsylvania[7] and subsequently he had 2,000 "hand bills to emigrants" printed in Philadelphia.[8] In 1830, when making arrangements to return to Europe, List applied for a post in the American consular service and informed Secretary of State van Buren that if he were appointed he would encourage Germans to emigrate to the territory of Michigan.[9] Back in Europe he corresponded with his business partner Isaac Hiester on the possibility of securing German miners for the colliery in which they both had an interest. He wrote:

> In respect of your desire to send coalminers from this country to Pennsylvania I have inserted some articles into the news-papers but I don't think that they will effectuate much, as the miners of this country are too poor to pay the passage to the United States. I will propose to you another plan. Several or all of the coal companies ... ought to combine for the purpose of importing miners. The passage might well be effectuated for 35 dollars a head. It therefore would require no greater advance than about 10,000 dollars to import 300 men, which might be recovered by deducting the advances afterwards from their wages.[10]

When he held office as American consul in Saxony List received an official enquiry concerning the transport of paupers from Germany to the United States. He replied that it had become

> a general practice in the towns and boroughs of Germany to get rid of their paupers and vicious members, by collecting the means for effectuating their passage to the United States among the inhabitants, and supporting them from the public funds. This practice is not only highly injurious to the United States, as it burdens them with a host of paupers and criminals, but it also deters the better and wealthier class of inhabitants of this country from emigrating to the United States.[11]

In the 1830s much of List's time and energy was devoted to promoting the construction of a network of railways in Germany. His writings on railways, however, throw little light on his views on the social question. He argued that the railways would create far more jobs than they would destroy and he appealed to rail-way companies to introduce cheap fares so as to give workers opportunities to travel that they had never enjoyed before. At this time List was involved in launching a new encyclopaedia to which he contributed articles on the workers and on labour-saving machinery. Here he attacked those who criticised the establishment of factories with machinery driven by steampower because they would throw domestic craftsmen out of work. List insisted that factories, like railways, eventually increased the number of jobs available. In his view the decline of job oppor-tunities was only a temporary phenomenon.[12]

III

List's attitude towards the social question in the 1840s may be gathered from articles which appeared in the *Zollvereinsblatt* and other journals. In a prospectus List promised that methods of alleviating distress among the workers would be discussed in the *Zollvereinsblatt*.[13] And in 1844 he printed an article from the *Trier'sche Zeitung* on a Society for the Welfare of the Working Classes which had recently been founded in Berlin.[14] List wrote many of the articles which appeared in the *Zollvereinsblatt*. Others were written by various contributors or were reprinted from German and foreign newspapers and weeklies. The contributors to the *Zollvereinsblatt* cannot always be identified but as List was the editor it may be assumed that he agreed with the opinions expressed in its pages.

List examined the condition of various types of workers – factory workers, smallholders, and domestic craftsmen – whose incomes were so low that they could not provide for themselves and their families. When dealing with the grievances of factory workers List faced a dilemma. He advocated the extension of the factory system and he believed that the establishment of an industrial economy would increase a country's wealth, enhance its power, and raise the standard of living of its people. In 1843 he declared that the factory system, far from impoverishing the workers provided them with higher earnings than they had obtained as peasants or domestic craftsmen. "It is not the factories that have created the poor, but the poor who have created the factories."[15]

Dr. Tögel, one of List's closest collaborators, declared that "wherever production by machinery flourishes, more workers are employed than were previously to be found in domestic workshops". And he considered that the workers had been relieved by machines of much heavy manual labour. Moreover workers were not only producers of goods. They were also consumers. And, as consumers, they could now buy a wider range of cheap manufactured products than before, because the output of factories was much greater than that of small workshops. Dr. Tögel denied that industrialisation had created "a great new proletariat" or that "despotic masters" were exploiting factory workers.[16]

It was not easy for List to reconcile his belief that the rise of modern industry benefited the labour force with the fact that there was serious unrest among many factory workers in the 1840s since men, women, and children worked long hours for low pay. He had to answer those who claimed that the workers were being exploited by the factory owners and were worse off than under the domestic system.

One argument that he put forward was that bad conditions of work were not an inherent characteristic of the factory system. He quoted in the *Zollvereinsblatt* an account by Charles Dickens of conditions in a cotton mill in Lowell (Massachusetts). He had written that the factory girls

> were all well dressed ... they had serviceable bonnets, good warm cloaks and shawls; and were not above clogs and pattens ... They were healthy in appearance, many of them remarkably so, and had the manners and deportment of young women; not of degraded brutes of burden ... The rooms in which they worked, were as well ordered as themselves. In the windows of some, there were green plants, which were trained to shade the glass; in all, there was as much fresh air, cleanliness and comfort, as the nature of the occupation would possibly permit of.

Dickens added that the girls lived in well conducted boarding houses near the mill.[17]

List also printed an article from the *Deutsche Gewerbezeitung* describing conditions in the Hammerstein cotton mill near Elberfeld. The most modern machinery, operating 24,000 spindles, had been installed in nine large workrooms which were well ventilated and spotlessly clean. Fire precautions included the construction of an outside fire escape built of stone. The labour force consisted of 400 operatives and some ancillary workers such as mechanics and carpenters. Power was supplied by a "gigantic iron waterwheel" and by a steam engine. Among the welfare services provided for the workers were houses, an elementary school, a sewing class, a savings bank, and a health insurance scheme. The millowner had built 18 blocks of flats for 75 families for which the workers paid much lower rents than those charged in neighbouring towns. Each flat had its own vegetable garden. Factory children received an hour's schooling a day, as well as religious instruction, while a sewing class for young women was held after working hours in the summer. The health insurance scheme was subsidised by the management, though the workers had to pay a small weekly contribution. The local medical officer had reported favourably on the health of the operatives. The article attacked critics of industrialisation who painted a gloomy picture of factory workers being treated like slaves by heartless employers. A visit to the Hammerstein mill would cause them to take a more favourable view of the social consequences of industrialisation.[18]

Although there were modern factories run by enlightened employers it was obvious that widespread distress existed in many factory towns. The passing of a Factory Act in Britain in 1844 gave List an opportunity to explain his attitude towards the evils of the factory system. He argued that the situation in Britain was an exceptional one which need not be repeated when other countries became industrialised. During the industrial revolution large numbers of workers had left the land for centres of industry. Manufacturers had made large profits. The great landowners had also enjoyed high incomes because they had been able to use their political influence to secure the maintenance of high import duties on cereals. The policy of protection raised the cost of living for the workers. List thought that the workers had earned high wages in the early phase of the industrial revolution – certainly more than they had earned as farm workers or domestic craftsmen. But circumstances were changing. Since 1815 the output of British industry had greatly expanded with the erection of new and bigger factories and the introduction of more efficient machines and processes. Competition among manufacturers coupled with a fall in the level of prices had reduced profits. The factory owners had reacted by reducing wages. But there had been no corresponding fall in the prices charged for food or consumer goods. A great tariff wall – particularly the Corn Laws – kept prices high. So in List's view it was a decline in the standard of living that had caused unrest in England in the 1840s.

List thought that the Factory Act of 1844, which reduced the hours worked by women in textile mills, failed to deal with the real cause of labour unrest. In his opinion workers in England were more concerned with the high price of food than with long hours. He proposed that landowners and manufacturers should make financial sacrifices to solve the problem – the former by agreeing to free trade (including the repeal of the Corn Laws) and the latter by increasing wages even if this meant lower profits. Only such a policy would reduce the cost of living for the workers and bring about industrial peace. He thought that Peel had been right to introduce an income tax since this would, to some extent, shift the burden of taxation to the shoulders of the wealthier classes. At the same time a reduction in the tariff would bring down the cost of food and consumer goods.

It has been seen that List regarded emigration as a cure for pauperism. In the early 1840s he wrote articles in the *Zollvereins-blatt* and the Augsburg *Allgemeine Zeitung* on this subject.[20] He advocated the establishment of a joint stock company to buy land in North America and to be responsible for settling Germans there. He praised a suggestion by Gladstone that the British government should make loans available to enable 20,000 persons a year to emigrate. But List thought that this scheme was far too modest to make a substantial impact on the problem that it was designed to solve.[21]

List had less difficulty in dealing with distress among domestic workers who could not compete with new factories and among peasants who could not make ends meet because their farms were very small. He considered that both groups belonged to a phase of economic development that was passing away. In his view the future lay with large factories and large farms which would be much more efficient than domestic workshops and tiny smallholdings. The creation of an industrial economy involved the transformation of rural craftsmen into urban factory workers and the establishment of large farms to feed the growing factory towns. List admitted that the transition from one type of economy to another might lead to temporary unemployment but eventually the workers would be better off in the new urban industrial society than they had been in the old rural society.

Since small workshops could not compete with factories, the fortunes of domestic craftsmen declined in the first half of the nineteenth century, particularly in the textile industries. In England the handloom weavers sank into a condition of abject poverty and by 1850 only 50,000 of them survived. In Germany the handloom weavers of Silesia were in a similar plight. By the 1840s piecework rates were so low that many weavers could not make ends meet, even though they often had smallholdings on which to grow their own vegetables. To make matters worse, feudal dues survived in Silesia, the weavers paying a special tax instead of working on their lord's farm. Yet there were those who argued that to some extent the weavers had only themselves to blame for their misfortunes. One contemporary writer accused them of "idleness, obstinacy, and conservatism"[22] because they refused to move with the times and rejected opportunities to enter a factory as full-time machine weavers, since that would involve giving up their smallholdings.

In June 1844 there were serious disturbances in the mountain villages of Silesia and mobs attacked the warehouses and homes of unpopular employers. The authorities called in troops to restore order. These events came as a shock to the public and many articles and pamphlets discussed the cause of poverty and suggested ways in which the situation might be remedied. An article by List on the Silesian weavers appeared in the *Zollvereinsblatt* in July 1844.[23] He contrasted the disturbances in Silesia with those in the English factory districts. He observed that the unrest in England had been due to the grievances of factory workers while in Silesia it was due to the grievances of handloom weavers. He argued that in England machinery had been adopted too quickly, while in Silesia it had not been adopted quickly enough. In England the recent slump had been caused by over-production and the inability of foreign markets to absorb all the goods that English manufacturers wished to sell. The Silesian economy, on the other hand, was depressed because markets had been lost owing to the imposition of hostile tariffs by foreign countries and to the greater efficiency of foreign manufacturers. The British tariff gave industrialists protection in the home market: the Zollverein tariff did not.

List declared that it had long been recognised that the manufacture of linen – once Germany's greatest export industry – would continue to decline unless more machinery was introduced. The Overseas Trading Corporation (*Seehandlung*), a Prussian state institution, had established some mechanised mills in Silesia[24] but List considered that they provided no answer to the problem. He argued that nationalised factories controlled by bureaucrats were never as successful as those run by private entrepreneurs. An official Prussian report had stated that in the past six months the *Seehandlung* had provided work for 1,200 weavers and their families and had paid them 6,722 thalers in wages.[25] List declared that this was an admission of failure. On the other hand he praised the Württemberg government which had granted a loan to enable a mechanical flax spinning mill to be established in Urach.[26] He thought that it was right for the state to assist private enterprise in this way but wrong for the state to set up its own nationalised enterprises.

The situation in Silesia could be remedied in two ways. The first was that the Zollverein should levy a high import duty on foreign linen yarn and cloth so as to give German manufacturers and workers an assured market at home. The second was that the Prussian government should grant subsidies and loans to entrepreneurs to enable them to establish factories with modern machines driven by steam power. As a temporary measure List advocated the introduction into Silesia of an improved handloom constructed by Claussen, a Belgian inventor.[27]

List also discussed the fate of peasants who practised what he called a "dwarf economy" and were condemned to a life of poverty because their holdings were too small to support a family. He argued that one cause of poverty in Ireland was early marriages and large families which were encouraged by the ease with which tiny plots of land could be rented. No wonder that the population of the country had doubled in 50 years.[28] List also discussed the causes of poverty among the peasants in the valleys of the Main and the Neckar. Like the Irish they cultivated minute smallholdings but while the Irish peasants were tenants, many of the peasants in south west Germany were freeholders. Their plots of land were continually being reduced in size because in that part of the country an estate was divided equally among the heirs when a peasant died. List argued that where a "dwarf economy" existed, the smallholdings should be combined to form larger farms and that displaced peasants should be encouraged to emigrate or to look for work in factories.[29]

IV

It has been seen that List did not put forward a doctrine of social development to supplement his theories of productive forces and phases of economic growth. His critics suggested that he was too preoccupied with his advocacy of industrialisation to concern himself with the social question and that he was more interested in the rôle of the middle classes in promoting economic expansion in Germany than in the fate of the workers in the new factories. List admired Defoe's "honest projector" and believed that the middle classes would provide the dynamic drive towards industrialisation. From their ranks would come the architects of the new economy – the scientists, the inventors, the entrepreneurs, and the managers. The factory workers no doubt had a part to play in the process of industrialisation but their rôle would be a subordinate one. And as for peasants, smallholders, and domestic craftsmen, List considered that they belonged to an age of economic development that was soon destined to give way to a predominantly industrial economy. It has been suggested that List's attitude towards the social question explains his failure to examine in any detail the doctrine of the early socialists. He showed some interest in the communities established by Robert Owen and the Rappists in America but he does not seem to have taken the socialist doctrines of Fourier, Weitling and Marx very seriously.

It has been observed that List and Marx were the leading exponents of two diametrically opposed views on the future development of society.[30] They agreed that the old feudal agrarian society was giving way to a new industrial society in which the middle classes would play a dominant role. But while List apparently assumed that the triumph of the middle classes would last for ever, Marx was confident that it would be shortlived. Before long the workers would overthrow the bourgeoisie to become the dominant class in society. Another fundamental difference between List and Marx was that List was a nationalist who devoted his energies to promoting the economic expansion and political unification of Germany while Marx believed that his doctrines were of universal application and he appealed to the workers of the world to unite to destroy the capitalist system and to replace it by a dictatorship of the proletariat.

In the twentieth century the leaders of communist states paid homage to Marx, whose doctrines had inspired the revolutions that had brought them to power. The capitalist world, however, largely forgot List's powerful advocacy of industrialisation and free enterprise. One reason for this may be his failure to place a greater emphasis on the rôle of the vast mass of the workers in the industrial society that he wished to promote.

NOTES

1. See also F. Seidel, *Das Armutsproblem im deutschen Vormärz bei Friedrich List* (1971) and *Die soziale Frage in der deutschen Geschichte* (1964).
2. *Mitteilungen der List-Gesellschaft*, No. 29 (May 5, 1935), p.554.
3. Hilde Rigaudias-Weiss, *Les enquêtes ouvrières en France entre 1830 et 1848* (1936), p.33. Pierre Leroux argued that the official figures were too low and he estimated there were 1,831,000 paupers in France in 1833.
4. The manuscript of List's record of his interviews in Heilbronn, Weinsberg, and Neckarsulm is in the List archives (Fasc. II/4) and part of a draft of his report to the Ministry of the Interior is printed in F. List, *Werke*, Vol. VIII, pp.104–8. See also T. Steimle, "Friedrich List und die Auswanderung aus Württemberg" in *Mitteilungen der Friedrich List Gesellschaft*, 1921, pp.444–8; M. Miller, "Ursachen und Ziele der schwäbischen Auswanderung" in *Korrespondenzblatt des Gesamtvereins der deutschen Geschichts- und Altertumsvereins*, Vol. 81 (1933) and G.P. Bassler, "Auswanderungsfreiheit und Auswanderfürsorge in Württemberg" in *Zeitschrift für Württembergische Landesgeschichte*, Vol. 33, 1974, pp.117–60.
5. F. List, *Werke*, Vol. VIII, pp.867–7.

6. *Readinger Adler*, September 26, 1826, in F. List, *Werke*, Vol. II, p.240.
7. J. Ridgway to F. List, April 23, 1828: "Dr. Rush handed to me your letter to him on the subject of a German settlement in Lycoming County" (List archives, Fasc. 41/47 and *Werke*, Vol. II, p.485).
8. F. List, *Werke*, Vol. II, p.485.
9. F. List to Martin van Buren, October 21, 1830 in *Werke*, Vol. II, pp.302–3.
10. F. List to Isaac Hiester (probably 1832) in *Werke*, Vol. II, pp.486–7.
11. F. List to Levy Woodbury (secretary to the Treasury), March 8, 1837 in *Werke*, Vol. II, pp.332–3.
12. Rotteck and Welcker, *Staatslexikon oder Encyklopädie der Staatswissenschaften*, Vol. I (1832) and F. List, *Werke*, Vol. V, pp.30–5.
13. F. List to the J.G. Cotta publishing house, November 19, 1842 in F. List, *Werke*, Vol. VIII, p.656.
14. "Der Verein für das Wohl der Hand- und Fabrikarbeiter" in *Das Zollvereinsblatt*, No. 47, November 18, 1844, pp.924–8. The correct name of the society was *Verein für das Wohl der arbeitenden Klassen*. See Adolf Schmidt: *Die Zukunft der arbeitenden Klassen und die Vereine für ihr Wohl* (1845), *Der Centralverein für das Wohl der arbeitenden Klassen in fünfzigjähriger Täthigkeit 1844–94* (1894), H.R. Schmeider, "Bürgerliche Vereinsbestrebungen für das Wohl der arbeitenden Klassen" (University of Bonn dissertation, 1967).
15. List to King Wilhelm I of Württemberg, April 9, 1843 in F. List, *Werke*, Vol. IX, pp.1–15.
16. "Die Organisation der Arbeiter und die heutige Industrie" in *Das Zollvereinsblatt*, February 11, 1845 (signed 'T').
17. "Die Factorybill" (second article) in *Das Zollvereinsblatt*, April 22, 1844, pp.313–22. See Charles Dickens, *American Notes and Pictures from Italy* (reprint of the first edition, 1893), pp.57–9.
18. "Die Spinnerei zu Hammerstein bei Elbefeld" in *Das Zollvereinsblatt*, March 25, 1845.
19. The Factory Act of 1844 gave women of all ages the same protection as that granted to young persons (aged 13 to 18) in 1833. Their hours of work were reduced to 12 a day and they were not allowed to work at night. Children under 13 were to attend school for 3 hours a day and their daily hours of labour were reduced to 6½. Dangerous moving machinery had to be fenced. The Act applied to textile factories.
20. F. List, "Über die Auswanderung nach Nordamerika" in *Das Zollvereinsblatt*, July 24, 1843, pp.603–4 and 622–3. A book on emigration to Texas (by G.A. Scherpf) was advertised in *Das Zollvereinsblatt*, October 23, 1843. On March 15, 1843 W.L.I. Kiderlin wrote to List: "I see from several articles in the (Augsburg) *Allgemeine Zeitung* that you are at present concerned with a plan to promote emigration" (List archives, Fasc. 41/2 and F. List, *Werke*, Vol. II, p.487).
21. F. List, "Die Factorybill" (first article) in *Das Zollvereinsblatt*, April 8, 1844, pp.281–9. A second article appeared on April 22, 1844 (pp.313–22).
22. Alexander Schneer, *Über die Not der Leinen-Arbeiter in Schlesien und die Mittel ihr abzuhelfen* (1844).
23. F. List, "Die Noth in Schlesien und die Handelspolitik des Zollvereins" in *Das Zollvereinsblatt*, July 8, 1844, pp.537–47 and in F. List, *Werke*, Vol. VIII, pp.397–403. At the end of this article List printed an extract from the *Weser-Zeitung*, June 26, 1844 (pp.544–7) which is not reproduced in *Werke*.
24. For the industrial enterprises of the Overseas Trading Corporation see Christian von Rother, *Die Verhältnisse des Königlichen Seehandlungs-Institut und dessen Geschäftsführung und industrielle Unternehmungen* (1845).
25. Article in the *Vossiche Zeitung* quoted in F. List, "Die Noth in Schlesien ..." in *Das Zollvereinsblatt*, July 8, 1844, p.540 (note).
26. Escher Wyss of Zürich received a loan of 150,000 florins to build a flax spinning mill

at Urach and to instal 20 spinning machines. See P. Borscheid, *Textilarbeiterschaft in der Industrialisierung* (1978), p.113.

27. For Claussen's handloom see "Der neue Handwebstuhl" in *Das Zollvereinsblatt*, 1846, p.577.

28. F. List, "Das Eisenbahnsystem in Irland" in the Augsburg *Allgemeine Zeitung*, No. 169 and No. 170, 1839 and *Werke*, Vol. VII, p.374.

29. F. List, "Die Ackerverfassung, die Zwergwirtschaft, und die Auswanderung", in the *Deutsche Vierteljahrschrift*, 1842, Heft IV, pp.106–191 and in *Werke*, Vol. V, pp.418–547 and comments by the editors, pp.640–91. See also Gertrud Mayer, *Friedrich List als Agrarpolitiker* (1938).

30. J. Plenge, *Die Stammformen der vergleichenden Wirtschaftstheorie* (1919), A. Meusel, *List und Marx* (1928), and F. Lenz, *Friedrich List: die 'Vulgarökonomie', und Karl Marx* (1930). Marx criticised List's *National System of Political Economy* in an essay probably written in 1845. The essay was not published in Marx's lifetime but 39 pages of the manuscript have survived. Pages 10 to 21, however, are missing. The manuscript was published under the title "Über Friedrich Lists Buch *Das nationale System der politischen Ökonomie*" in *Beiträge zur Geschichte der Arbeiterbewegung*, June 1972, Heft iii. See Carl-Erich Vollgraf, "Karl Marx über die ökonomische Theorie von Friedrich List" in *Wirtschafts Wissenschaft*, 1977, Vol. 7, pp.991–1010.

9

FRIEDRICH LIST AND THE FRENCH PROTECTIONISTS

In the nineteenth century few economists had travelled as widely as Friedrich List. In Germany he lived in his native Württemberg and in Baden, Saxony, and Bavaria. Abroad he made his home first in America and then in France. He visited Austria, Hungary, England and Belgium. It is hardly surprising that his doctrines should have been influenced by ideas on economics prevalent in the countries in which he lived. When he was in the United States in 1825–1830 he was a leading advocate of the "American System" which was supported by Henry Clay, Mathew Carey, and Charles Ingersoll, who urged Congress to impose high import duties to safeguard "infant industries" from foreign competition.[1]

While List's debt to American protectionists is well known his debt to French protectionists has sometimes been overlooked.[2] His ideas were in no small measure derived from those put forward by an influential group of French economists who rejected the principles of laissez-faire and free trade advocated by Adam Smith and his French disciples, such as J.B. Say and Bastiat. The leaders of the French protectionists in the early nineteenth century – Jean Antoine Chaptal and Charles Dupin – considered that France should adhere to her traditional economic policies, once successfully pursued by Colbert, with such modifications as were necessary in view of changes in the economy that had taken place since the seventeenth century.

These economists, and the governments which followed their advice between 1815 and 1848, believed that it was the duty of the state to encourage farming, industry, and commerce by every means in its power. They considered that a high tariff should be imposed to safeguard native industries, that exports should be stimulated to earn foreign currencies, and that shipping should be protected by navigation laws. They believed that the state should promote economic growth in various ways – by organising industrial exhibitions, by encouraging inventors, by attracting skilled foreign artisans to the country, and by founding technical colleges and scientific academies.

J.A. CHAPTAL

One of the first works by a French economist that influenced List was Chaptal's account of France's national wealth which appeared in 1819.[3] In the following year List referred to this book in a memorandum which he submitted to Metternich on behalf of the German Union of Merchants.[4] List admired Chaptal not only as an economist but as a scientist, a statesman, and a practical man of affairs.[5]

J.A. Chaptal was a man of exceptional gifts who had a remarkable career. In 1781 the Languedoc Estates established a chair of chemistry at the medical academy of Montpellier and appointed Chaptal, then aged 25, to be the first professor. Five years later he was also running a chemical factory producing sulphuric acid and alum.

During the revolution the Committee of Public Safety enlisted the aid of leading scientists to stimulate industrial expansion. France was threatened by a hostile coalition and the armies of the Republic were short of ammunition. In this crisis Robespierre called upon Berthellot, Monge, and Chaptal to increase the production of gunpowder as quickly as possible. In seven months Chaptal set up saltpetre works in 11 Departments. Although a large powder mill at Grenelle (a suburb of Paris) blew up with heavy loss of life, sufficient gunpowder was produced to enable a successful offensive to be launched in the Austrian Netherlands. At the same time Chaptal was involved in the founding of the *Ecole Polytechnique* in Paris to ensure a supply of well trained scientists and engineers in the future. This institution became one of the leading technical colleges in Europe.[6]

On becoming First Consul Napoleon placed Chaptal in charge of the Ministry of the Interior, which was responsible for economic affairs and education. List regarded this as an imaginative appointment, since although Chaptal was a "mere chemist", he filled the post "with great success".[7] Years of conflict at home and abroad, the collapse of the currency, and the loss of overseas markets had left the economy in a deplorable state. And during Chaptal's term of office France was at war with Britain, except for a brief interlude of 14 months when the Treaty of Amiens was in force. Chaptal realised that some of the changes which had occurred during the revolution favoured the revival of agriculture and industry. Internal tariffs had been abolished, restrictions on industry imposed by the gilds and local authorities had disappeared, and the peasants had been freed from feudal obligations. In the circumstances Chaptal was confident that, aided by government assistance and encouragement, the French economy could quickly recover from its recent decline.

Chaptal's policy of reconstruction included installing new machines in French workshops, making practical use of new scientific discoveries and introducing substitutes for products which were in short supply because of the British blockade. Woad replaced indigo, beet sugar replaced cane sugar while improvements were made in the purification of alum and in the manufacture of sulphuric acid, gunpowder, and dyestuffs. Chaptal disseminated information concerning improved processes and machinery through over twenty newly established advisory chambers of commerce as well as through consultative councils of manufacturers, industrial exhibitions,[8] and the influential Society for the Encouragement of National Industry.[9]

As Minister of the Interior Chaptal generally devoted one day a week – sometimes accompanied by Napoleon – to visiting industrial establishments in and around Paris to encourage managers and workers to achieve greater efficiency in production. He also accompanied Napoleon on tours of inspection further afield. In his memoirs he mentioned visits to Lyons, Normandy, and Belgium.[10] Chaptal was also responsible for constructing public works in Paris. Waterways were improved by constructing the Ourcq canal; an extension to the Louvre was built; and the quays of the River Seine were extended.

The poor in Paris were assisted by the establishment of a public granary, new almshouses, and a maternity hospital. Another of Chaptal's achievements was the inauguration of an economic survey of the whole of France. Prefects were made responsible for the collection of statistics on the output of agriculture and industry in their Departments and this information was sent to the Ministry of the Interior. The survey was not completed but it was the first attempt since Louis XIV's reign to make an estimate of the output of the whole economy.

In 1803 Chaptal persuaded the Scottish engineer William Douglas to migrate to France. Assisted by a government grant Douglas set up a woollen cloth mill on the Ile de Cygnes in Paris in which he installed the newest carding and spinning machines. Then he turned his attention to the manufacture of textile machinery and within a few years he had supplied nearly a thousand machines to a hundred factories.[11] The introduction of improved machinery into French workshops was an essential feature of Chaptal's policy. He accepted that this might cause temporary unemployment but he had no sympathy with workers – such as the hand-shearers of Sedan – who resisted the installing of new machines.[12]

When Chaptal left the Ministry of the Interior in 1805 with the reputation of "a Colbert of the nineteenth century"[13] he was appointed a member of the Senate and continued to act as one of Napoleon's advisers on economic affairs. In 1810, when he became a member of the Superior Council of Manufactures and Arts, he was given responsibility for industrial affairs. In the following year he was ennobled and took the title of Comte de Chanteloup. He remained faithful to Napoleon during the Hundred Days, holding office as Director of Trade and Industry. Between 1804 and 1814 he was engaged in public duties, in running his chemical works, and in continuing his scientific researches. As early as 1802 Chaptal had claimed that there was a great difference "between the present state of our industry and that in which it has been in all former times".[14] Later, in his memoirs, he confidently asserted that under Napoleon "we freed ourselves from the tribute which we had up to that time paid to foreigners. It was during his rule that we saw for the first time all our industrial products compete favourably, both as to price and to quality, with the goods of the most advanced industrial nations in all the markets of Europe".[15]

After Napoleon's fall Chaptal did not hold public office again but his services to his country were recognised by his elevation to the *chambre des pairs*. He extended his business interests by establishing a beet-sugar refinery at Chanteloup and by becoming an investor in the Le Creusot ironworks. In 1819 he completed his major work, *De l'industrie françoise*, which was soon recognised as a standard work on the changes that had occurred in the French economy between 1789 and 1819. But Chaptal would have been surprised had he realised that his book was to have an influence far beyond the frontiers of France. It was to inspire the thinking of a young man who was to become one of the leading economists in Germany. It has been seen that List had read Chaptal's book soon after it appeared. In Chaptal's discussion of national wealth, economic growth and the role of the state in promoting the expansion of agriculture and industry List found many of the ideas which were to form the basis of his own economic theories. But he did not follow Chaptal slavishly.

It has been observed that Chaptal "defended not merely protective tariffs but prohibitions (which, he claimed, had alone enabled French industry to prosper) and even duties on imported raw materials".[16] List, on the other hand, argued that import duties were normally preferable to prohibitions and that raw materials and agricultural products should be admitted duty free.[17]

Chaptal's book was not a treatise on economics but a survey of France's economic development and commercial policy between 1789 and 1819. It was (in List's view) "nothing less than a defence of the French commercial policy, and an exposition of its results as a whole and in every particular".[18] In his introduction Chaptal summarised the fortunes of the French economy, with particular emphasis on the way in which Sully and Colbert had promoted the expansion of industry in the seventeenth century. Chaptal then examined France's commercial relations with foreign countries before 1789 and gave detailed statistics of imports and exports in the three years before the revolution. He criticised the Eden Treaty of 1786 on the ground that Britain had secured the best of the bargain. There followed an examination of recent progress in France of various branches of agriculture and industry. Chaptal considered that important factors in stimulating the expansion of manufactures were the adoption of new machines and the introduction of new processes based upon scientific discoveries. In conclusion he discussed the "administration of industry". He considered that "commerce, agriculture, and industry are the basis of a nation's wealth and governments should have but one aim, namely to protect them and to encourage them".

In List's writings there are numerous references to *De l'industrie françoise* and there are also passages which, though Chaptal's name may not be mentioned, are clearly based on Chaptal's book. In two pamphlets, published in the United States in 1827, List declared that Chaptal was "a chemist and statesman, who by his researches in chemistry as well as by his political exertions did more for the promotion of the industry of France than ever one man did in any other country". He praised Chaptal's chapter on tariffs which, in his view, was "a most practical and material refutation" of the doctrine of free trade.[19]

In *The Natural System of Political Economy*, written in 1837,[20] List quoted with approval a statement by Chaptal defending France's traditional economic policy. Chaptal had explained that

instead of becoming lost in a labyrinth of metaphysical abstractions, we would maintain the existing state of affairs and endeavour to improve it. A sound tariff is a real protection for agriculture and industry. Its duties are raised or lowered in accordance with circumstances and needs. It compensates manufacturers for high wages and the high cost of fuel. Its prohibitions protect infant industries until they are strong enough to face foreign competition. It ensures the industrial independence of France and enriches the state by the labour of its workers which, as I have frequently observed, is the chief source of national wealth.[21]

List also named Chaptal as one of the writers whose views on "productive forces" had influenced him in enunciating his own theory on this subject. He observed that Chaptal had shown how much the growth of the French economy owed to the efforts of the government to stimulate agriculture and industry and to promote foreign trade.

List's principal work, *The National System of Political Economy,* published in 1841, also contained references to Chaptal's book. List's discussion of England's commercial policy, of the Methuen and Eden treaties, of scientific advance as a factor promoting economic growth, and of the ability of agriculture to flourish without tariff protection were very similar to the views expressed in *De l'industrie françoise* 22 years before. But List complained that in one passage Chaptal had praised the policy of free trade which was in direct contradiction to his frequent advocacy of a protective tariff.[22] What List failed to appreciate was that when Chaptal supported "freedom of commerce" he did not have free trade between nations in mind but he was referring to freedom from the shackles imposed upon industry by the state and by the gilds in France under the ancien régime.

Moreover List failed to realise the drawback of placing so much reliance upon Chaptal's arguments. It has been seen that Chaptal had been Minister of the Interior when France was at war and that his policy had been to promote economic growth at a time when France was cut off from her colonies and other overseas markets — though she was able to exploit the resources of neighbouring countries which had been overrun by Napoleon's armies. In these circumstances it was natural that the French government should (regardless of cost) foster the establishment of industries which would provide substitutes for products — such as sugar and soda — which were in short supply because of the British blockade.

Writing in 1819 Chaptal not only defended Napoleon's economic policy in time of war but argued that France should continue to pursue the same policy in time of peace. It has been seen that List's main works were written in 1837 and in 1841 when economic conditions in Europe and North America were very different from what they had been a quarter of a century before. Some of the policies which Chaptal had advocated in 1819 had little relevance in a world which was being rapidly changed by advances in science and technology, by the expansion of industry and banking, and by improvements in communications. Moreover Chaptal's statistics were out of date by the time that List was writing. For example in 1831 List wrote an article in which he discussed Chaptal's views on the tobacco régie in France.[23] Chaptal had argued that the régie had failed to revive tobacco cultivation since between 1812 and 1816 – the first four years when it was in operation – there had been a sharp decline in the number of tobacco factories.[24] He had advocated the imposition of an excise on tobacco which he believed would produce a larger revenue for the state than the profits from the régie. But the statistics used by Chaptal to support his argument – and quoted by List – had little relevance in 1832.

CHARLES DUPIN[25]

In a series of letters to Charles Ingersoll, published in 1827, List urged the American Government to impose a high tariff to stimulate industrial growth.[26] To mark the success of the pamphlet in which the letters were printed the Pennsylvania Society for the Encouragement of Manufactures – a leading protectionist association – gave a dinner in Philadelphia in honour of the author. In his speech on this occasion[27] List declared that "the days of the *laissez faire* theory are numbered even in France, since the celebrated Charles Dupin wrote his *Situation Progressive des Forces de la France depuis 1814* (1827)". This pamphlet was the introduction to Dupin's *Forces productives et commerciales de la France*. His views on the productive forces of France coincided with those expressed by List in his letters to Ingersoll. He admired Dupin as a scholar and practical man of affairs – mathematician, engineer, economist, writer, official, and politician – who was one of the leading authorities on the French economy.

Charles Dupin was born in 1784. He studied mathematics and engineering at the Ecole Polytechnique in Paris and then joined the corps of naval engineers in 1803. He worked on the construction of fortifications at Boulogne, Antwerp, and the Dutch coast. Next he served in the Ionian Islands, Italy and Toulon. After Napoleon's fall Dupin, now a captain, paid several visits to Britain and submitted a report to the French Academy of Sciences on the ports and high-ways of that country.[28] A long account of his travels appeared in 1820.[29] He was now teaching geometry and mechanics at a college associated with the Conservatoire des arts et métiers,[30] and his major work on the economic recovery of France after the Napo-leonic wars was published in 1827.[31]

In the same year Dupin was elected to the Chamber of Deputies. He supported the critics of the restored Bourbons and denounced the reactionary policy of Joseph Villèle, the ultra-royalist president of the Council of State from 1821 to 1828. Dupin was also one of the most effective champions of the protectionist cause in the chamber.[32] The aims of the supporters of the more liberal July Monarchy were more to Dupin's liking than those of Villèle. Louis Philippe appointed Dupin to several public offices – the Council of State, the Admiralty Council, the Commission of Finances, the Agricultural Council, and the Academy of Sciences. Dupin also served as rapporteur on the naval estimates. In 1832 he was appointed a commander of the Legion of Honour. Two years later he was responsible for the report of the jury on the manufactures shown at the Paris industrial exhibition.[33] He was appointed a member of the upper chamber of the legislature (*chambre des pairs*). Here he supported a bill to regulate the hours of children under the age of 16 in workshops.[34] In the following year he advocated the establishment of a factory inspectorate, a reduction in the hours worked by women in factories, and an extension of the regulations to establishments employing more than ten workers.

Although Dupin was moving to the right in politics he was elected to the Constituent Assembly in 1848 and was appointed president of its Admiralty Committee (*Comité de la Marine*). He was a member of the committee which recommended the dissolution of the National Workshops.[35] In 1849 he was elected to the Legislative Assembly. He supported Louis Napoleon's coup d'état and was later rewarded with a seat on the Senate. During the Second Empire he devoted his energies to stimulating the growth of French manu-factures by promoting industrial exhibitions. In 1847 he had advo-cated the holding of an international (as distinct from a national) industrial exhibition[36] and in 1851 he was president of the French jury at the Great Exhibition in London. In 1855 he served on the commission responsible for organising the industrial exhibition in Paris.

Dupin laid no claim to be an original thinker or a propounder of new economic theories. He regarded himself as a "narrator" and a "statistician".[37] His major work on *Forces productives et commerciales de la France* might be regarded as a sequel to Chaptal's *De l'industrie françoise*. While Chaptal had dealt with the period 1789–1819 Dupin examined France's recovery after the Napoleonic wars and covered the period 1818–1827. He estimated that during the recent wars France had lost 1,500,000 men. She had lost rich colonies in the West Indies while her overseas trade had suffered from the British blockade. After the war provision had been made for 300,000 soldiers returning to France from serving abroad. Money had to be found to pay an indemnity and to defray the costs of an army of occupation. Yet in the twelve years that followed the Congress of Vienna France had made an astonishing recovery. Dupin declared that "l'oeil cherche en vain nos cicatrices; la patrie a réparé ses immense malheurs; elle est sortie de son épuisement, et, grâce à son énergie morale, fruit heureux de ses libertés, la voila plus robuste, plus active et plus imposante que jamais".

Dupin believed that encouragement by the state had been a major factor in promoting the economic recovery of France after 1815. A high tariff had protected manufactures from foreign competition. A navigation code had safeguarded shipping interests. Grants had been made to foster new industries and new inventions. Technical schools and colleges had provided industry with well educated skilled workers and managers. Industrial exhibitions had been held. Policies once practised by Colbert had been revived and adapted to the needs of a country which was becoming industrialised. The policy that Dupin believed to be right to promote the development of France's "productive forces" was the policy that List believed would be right for Germany.

While List's doctrines had undoubtedly been influenced by Chaptal's *De l'industrie françoise*, published in 1819, they had not been influenced by Dupin's *Forces productives et commerciales de la France* which appeared after List had written his letters to Ingersoll. List did not see himself as one of Dupin's disciples. He regarded Dupin as a colleague with whose views he agreed and whose book provided evidence of the success of the policy of promoting economic growth by state action. He used Dupin's statistics on several occasions in articles written for French periodicals in the

1830s and in his contributions to the Augsburg *Allgemeine Zeitung* in the 1840s. List saw Dupin as one who – in his writings and speeches – was advocating in France the same policy that he was trying to persuade the Germans to adopt. He regarded Dupin as a powerful ally who was energetically attacking the free trade and laissez faire notions of the English classical economists and their disciples in France. Dupin and List agreed that the liberal economic doctrines of J.B. Say were erroneous and should be refuted on every possible occasion.

Dupin had a considerable influence over List's first detailed statement of his economic theories. This was *The Natural System of Political Economy* which he wrote shortly after settling in Paris in the autumn of 1837.[38] The essay was written in the hope of winning a prize offered by the French Academy of Moral and Political Sciences. Three years previously the Academy had proposed the following subject for a prize essay: "Lorsqu'une nation se propose d'établir la liberté du commerce ou de modifier sa législation sur les douanes, quels sont les faits, qu'elle doit prendre en considération pour concilier de la manière la plus équitable les intérêts des producteurs et ceux de la masses des consommateurs?" None of the four essays submitted received a prize and in December 1836 the Academy again offered a prize for an essay on the same subject.[39] This time some guidance to the candidates was offered by the Academy in a report drawn up by Dupin. An examination of the essay submitted by List shows how closely List followed Dupin's advice.[40]

In his "programme" Dupin had raised a number of questions which he hoped that the competitors would answer in their essays. Was it right that cheap imports from abroad should be allowed to ruin a branch of industry at home in the name of free trade? Should industries that had developed during a war (to produce goods in short supply) be allowed to sink into oblivion when hostilities ceased? Would it be in the national interest to protect an industry which could not compete with a foreign rival because that rival had gained an advantage by using a newly invented efficient machine? And should the state foster the growth of a new industry by a tariff and by encouraging skilled foreign mechanics to settle in France? In his essay List attempted to answer these – and other – questions posed by Dupin.

List was angry when the Academy for the second time declared that none of the essays submitted was good enough to be awarded the prize but he did not blame Dupin for his disappointment. In *The*

National System of Political Economy, his major work published in 1841, he again praised Dupin for "throwing such a clear light on the commercial policy which France has followed since the Restoration". And he again urged his compatriots to adopt the policy of protection which, in his view, had brought prosperity to France.

Dupin for his part continued to appreciate the significance of List's work in the cause of protection. In 1846 he gave Freiherr von Varnbüler a copy of a recent speech that he had made on fiscal policy and asked him to pass it on to List. And List published the speech in his periodical, the *Zollvereinsblatt*.[41] This was his last tribute to a statesman and scholar whom he had admired for nearly twenty years.

F. L. A. FERRIER

If Karl Marx had not declared that a book by F. L. A. Ferrier was "the main source" from which List had derived his economic theories no one would for a moment have associated List with one of the least known French economists of the early nineteenth century.[42] Marx's assertion – unsupported by any evidence – was however sufficient to encourage Ladenthin to comb the works of Ferrier and List in the hope of finding some similar passages in the writings of the two economists.[43] But his researches provided no satisfactory evidence that List was in any way indebted to Ferrier.

Ferrier, an official in the customs administration, rose to be the Director of Customs in 1812, a post which he lost when Napoleon fell from power. He was subsequently Director of Customs in Dunkirk and wrote several reports, the most important being *Du gouvernement considéré dans ses rapports avec le commerce*. The first edition of 1802 was followed by a second in 1820 and a third in 1822. The third edition was considerably longer than the first – 587 pages as against 397 pages. The main difference between the two editions was that in the first Ferrier argued that "l'argent est le grand instrument, l'instrument indispensable de la circulation et de la reproduction" whereas in the second he declared that "la richesse des peuples consiste dans l'abondance des choses consommables". Ferrier, like Chaptal and Dupin, supported the economic policy pursued by Napoleon and argued that it was the duty of the state to promote the expansion of agriculture, industry, and commerce by every means in its power.

In their introduction to List's *The Natural System of Political Economy* Edgar Salin and Artur Sommer discussed at great length the alleged influence of Ferrier upon List. After exhaustive researches they could find only three possible links between the two economists. First, there is a scrap of paper in the List archives in Reutlingen[44] on which List had written "Ferrier commerce français" on one side and "Paris, September 15, 1831" on the other. But the fact that a scholar makes a note of the title of a book is no evidence that he has read the book. Secondly, in the introduction to *The Natural System of Political Economy* List referred with approval to the doctrines of "a French writer". In the margin of the manuscript List identified the writer as "M. Ferrier". This is evidence that List was aware of Ferrier's existence but it does not prove that Ferrier exercised any influence over List.

Thirdly, there is a passage in *The National System of Political Economy* which closely resembles a passage in the third edition of Ferrier's book. List wrote that there were people who had argued that economics could not yet be regarded as an exact science. In the meantime "what goes by its name is merely an astrology – but it is possible and desirable to produce an astronomy out of it".[45] In a similar passage Ferrier had observed that in the seventeenth century the French Academy had warned astronomers not to dabble in astrology and had urged chemists to stop looking for the philosopher's stone. "La pierre philosophale de l'économie politique, c'est la liberté illimitée du commerce. Espérons qu'elle y renoncera aussi et qu'elle deviendra enfin une science utile, comme cela est arrivé de l'astronomie et de la chimie depuis que la première a méprisé l'astrologie et la seconde le grand-oeuvre".[46] The reference to astrology and astronomy in both passages makes it possible to argue that List had read Ferrier's book. But the evidence is not conclusive and it is quite clear that List's doctrines were not influenced by Ferrier's book in the same way that they were influenced by the works of Chaptal and Dupin. And it is not known why Marx, who had a detailed knowledge of the history of economic thought, should have regarded Ferrier's book rather than the works of Chaptal and Dupin as the "source" of List's economic doctrines.

It would be unfortunate if the search for the "sources" of List's doctrines were to detract in any way from an appreciation of List as an original thinker. List had read the works of the leading American and French protectionists of his day and he used the material that they had assembled to support his own arguments. But his doctrines were not derived from those of earlier economists. List's theories of productive forces and stages of economic growth were his own and were a significant contribution to the development of economic studies in the 1830s and 1840s. And his views reached a wide public in Germany, since they appeared not only in *The National System of Political Economy* but in newspapers (such as the Augsburg *Allgemeine Zeitung*) and in his own periodicals – the *Eisenbahnjournal* and the *Zollvereinsblatt*.

NOTES

1. W. Notz, "Friedrich List in America" in *American Economic Review*, XV (2), June 1926, and the same author's introduction to F. List, *Werke*, Vol. II.
2. For the French protectionists in the first half of the 19th century see R. Maunier, "Les économistes protectionnistes en France de 1815 à 1848" in *Revue Internationale de Sociologie*, XIV, pp.485–510.
3. J.A. Chaptal, *De l'industrie françoise* (2 vols, 1819). An English translation of one chapter – *Essay on Import Duties* – was published in Philadelphia in 1821.
4. List to Metternich, 18 Feb. 1820 in F. List, *Werke*, Vol. I (2), p.551. There are also references to Chaptal in articles by List in *Organ für den deutschen Handels- und Gewebestand*, 1820, p.37 and 1821, p.93 and p.143 and in the *Allgemeine Anzeiger der Deutschen*, 1822, No. 169 ("Das verarmende Deutschland").
5. See J.A. Chaptal, *Mes souvenirs sur Napoléon* (1893), M.J. Flourens, *Eloge historique de J.A. Chaptal* (1835), and J. Pigeire, *La vie et l'oeuvre de Chaptal, 1756–1832* (1932).
6. J.P. Callot, *Histoire de l'école politechnique* (1958). The Paris polytechnic was established by a decree of 11 March 1794 (the original name being Ecole centrale des travaux publiques) and was opened on 28 Sept. 1794. Chaptal lectured on "vegetable chemistry" at the Paris polytechnic. Charles Dupin, writing in 1827, declared that "depuis trente trois ans, l'école politechnique a répandu sur tous les points de la France, près de quatre mille officiers des travaux publics" (*Forces productives et commerciales de la France* (2 vols, 1827, introduction, p.xxiii).
7. F. List, "Der Kampf um die württembergische Verfassung" (1822) in F. List, *Werke*, Vol. 1 (1), p.472.
8. Industrial exhibitions were held in the Champ de Mars in 1798 and in the Louvre in 1801 and 1802.
9. The *Société d'encouragement pour l'industrie nationale* was founded in 1801.
10. See the chapter on "Mes voyages avec Napoléon" in J.A. Chaptal, *Mes souvenirs sur Napoléon* (1893), pp.367–78. On a visit to a cotton mill in Rouen Chaptal showed a dyer how to produce "des couleurs unies".
11. J.A. Chaptal, *De l'industrie françoise* (2 vols, 1819), Vol. II, p.16.
12. H. Sée, *Histoire économique de la France*, Vol. II, *Les temps modernes* (1951), p.103. The riots in Sedan occurred in 1803.
13. Lujo Brentano to Charles Gide in J.A. Chaptal, *Mes souvenirs sur Napoléon* (1893), p.51 (note).
14. Quoted by S.B. Clough, *France. A History of National Economics* (1939), p.63.
15. J.A. Chaptal, *Mes souvenirs sur Napoléon* (1893), p.279.
16. B.M. Ratcliffe, "The Tariff Reform Campaign in France, 1831–6" in *Journal of European Economic History*, VII, p.61–138.
17. In 1845, in reply to Richelot's criticism of his views on agriculture, List accepted that, in certain circumstances, tariff protection might be extended to farm produce.
18. F. List, *The National System of Political Economy* (1841; English translation by S.S. Lloyd, 1885 and 1966), p.375. In 1837 in *The Natural System of Political Economy* (translated by W.O. Henderson, 1983) List had written that "Chaptal's

book on French industry champions the policy of protection from cover to cover and gives numerous details of the success achieved by this policy" (p.150).

19. F. List, *The Outlines of American Political Economy* (1827), reprinted in F. List, *Werke*, II, p.111. In November 1829 in the *Readinger Adler*, which he edited, List mentioned a book by Chaptal on the wine industry.

20. First published in F. List, *Werke*, IV.

21. J.A. Chaptal, *De l'industrie françoise* (2 vols., 1819), II, p.417 quoted by List in *The Natural System of Political Economy* (1837; English translation 1983), p.150. In this book List referred to Chaptal's work in footnotes on pp.61, 65, 66 and 87.

22. F. List, *The National System of Political Economy* (1841; English translation, 1885), p.359. Chaptal had written: "Livrez le commerce à lui même, laissez lui la liberté de ses opérations et vous verrez bientôt s'établir l'équilibre entre les besoins et les ressources" (J.A. Chaptal, *De l'industrie françoise* (1819), II, p.244).

23. F. List, "Idées sur les réformes économiques, commerciales et financières, applicables à la France" in the *Revue Encyclopédique*, March, April and Nov. 1831 (reprinted in F. List, *Werke*, V), p.59.

24. The output of tobacco in France had been only 5.7 million kgm in 1816 but it rose to an average of over 12 million kgm between 1831 and 1836.

25. For Charles Dupin see the *Biographie nouvelle des contemporains*, XV, 1922, pp.299–303, H. Bertrand, *Eloges académiques*, I, pp.225–46, and an article in the *Dictionnaire de biographie française*, XII, 1970, pp.358–62.

26. F. List, *Outlines of American Political Economy* (1827). The pamphlet included 11 letters. A twelfth letter, dated 27 July 1827, appeared in the *Philadelphia National Gazette* on 27 Nov. 1827. It is reprinted in F. List, *Werke*, II, pp.155–6.

27. List's Philadelphia address is printed in F. List, *Werke*, II, pp.157–72.

28. C. Dupin, *Mémoire sur la marine et les ports et chaussées de la France et d'Angleterre* (1818): English translation – *Narratives of two Excursions to the Ports of England, Scotland and Ireland* (1819).

29. C. Dupin, *Voyages en Grande Bretagne de 1816 à 1819* (6 vols., 1820–24).

30. This was the *Haute école d'application de la science au commerce et à l'industrie*.

31. C. Dupin, *Forces productives et commerciales de la France* (2 vols., 1827). The introduction was published separately as a pamphlet – *Situation progressive des forces de la France* (1827). See also C. Dupin, *Progrès de l'industrie française depuis le commencement du XIXe siècle* (*Discours prononcé le 29 novembre 1823 pour l'ouverture du cours de méchanique appliquée aux arts* (1824).

32. Extracts from Dupin's speech of 14 April 1836, in which he supported protectionism are printed in F. List, *Werke*, IV, pp.59–60.

33. C. Dupin, *Rapport du jury central sur les produits de l'industrie française à l'exposition de 1834* (1836).

34. Dupin was the rapporteur of the committee of the upper house which examined a draft law to protect children employed in factories and workshops.

35. Shortly before his appointment Dupin had expressed his opposition to the national workshops.

36. C. Dupin, *Industries comparées de Paris et de Londres* (1852), p.32.

37. Dupin wrote in the introduction to his *Forces productives et commerciales de la France* (2 vols., 1827), Vol. I, p.ii: "Je ne suis pas un novateur; je ne suis pas un faiseur de systèmes; je n'offre pas de théories qui soient à moi; je n'ai pas l'orgueil insensé d'aspirer à voir mon pays conduit d'après les déceptions de mes pensées vagabondes. Je ne suis qu'un narrateur, et le plus souvent qu'un simple arithméticien. Je rapporte avec fidélité ce que j'ai vu, lu et compté. C'est une chronique, ou pour mieux dire, une statistique contemporaine."

38. List lived in Paris between August 1837 and May 1840. He contributed many articles on French affairs to the Augsburg *Allgemeine Zeitung*.

39. The only change made in the title of the essay was that the word "producteurs" in the original title became "producteurs nationaux" in the title of 1836.

40. C. Dupin, *Rapport sur le prix d'économie politique relatif aux moyens d'établir la liberté commerciale* (28 Dec. 1836) in F. List, *Werke*, IV, pp.29–44.
41. *Das Zollvereinsblatt*, 1846, No. 47, pp.749–52; No. 48, pp.758–9; No. 49, pp.773–84; and No. 50, pp.791–9.
42. Karl Marx, *Theorien über den Mehrwert* (Berlin, 1956), I, p.214.
43. E. Ladenthin, *Zur Entwicklung der nationalökonomischen Ansichten F. Lists von 1820–25* (1912).
44. List Archives (Reutlingen), Fasc. 22.
45. F. List, *The National System of Political Economy* (1841; English translation 1884 and 1966), p.361.
46. Quoted by Salin and Sommer in their introduction to F. List, *Werke*, VI.

10

FRIEDRICH LIST AND ENGLAND

I. INTRODUCTION

In the nineteenth century few economists were so widely travelled as Friedrich List, who lived for quite long periods in foreign countries.[1] In 1822 he fled from Württemberg to Strasbourg on learning that he had been sentenced to 10 months imprisonment for insulting the king and other offences. He was in France for nearly a year and then went to Switzerland where he stayed until July 1824.[2] On returning to Württemberg he was sent to a fortress but was released after serving only half his sentence on condition that he emigrated. List then migrated to the United States where he remained for 5 years.[3] He was back in Europe in 1830 living first in Paris,[4] then in Altona and Leipzig, then in Paris again, and finally in Augsburg. List lived long enough in the United States and France to gain a wide knowledge of political and economic affairs in those countries – as can be seen from many well informed articles which he contributed to the Augsburg *Allgemeine Zeitung,* the *Eisenbahn-journal*, the *Zollvereinsblatt* and other periodicals.

Although List never lived in England he was well informed on English affairs. He had a high opinion of English democratic institutions – the constitutional monarchy, the elected House of Commons, the free press and the jury system. He had made a detailed study of the works of the English classical economists and he had read the standard accounts of English commercial, industrial and agricultural developments. He regularly read English newspapers and periodicals. He met and corresponded with men like Dr. Bowring and Poulett Thomson who were eminent in public life.

List both admired and envied England's success in promoting industrial growth and in establishing a great empire overseas. He recognised the skill of English ministers in negotiating favourable commercial treaties with foreign countries, such as the Methuen treaty with Portugal (1703), the Asiento agreement with Spain (1713), and the Eden treaty with France (1786).[4a] List paid only two visits to England.[5] Little is known of his first visit in the spring of 1824. He met Dr. John Bowring[6] and Poulett Thomson[7] and he later stated that it was in England that he first became interested in railways. List's second visit was in 1846 when he stayed in London from June 19 to August 26, attempting to interest English politicians in his plan for the establishment of an Anglo-German alliance. Ludwig Häusser, List's first biographer, considered that the visit to London completely refuted the charge that List regarded the English with "a blind hatred". He declared that List had repeatedly called upon his countrymen to emulate the pragmatism and the ruthless egoism of the English people.[8]

II. LIST ON ENGLAND'S COMMERCIAL POLICY, 1819–20

While the Easter fair was being held at Frankfurt am Main in 1819 the city was visited by List, a recently appointed professor at the university of Tübingen, then aged 30. He stated that he was passing through Frankfurt on his way to Göttingen where he would be engaged on academic business. But as it turned out, his activities in Frankfurt were far from being academic since, at the request of a group of merchants, he drew up a petition to the Federal Assembly of the German Confederation (*Bund*) urging the establishment of a German customs union. Shortly afterwards a Union of Merchants[9] was established to urge upon the Confederation and the govern-ments of the German states the adoption of the proposals made in the petition. List gave up his chair at Tübingen and became the secretary (*Konsulent*) of this organisation. Hitherto List had made a name for himself in his native Württemberg as a civil servant, a university professor and a journalist. His sharp criticisms of the Württemberg bureaucracy had made him powerful enemies in the ranks of some senior civil servants. Now he intensified his study of economics and he became known all over Germany as the leader of a campaign in favour of the establishment of a German customs union. His petitions to the Confederation and to the rulers of German states and his articles in the weekly periodical *Organ*[10] brought his name to the attention of the German public.

Two of List's numerous writings at this time throw light upon his views on England's commercial policy after the end of the Napoleon wars. They were the "Letters on the German Economy", published in *Organ* in 1819,[11] and the "Vienna Memorandum", which was a petition presented to Metternich in February 1820.[12] In his article on the German economy List declared that Germany's national wealth was declining since imports from England greatly exceeded exports to England. Official statistics showed that great quantities of manufactured goods and colonial produce (sugar, tobacco, coffee) left English ports every year for Germany while England's imports from Germany were confined to rags for her paper mills and also a little wool.[13] List claimed that the situation had deteriorated in recent years. When the Continental System had been in force new industries had developed in Germany to fill the gap caused by the exclusion of English manufactured goods. After the war, however, English goods had quickly appeared in Germany again and there was soon an unfavourable balance of trade with England. For a time the balance was covered by English subsidies and loans but by 1819 this temporary alleviation of the situation had come to an end. List observed that English manufacturers had greater experience and greater access to new capital than their German competitors. Moreover they enjoyed the support of a strong national government. When the Continental System came to an end English merchants dumped large quantities of manufactured goods onto the German market at low prices. Their aim – wrote List – was to destroy Germany's manufacturing capacity and when they had secured a dominant position in German markets they would raise their prices. To remedy this state of affairs the members of the German Confederation should unite to establish a customs union with a high tariff to protect German industry.

List put forward similar arguments in the Vienna memorandum of 1820 presented to Metternich on behalf of the Union of Merchants. He stated that Germany's former export trade had been virtually destroyed to the great detriment of the country's prosperity. Cheap foreign imports were to blame. England virtually prohibited the import of cereals,[14] hops and wool. German manufactured goods were either banned from the English market or admitted only on payment of high duties. There was, for example, an import duty of 200 per cent on Bohemian mirrors and other types of glassware. List alleged that England was on the point of taxing German linens which would ruin this branch of German industry and cost the jobs of thousands of domestic spinners and weavers. Meanwhile England was sending to Germany vast consignments of manufactured goods of all kinds as well as tropical products. The situation had worsened when German ports were opened to international trade after the collapse of the Continental System. Now large quantities of cheap English goods were flooding the German market. As usual List pleaded for the establishment of a German customs union. He recognised that if such a union were founded it might be difficult to persuade Hanover to join it. This was because at that time Hanover was in personal union with England. But he hoped that Hanover would resist pressure from England to refrain from joining a German customs union.

III. OUTLINES OF AMERICAN POLITICAL ECONOMY

It has been seen that List spent five years in the United States. He settled in Reading (Pennsylvania) in 1825 earning his living first as a farmer and then as an entrepreneur engaged in opening up a coalfield near Tamaque and in constructing a colliery railway from the mine to the Shuylkill canal. At the same time he edited a weekly newspaper (the *Readinger Adler*) which was widely read by members of the local German community. No wonder that he claimed to be a practical man as well as an economist. In addition List found time to become involved in the controversy between the free traders and the protectionists in the United States.

At the request of District Attorney J.C. Ingersoll[15] he-wrote 12 letters in favour of the policy of protection. They appeared in the *National Journal* (Philadelphia) and − with one exception − were reprinted in two pamphlets entitled *Outlines of American Political Economy*.[16] In the letters List attacked the doctrines of Adam Smith and his followers which were being promulgated in the United States by Thomas Cooper.[17] List argued that only by introducing a high tariff − particularly on iron products and textiles − could the United States promote the growth of its own industries. While List's earlier writings on fiscal policy had been addressed to his fellow countrymen, the letters to Ingersoll dealt with the fiscal controversy in the United States.

List's letters included several references to England and to English commercial policy. He argued that England was pursuing a ruthless policy aimed at maintaining her position as the most advanced industrial country in the world. He claimed that "English national economy has for its object to manufacture for the whole world, to monopolise all manufacturing power ..., to keep the world and especially her colonies in a state of infancy and vassalage by political management as well as by the superiority of her capital, her skill and her navy".[18] After the collapse of the Continental System English merchants had ruined many branches of German industry by flooding the German market with cheap manufactured goods while at the same time levying high import duties on foreign cereals and wool – thus making it difficult if not impossible for the Germans to pay for the goods that they imported. List denounced Canning[19] for paying lip service to the doctrine of free trade while continuing to protect English industry and agriculture by a high tariff. He considered that Huskisson's modification of the tariff did little to lessen the protection afforded to English manufacturers and landowners.[20] List congratulated the French government, led by Villèle,[21] for resisting Canning's offer to lower English duties on wines and spirits in return for a reduction in the French duties on English manufactured goods. Had Villèle accepted Canning's proposal France would have shared the fate of Portugal which, as a result of the Methuen treaty (1703), had secured a market for her wine at the expense of becoming entirely dependent upon England for manufactured goods. List went on to denounce Canning for attempting to monopolise the trade of a vast region by recognising the independence of Spain's former colonies in South America.

List argued that the United States should have followed the example of France by safeguarding her industries from English competition. He considered that, since the American tariffs of 1816 and 1824 had failed to give manufacturers the protection that they needed, those industries which had grown up during the era of the Embargo and Non-Intercourse Acts were not likely to survive. List thought that it was absurd that the United States should export raw cotton to England and then purchase from Lancashire some of the cloth made from that cotton. The Americans should develop their own cotton industry to manufacture cotton cloth and cotton garments. He denounced the selfish commission agents and southern planters who were resisting the demands of the protectionists. He considered that if they were sheltered by a high tariff American manufacturers would be able not only to capture their own home market but to compete successfully with England in the markets of South America.

IV. TWO SYSTEMS OF POLITICAL ECONOMY, 1837–41

Between 1837 and 1841 List wrote two books in which he set forth his economic doctrines in a systematic manner. The first was not published in his lifetime. Indeed it was not published until 1927. The second work appeared in 1841 and established List's reputation as one of the leading economists of his day. Both books contained chapters on Britain's commercial policy.

When List returned to Europe from the United States he devoted much of his time to the promotion of railways in France and Germany. His greatest success was the construction of the line between Leipzig and Dresden, in which he played a leading role. In his articles in the *Eisenbahnjournal* and the Augsburg *Allgemeine Zeitung* there were frequent references to the progress that was being made in the construction of railways in the British Isles. Disappointed at having failed to secure a post in a railway administration in Germany List moved to Paris in the autumn of 1837 in the hope of interesting the French authorities in railway developments. However his attention was diverted from railways to economics when he learned that the Academy of Moral and Political Sciences was offering a prize for a treatise answering the question: "If a country proposes to introduce free trade or to modify its tariff, what factors should it take into account so as to reconcile in the fairest manner the interests of producers with those of consumers?" List decided to compete for the prize and wrote a treatise on *The Natural System of Political Economy*.[22] This was List's first attempt to explain his economic doctrines in some detail.

In a chapter on the history of England's commercial policy List dealt at greater length with a topic that he had previously discussed only briefly.[23] He began his survey in the twelfth century when England had been "a very poor and primitive agricultural country". Much of her foreign trade was in German hands, represented by the powerful Hanseatic League. The Hansa merchants sent English wool to Flanders and Germany where it was spun and woven. In return they sent manufactured goods (particularly woollen cloth) – and luxuries for the wealthy – to England. "But in Edward III's reign the government realised that England could do better than to export wool in order to import cloth. Edward III invited weavers from Flanders and Brabant to settle in England." Later English monarchs promoted the expansion of the manufacture of cloth by insisting that "foreign merchants had to export English manufactured goods of equal value to the goods which they had brought to England from abroad". In the Tudor period England had become strong enough to dispense with the services of the Hanseatic merchants and Elizabeth deprived them of all their privileges.[24] In the seventeenth century England fought three wars against the Dutch to establish her position as the world's leading naval and commercial power. The eighteenth century saw the conclusion of the Methuen and Eden commercial treaties with Portugal and France which opened up new markets to English manufactured goods. And List repeated his earlier attacks upon these agreements as being harmful to the economic development of Portugal and France. He also drew attention to the significance of the development of the coal industry in England in the seventeenth and eighteenth centuries. "The mineowners opened up new collieries and were able – in addition to supplying the home market – to export large quantities of coal. This led to a remarkable expansion of coastal and overseas shipping."

List repeated his condemnation of England's commercial policy after the Napoleonic wars. Although England had become the world's greatest exporter of manufactured goods she had placed prohibitions or high duties on the agricultural products which might pay for those goods. List complained that "free trade for the English means that foreign farm products may be imported only when the country is threatened with famine. As for manufactured goods Huskisson was steadfast in his support of the policy of protection while in his speeches he was always prepared to use the catchwords of the free traders." List again congratulated the French for rejecting Canning's plea for lower import duties on English manufactured goods. But List failed to mention that in 1836 France had made some modest concessions to England by removing the prohibition on the export of raw silk and certain cotton yarns and by reducing import duties on iron goods and on coal arriving by sea.[25]

When the jury of the academy decided that none of the candidates merited the prize List decided to write a comprehensive work on his economic doctrines. And this major work – *The National System of Political Economy* – appeared in 1841. List had originally planned to discuss international relations and foreign policy in a final volume but his long-standing feud with the English free traders caused him to change his mind and to write his last volume at once.

What happened was that Dr. Bowring had been instructed by the British Foreign Office in July 1839 "to report on the progress, present state, and future prospects of the Prussian Commercial League".[27] He was in Berlin – lobbying on behalf of British interests – at the third Zollverein congress. List later complained that Bowring had been welcomed like a messiah in the Prussian capital.[28] Bowring tried to persuade the Prussian officials responsible for Zollverein affairs and also German manufacturers to maintain the existing moderate tariff and to resist the demands of the protectionists for the introduction of higher import duties.

When he returned to England Bowring addressed several meetings of chambers of commerce on his mission.[29] They were reported in the press in England and in Germany. List promptly replied to Bowring's arguments in a number of articles in the Augsburg *Allgemeine Zeitung* and the *Zollvereinsblatt*.[30] List declared in a letter to Robert Mohl that he had "bombed" Dr. Bowring before he came to Berlin, when he arrived in Berlin, and when he had returned to his island.[31] But this was not enough. List decided that his work on economics should start with a volume on *The National System of Political Economy* – a comprehensive refutation of the views of Dr. Bowring. The subtitle of the book – "International Trade, Commercial Policy and the German Zollverein" – made his intention quite clear.

This is not an occasion on which to attempt to discuss the significance of List's doctrines of productive forces and of stages of industrial growth which made *The National System of Political Economy*[32] one of the major works on economics written in the nineteenth century. In writing of England as the workshop of the world and England as the greatest naval and colonial power he was covering familiar ground. He had in the past frequently praised England's restrictive fiscal and commercial policy in the seventeenth and eighteenth centuries and he had often criticised her failure to adopt a more liberal policy after 1815. Nor was there anything new in his attack on England's policy towards the Zollverein – her opposition to those who pressed for a higher Zollverein tariff and her support for those north German states which refused to join the customs union.

There was, however, something new in List's attitude towards England. A proposal which had been discussed in a couple of paragraphs in *The Natural System of Political Economy*[33] was now discussed in greater detail. He argued that what he called England's "insular supremacy" should be challenged by countries on the Continent which should co-operate to restrict the flow of English manufactured goods and colonial products to their territories. List believed that Napoleon's Continental System had given industries on mainland Europe an opportunity to expand without having to meet English competition. The same result would be obtained by setting up a new Continental System. But while Napoleon's Continental System had been dominated by France, List's system would be an alliance of equal partners.

V. MEMORANDUM ON AN ANGLO-GERMAN ALLIANCE, 1846[34]

The early 1840s saw a dramatic change in List's attitude towards England. In *The National System of Political Economy* he had urged the states on the Continent to unite to challenge England's "insular supremacy". In 1845 and 1846, however, he advocated something very different – the conclusion of the Anglo-German alliance.[35] In 1846 List informed Karl von Abel, the Bavarian minister of the interior, that – in view of the forthcoming repeal of the Corn Laws in England – he proposed to write a memorandum suggesting that there should be an alliance between England and Germany. He would cross the Channel to give a copy to the prime minister Sir Robert Peel.[36] Some manufacturers in Württemberg contributed to a fund (6,000 gulden) to defray List's expenses but it appears that he left the money on deposit in a bank.[37]

This was not the first time that List had attempted, as a private individual, to play an active part in international diplomacy. Acting on behalf of the Union of Merchants he had been in Vienna for five months in 1820 lobbying German ministers assembled there for a conference. In April 1844 he had turned up in Brussels in the hope of influencing commercial negotiations then in progress between Prussian and Belgian diplomats. And in the winter of 1844–5 List had been in the Habsburg dominions to promote the establishment of a central European customs union and the creation of German settlements in Hungary. None of these ventures had been successful and Dr. Kolb warned List that his visit to London would also be doomed to failure. But List was determined to embark upon what he claimed would be "the most glorious mission of his career".[38] He arrived at the Royal Hotel in Bridge Street, Blackfriars, on 19 June 1846 well provided with letters of introduction from distinguished persons. He regarded the English as "silly fellows" who would be greatly impressed if he could claim to number princes and dukes among his acquaintances.[39] His visit to London lasted until August 26.[40] In official circles in London[41] he was at first regarded with some suspicion but he was nevertheless cordially received by several politicians.

Since Prussia was the leading state in the Zollverein it was natural that List should endeavour to interest Freiherr Josias von Bunsen, the Prussian ambassador in London, in his project. But Bunsen had been warned by Freiherr von Canitz, the Prussian Foreign Minister, that List was a trouble-maker who was meddling in diplomatic affairs at the very time that delicate negotiations concerning the renewal of the Anglo-Zollverein commercial treaty of 1841 were in progress. It was even suggested that List was planning to wreck the Zollverein at the behest of his paymasters in Vienna and Munich.[42] However when Bunsen met List in June 1846 he soon recognised the absurdity of these allegations. While not sharing List's views on protection and deploring List's recent attack upon Ludwig Kühne[43] he did accept that List was "a sincere German patriot".[44] He reported favourably on List's character and conduct in reports to the Prussian Foreign Office and to Frederick William IV.[45] Before long List was a regular visitor to the Prussian embassy in Carlton Terrace where he was "treated as one of the family".[46] Bunsen introduced him to the Athenaeum and secured a seat for him in the strangers' gallery in the House of Commons. But Bunsen failed to appreciate how passionately List was devoted to the causes that he championed. It was naive of him to hope that List's visit to England would "modify or at least moderate his exclusive views".[47]

List was also in contact with leading free traders such as Dr. Bowring, Richard Cobden, J. MacGregor and G.R. Porter. Bowring, who had met List in 1824 and had subsequently corresponded with him, now introduced him to the Travellers Club.[48] In his memoirs Bowring wrote: "It was not long before List's death that I discussed some of his opinions with him. He was what the world calls a jolly jovial fellow, and had certainly the virtue of not taking offence at pretty severe criticism."[49] A week after arriving in London List was taken to the Houses of Parliament by Dr. Bowring and introduced to Cobden, MacGregor and Lord Monteagle. He was in the House of Lords when the bill repealing the corn laws received its third reading without a division – a bill from which the landowners and farmers of north Germany would be among the first to benefit. And a little later List was in the House of Commons when Peel's administration was defeated on the Irish Coercion Bill.[50]

List was also assisted by two influential members of the Bavarian aristocracy – Prince Ludwig von Öttingen-Wallerstein (a former Minister of the Interior)[51] who gave him letters of introduction and Prince Karl von Leiningen (president of the Bavarian chamber of notables) who was on his annual visit to London at this time. Leiningen was Queen Victoria's half brother and Prince Albert's cousin.[52] On Leiningen's recommendation Dr. Karl Mayer, the Prince Consort's private secretary, gave List all the assistance he could.[53] List was also in touch with the Belgian court and it was through Baron Stockmar that a copy of List's memorandum reached the Prince Consort. Albert suggested that an English version of the memorandum should be sent not only to Sir Robert Peel but also to two leading Whigs — Lord Palmerston and Lord Clarendon. While actively engaged in making his proposals as widely known as possible, List still found time to write several articles on the political and economic situation in England in 1846.[54]

In his memorandum[55] List argued that the repeal of the corn laws was more than a change in fiscal policy. It marked a watershed in Britain's economic and political evolution. It opened a new era in Britain's role as the world's leading industrial nation. But Britain's position as the workshop of the world could not last for ever. In List's view the main threats to Britain's economic supremacy would come from the United States and Russia. List considered that the population and wealth of the United States were growing in geometrical progression while those of Britain were growing only in arithmetical progression. Inevitably a time would come when the United States would challenge Britain's position as the workshop of the world. List regarded Russia as "a mass of barbarous hordes" ruled by an autocratic czar. Russia posed a threat to Britain because of her plans to expand in the Balkans and in Asia. In the future Russia might be able to challenge Britain's hold over India. And Russia threatened not only India but the German states as well. In alliance with France she might be able to satisfy her territorial ambitions on the Continent.

In the circumstances List offered England two pieces of advice. First, she should expand her existing colonial possessions, particularly in those regions which were suitable for white settlement and had a great potential for future trade expansion. Secondly, she should safeguard her route to India by establishing a new "central empire" (*Mittelreich*) in Asia Minor and Egypt as her share of a future partition of the Ottoman empire. Such a partition had already been discussed by the great powers and List considered that the Ottoman empire would soon collapse. But there was a danger that an attempt to extend British influence in the Middle East might be frustrated by Russia, which had designs in the Balkans, and by France, which had long established interests in the Mediterranean. List argued that these dangers might be averted by the conclusion of an Anglo-German alliance. Moreover List believed that Russia and France might be plotting to dismember Germany. In his view the recent attempt by France to form a customs union with Belgium posed a threat to the independence of the north German states.

Since Britain and Germany were threatened by the same powers it was in their interests to form an alliance.

List complained that England had adopted a short-sighted policy with regard to the Zollverein. England had supported the merchants of Hanover and the Hansa Towns – "those hucksters of English manufactured goods" – in their refusal to join the Zollverein. In 1844, for example, England had signed a commercial treaty with Hanover which prevented Hanover from joining the Zollverein until 1854. And at congresses of the Zollverein British diplomats had been very active behind the scenes in frustrating the efforts of the protectionists to secure the imposition of higher import duties on textiles and iron products.[56] List argued that England's policy was harming Germany in various ways. England was checking Prussia's efforts to include all the German states (except Austria) in the Zollverein. England was checking Germany's industrial growth by supporting the German free traders. And England was supporting the powerful civil service in Prussia which not only prevented the adoption of a liberal constitution in that state but also checked the movement to bring all the German states together in a united democratic country.

List summarised his oft repeated arguments in favour of promoting the growth of "infant industries" by protective duties. When these industries were fully developed it would no longer be necessary to protect them. List concluded his memorandum by urging the British government to change its policy towards the Zollverein and to accept the fact that the customs union needed to raise its tariff in order to foster the expansion of manufactures. He claimed that England needed Germany as an ally but if she wanted to have a strong partner she would have to help Germany to become an industrial state. And that help involved withdrawing her opposition both to an increase in the Zollverein tariff and to the incorporation of the North Sea states in the Zollverein.

Anyone reading List's memorandum over 100 years after it had been written must be struck by the author's uncanny ability to look into the future. He foresaw the outbreak of the Crimean war (1854), the construction of the Indo-European telegraph (1870), and the building of the Berlin–Baghdad railway (which reached Nusaybin in 1918). Above all he – like de Tocqueville – foresaw the decline of the great powers of western Europe and the emergence of the United States and Russia as super-powers. Of course not all of List's predictions proved to be correct. The United States, for example, never annexed Canada or the whole of Mexico. List's hopes for co-operation between Britain and a future united Germany were dashed long after his death by Germany's rejection of Joseph Chamberlain's offer of an alliance in 1898. It was only after two world wars that Britain and West Germany became partners both in the North Atlantic Treaty Organisation and the European Economic Community.

The fundamental weakness of List's memorandum was that when he wrote about "Germany" he was not referring to any existing institution such as the Confederation or the Zollverein. He was referring to a united Germany which he was confident would be established at some time in the future.[57] He admitted that his proposal depended upon the creation of "a Germany that will have those powers of a nation which are derived from the existence both of free institutions and of a truly national central authority". It was naive of List to imagine that any English politician would consider making immediate concessions to the Zollverein − such as a revision of the recently signed commercial treaty between Britain and Hanover − in the hope of one day receiving some return from a future united Germany. It was not until 1871 that Germany was united, so England would have waited for 25 years to secure any advantage from arrangements made in 1846. Another weakness of List's memorandum was his assertion that his views represented "the opinion of all the enlightened politicians of Germany". But he produced no evidence to support this statement. Presumably the merchants of Elbing who congratulated Peel on the repeal of the corn laws in 1846 and the free traders of Berlin who gave Cobden an enthusiastic welcome in July 1847 considered themselves to be just as enlightened as List.[58]

The comments which Peel and Palmerston made on List's memorandum were what might have been expected. Peel wrote that the sentiments expressed by List "in favour of the policy and reciprocal advantage of an intimate union between this country and Germany have my cordial concurrence, a concurrence as complete and unqualified as is my dissent from your views as to the mode by which that intimate union can be most effectually promoted". Peel denied that high Zollverein import duties would benefit the German people. On the contrary he believed that it would be of great advantage to them to have "free access to the products of English industry in exchange for their own".[59]

Lord Palmerston discussed List's memorandum at greater length. Though no economist he was familiar with the arguments in favour of free trade. He observed that the founding of the Zollverein had established free trade within most of Germany and he argued the Zollverein should now "give Germany the further advantage of free trade abroad". He accepted that import duties might properly be levied to raise revenue but he objected to the imposition of duties "for protection and therefore fixed in contemplation of a restricted or extinguished commerce". He declared that a high tariff would "diminish both the production and accumulation of wealth in a nation".[60] It may be added that Lord Clarendon acknowledged the receipt of List's memorandum and offered to grant him an interview.[61] When List realised that leading English politicians were not interested in his memorandum he reverted to his former plan for the establishment of an anti-English continental system.

List sent a copy of his memorandum not only to English politicians but also to the King of Prussia. In a covering letter he denied that he was an opponent of Prussia and declared that "only through Prussia can the German fatherland be born again". He concluded by offering his services to Frederick William IV.[62] This letter may be the key to the change in List's attitude towards England. In *The National System of Political Economy* he had argued in favour of a new continental system directed against English trade but in his memorandum of 1846 he advocated the establishment of an Anglo-German alliance. Although warmly welcomed in London as a distinguished visitor – he wrote to his wife that he was "completely satisfied" with his reception[63] – he must have appreciated that a private individual from abroad was hardly likely to exercise much influence on English politicians.

It may be that the real object of List's mission to London was not so much to convert influential people in England to his views on Anglo-German relations as to impress the King of Prussia and so secure an appointment in Prussia. At this time List's fortunes were at a very low ebb. He had given up all hope of ever securing reinstatement in the Württemberg civil service. His attempts to secure a permanent salaried post in Austria, Bavaria, and the Thuringian states had all failed. While the English freetraders were prepared to reward Cobden's services by presenting him with a testimonial of over £75,000 the sums given to List by the German protectionists were far too small to help him out of his financial difficulties. List made a precarious income by writing articles for the *Allgemeine Zeitung* and by editing the *Zollvereinsblatt*. Now even these sources of income were threatened by a dispute with Georg von Cotta, the publisher of these periodicals. Despite his friendship with Dr. Kolb (editor of the Augsburg *Allgemeine Zeitung*) there was a real danger that he would cease to be a contributor to the paper. One source of friction between Cotta and List was removed when List agreed to take full responsibility for publishing the *Zollvereinsblatt*. Now at the age of 57 he needed to secure a regular income. Having failed in several German states he now, in the last resort, turned to Prussia.

Bunsen forwarded List's letter to Frederick William IV and strongly recommended that Prussia and the Zollverein should make use of "the genius, the experience, and the political influence of the leading popular writer on economics and industry in Germany".[64] He considered List to be "au fond du coeur un très bon prussien" – a man well qualified to be put in charge of German settlements in Posen or to become Inspector of Railways and Factories in the Zollverein. Bunsen was a close friend of the king and his recommendation carried considerable weight. Frederick William IV for his part favoured the maintenance of good relations with England and he was impressed by List's views on Anglo-German relations.[65]

List, however, had many enemies – such as von Canitz[66] and Kühne – among the king's ministers and senior civil servants. Indeed Friedrich von Rönne (President of the short lived Prussian Board of Trade) was virtually List's only friend in Berlin and he received no offer of employment in Prussia. And this is hardly surprising since for years List had been criticising Prussia for failing to agree to an increase in the Zollverein tariff to protect German manufacturers from English competition. Moreover he had attacked Prussia for failing to adopt a liberal constitution under which an elected assembly would be able to curb the great influence wielded by a powerful bureaucracy. List was bitterly disappointed at his failure to secure an appointment in Prussia. He returned to Germany towards the end of August 1846 glad to escape from the English weather[67] and food. But he was no longer the "jolly jovial fellow" whom Bowring had met in London. The failure of his mission to England coupled with his failure to secure employment in Prussia contributed to the deep depression that led to his suicide in November 1846.

Shortly after List's death an article appeared in the influential London *Times* on Anglo-German commercial relations which denounced the protectionist views of List's followers. The writer considered that the merchants of northern Germany were "as well acquainted with sound principles of trade as any people on the continent". Hanover, the Mecklenburgs and the Hansa Towns were not members of the Zollverein and pursued a fiscal policy of free trade. But in south Germany "the pedants of Baden and Württemberg" were "discussing maritime interests as the blind might talk of colours and the deaf of sound". The writer congratulated the King of Hanover[68] on his "vigorous resistance to the Prussian commercial system" and Hamburg on its rapid recovery from the great fire of 1842. The article – in a newspaper with close links with government circles – suggests that List's plea that England should refrain from supporting the north German coastal states in their refusal to join the Zollverein and should accept a substantial increase in the Zollverein tariff had fallen on deaf ears.

NOTES

1. The first selection of List's works (F. List, *Gesammelte Schriften*, 2 vols, 1850) was edited by Ludwig Häusser. The first volume, a life of List, is cited as Häusser I. List's collected works (*Werke: Schriften, Reden, Briefe*, 10 vols, 1927–35; new edition, 1971) are cited as *Werke*.
2. Eugen Wendler, *Leben und Wirken von Friedrich List während seines Exils in der Schweiz und sein Meinungsbild über die Eidgenossenschaft* (1984).
3. H. Rickel, *Friedrich List whom American History forgot*. (Bulletin VI of the Concord Society, Detroit, 1926); W.F. Notz, "Friedrich List in America", in the *American Economic Review*, XV (ii), 1926, 249–265 and "Friedrich List in Amerika" in the *Weltwirtschaftliches Archiv*, XXI (ii), 1925 and XXII (i), 1925.
4. See Chapter 9 above.
4a. For the Anglo-French (Eden–Rayneval) treaty of 1786 see W.O. Henderson, *The Genesis of the Common Market* (1962), ch. 2.
5. The statement in *Werke*, V, 590 that List visited England "several times" is incorrect.
6. Dr. (later Sir John) Bowring was a leading Benthamite and editor of the *Westminster Review*. He wrote a *Report on the Prussian Commercial Union* (Parliamentary Papers, 1840, XXI).
7. C.E. Poulett Thomson (later Lord Sydenham) was Vice-President (1830–34) and then President of the Board of Trade (1834–39). He was appointed Governor of Canada in 1839. His name is incorrectly spelt by the editors of *Werke*, V, 573 (note 99) and 698.
8. L. Häusser, I, 379.
9. See Hans-Peter Olshausen, *Friedrich List und der Deutsche Handels- und Gewerbeverein* (1935).
10. The full title was *Organ für den Deutschen Handels- und Fabrikantenstand*.
11. F. List, "Briefe über den ökonomischen Zustand Deutschlands". In *Organ*, 1819, No. 6 and No. 9 and in *Werke*, I (ii) 570–578.
12. F. List, *Denkschrift, die Handels- und Gewerbeverhältnisse Deutschlands betreffend*, 1820. In *Werke*, I (ii), 527–547.
13. In fact there was a dramatic increase in England's import of German wool between 1814 and 1825 – from 3,432,455 lbs to 28,799,661 lbs (W. Cunningham, *The Growth of English Industry and Commerce*, 1925 (reprinted Frank Cass, 1968), III (ii), 645 (note).

14. The Corn Law of 1815 prohibited the import of foreign corn so long as the price of wheat did not rise above 80 shillings a quarter.
15. C.J. Ingersoll, Vice-President of the Pennsylvania Society for the Promotion of Manufactures and the Mechanic Arts, served as United States District Attorney for Pennsylvania from 1815 to 1829.
16. All 12 letters appear in *Werke*, II, 97–239: German translation – C. Köhler, *Problematisches zu Friedrich List* (1908).
17. See Thomas Cooper, *Lectures on the Elements of Political Economy* (1826). J.R. McCulloch considered Cooper's book to be "the best of the American works on political economy that we have ever met with".
18. *Werke*, II, 108.
19. George Canning was Foreign Minister 1822–27 and Prime Minister from February to August 1827.
20. William Huskisson was President of the Board of Trade 1823–27 and Colonial Secretary 1827–28.
21. Villèle was President of the Council, 1822–28.
22. F. List, *Le Système Naturel d'Economie Politique*, 1837 (in *Werke*, IV, 1927 and 1971 with German translation): English translation – *The Natural System of Political Economy* (1983 edited by W.O. Henderson).
23. F. List, *The Natural System of Political Economy*, 1837 (1983), ch. 27.
24. See E.M. Carus Wilson, "The German Hansa in the Economy of Medieval England". In Paul Kluke and Peter Alter (eds.), *Aspects of Anglo-German Relations through the Centuries* (1978), 14–23.
25. Barrie M. Ratcliffe, "The Tariff Reform Campaign in France 1830–1836", in *The Journal of European Economic History*, VII (i), spring 1978, 61–138.
26. F. List, *Das Nationale System der Politischen Ökonomie*, 1841 (in *Werke*, VI, 1971): English translation – *The National System of Political Economy*, 1885 (new edition, 1966).
27. Bowring's letters to the Foreign Office are in the Public Record Office (FO.97/326). See also his *Report on the Prussian Commercial Union* (Parliamentary Papers, 1840, XXI): German translation – *Bericht über den deutschen Zoll-Verband* (Berlin, 1840). Bowring was not the first English official to visit the states of the Zollverein. In the 1830s John MacGregor had visited Germany and had reported to the government on the early development of the customs union.
28. *Zollvereinsblatt*, 3 Feb. 1846 (No. 5), 68 and *Werke*, V, 587.
29. For example Manchester, 14 Nov. 1839 (special general meeting relative to the Prussian Commercial Union) and Hull (third annual report of the Hull Chamber of Commerce, 1840).
30. For example: "Dr. Bowring und der deutsche Zollverein". in *Werke*, V, 158–166 and 173–197.
31. List to Robert Mohl, January 1, 1846 in Häusser, I, 278 and *Werke*, VI, 512.
32. F. List, *The Natural System of Political Economy*, 1837 (English translation, 1983), ch. 8.
33. F. List, *The National System of Political Economy*, 1841 (English translation, 1885 and 1966), ch. 35.
34. List wrote two memoranda "On the Advantages and Conditions of an intimate Alliance between Great Britain and Germany". Memorandum I (in German) was sent to the King of Prussia and was printed (slightly abridged) in a supplement to the Augsburg *Allgemeine Zeitung*, 1847, 92–96. It appeared in full in Häusser II 435 and in *Werke*, VII, 267–296. An English translation of Memorandum I is preserved in the Peel Papers in the British Library (ADD.MS. 40.597). Memorandum II, which differs in some respects from Memorandum I, is preserved in the Royal Archives in Windsor Castle (*Werke* IX. 140–159). In a letter to Lord Clarendon, August 10, 1846 (*Werke*, VIII, 825) List described the second memorandum as "at the same time an extract and supplement of the first". A draft of the memorandum in English

is preserved in the List archives in Reutlingen (Fasz. 41/II/7). See L. Sevin, "Die Listsche Idee einer deutsch-englischen Allianz in ihrem Ergebnis für Deutschland", in *Schmoller's Jahrbuch für Gesetzgebung, Verwaltung und Volkswirtschaft*, XXXIV (i), 1910, 173–222.

35. *Zollvereinsblatt*, 1843 (35–40); No. 26 (484–489); No. 34 (952–943) and *Werke*, VII, 250–254, 263–267 and 620.
36. List to Abel, March 30, 1846 in *Werke*, III, 952–954 and VIII, 807–810.
37. Kolb (editor of the Augsburg *Allgemeine Zeitung*) to Häusser, 7 Feb. 1849 in *Werke*, VIII, 853–854. A small sum was also raised by Anton Bachmeier.
38. Gustav Kolb to Ludwig Häusser, 7 Feb. 1849 (*Werke*, VII, 854).
39. See extracts from Friedrich Bodenstedt's memoirs in *Werke*, IX, 201.
40. List to Kolb, June 20 and July 4, 1846 (*Werke*, VIII, 819 and 122).
41. In 1842 Lord Westmoreland (British ambassador in Berlin) had informed Lord Aberdeen that List was "a very able writer in the employ of the manufacturers" (*Werke*, VII, 556).
42. Alfred Zimmermann, *Geschichte der preussisch-deutschen Handelspolitik* (1892), 261.
43. Ludwig Kühne was the Director General of Taxes in Prussia.
44. Bunsen to Sir Robert Peel, 26 Aug. 1846 in *Werke*, VIII, 827.
45. Bunsen to the Prussian Foreign Office and to Frederick William IV (both 31 July 1846) in *Werke*, VII, 518–523.
46. List to Bachmeier, 2 July 1846 in *Werke*, VIII, 820–821.
47. Bunsen to Peel, 26 Aug. 1846 in *Werke*, VIII, 827.
48. List to Bowring, 1846 in *Werke*, VIII, 819. In 1831 List had asked Bowring and Poulett Thomson to use their influence to secure a modification in the English excise laws which would make it possible for him to market in England some inventions (for example a new method of making vinegar) in which he was interested. Nothing came of List's plans. See List to Poulett Thomson, September 1831 in *Werke*, VIII, 380–381 and Bowring to List, 3 Dec. 1831 in *Werke*, IX, 65. List declared in a letter to Robert Mohl that although he rejected his views on free trade he regarded Dr. Bowring as one of his friends (Häusser, I, 278).
49. *Autobiographical Recollections of Sir John Bowring* (1877), 88–90.
50. Augsburg *Allgemeine Zeitung* 1846 (1459) and *Werke*, VII, 627. The corn laws were not fully repealed in 1846. There was to be a sliding scale until 1849 and then a registration fee of one shilling per quarter was to be levied. The registration fee was abolished in 1869.
51. For Öttingen-Wallenstein see the *Allgemeine Deutsche Biographie*, XL, 736–747. He was Bavarian Minister of the Interior from December 1831 to October 1837.
52. List to Prince Karl von Leiningen, 2 July 1846 in *Werke*, VIII, 820. For Leiningen see *Neue Deutsche Biographie*, XIV, 145–146 and Veit Valentin, *Fürst Karl Leiningen und das deutsche Einheitsproblem* (1910). At the time of List's visit to London Leiningen was writing two memoranda on constitutional reform in Germany – "Zwei Denkschriften über Deutschlands Lage" – which may well have been influenced by List's views.
53. See Karl Mayer's obituary of List in the Augsburg *Allgemeine Zeitung*, 1846, No. 360 (*Werke*, IX, 203–207).
54. For example: "Der Economist gegen das *Zollvereinsblatt*" (*Zollvereinsblatt*, 1846, No. 38), "Richard Cobden ein falscher Prophet" (*Zollvereinsblatt*, 1846, No. 39) in *Werke*, IX, 160–164 and other articles cited in *Werke*, VII, 627–628.
55. F. List, *Über den Wert und die Bedingungen einer Allianz zwischen Großbritannien und Deutschland* (1846) in *Werke*, VII, 267–296 and English version in *Werke*, IX, 140–159.
56. In the previous year the seventh congress of the Zollverein had ended in deadlock and the protectionists had failed to secure any increase in import duties. Sir Alexander Malet, the English representative in Carlsruhe, had been delighted. See

Lord Westmorland to Lord Aberdeen, 15 Oct. 1845 (Record Office, F.O. 64/258).
57. List made this quite clear when he wrote that "the Germany, the alliance which alone can be of lasting benefit for this country, is not the Germany as it is, but as it will be and as it now exists only by anticipation, in the wishes and ideas of the patriotic and enlightened part of the German nation" (*Werke*, IX, 142).
58. For the Elbing address (14 July 1846) see J. Prince Smith, *Gesammelte Schriften* (3 vols, 1871–1880), III, 260. For Cobden's visit to Berlin in 1847 see John Morley, *The Life of Richard Cobden* (1881), 447.
59. Sir Robert Peel to List, 22 Aug. 1845 in *Werke*, VII, 526–527.
60. Lord Palmerston, "Memorandum on Dr. List's Pamphlet" (8. Sept. 1846) in *Werke*, VII, 524–526.
61. Lord Clarendon to List, 8 Aug. 1846 and List's reply, 10 Aug. 1846 in *Werke*, VIII, 824–825.
62. List to Frederick William IV, 31 July 1846 in *Werke*, VII, 633–634.
63. List to Caroline List, 30 July 1846 in *Werke*, VIII, 823.
64. Bunsen to Frederick William IV, 31 July 1846 in *Werke*, VII, 521.
65. Frederick William IV had been well received in England in 1842 when he had acted as godfather to Queen Victoria's eldest son.
66. In a marginal note to Bunsen's letter of 31 July 1846 to Frederick William IV von Canitz commented upon List's application for a post in Prussia: "Give him some money – and plenty of it – and it will be of little concern to him whether he runs railways or settlements in Austria or in Prussia" (*Werke*, VII, 523).
67. On August 1 in London List had experienced "the most violent and long continued storm of hail and rain, of which there is any record" (Thomas Tooke, *History of Prices*, IV (1848), 26).
68. *Times*, 16 Jan. 1847 and *Werke*, IX, 246–249. The writer of the article failed to mention that there had recently been negotiations between Prussia and Hanover concerning Hanover's adhesion to the Zollverein. The main reason for their failure was Prussia's refusal to pay the "preferential payment" demanded by Hanover as her share of the Zollverein revenues.

PART III

Frederick the Great

11

FREDERICK THE GREAT
AND ENGLAND

The relations between Britain and Prussia during the reign of Frederick the Great were generally far from satisfactory. It is true that between 1758 and 1760 the two countries were allies and the King of Prussia enjoyed a brief period of great popularity in England. But at most other times the two governments regarded each other either with grave suspicion or with positive hostility. Between 1746 and 1748, between 1751 and 1756, and again between 1762 and 1765 normal diplomatic relations virtually ceased to exist. There was no exchange of ambassadors and the legations were run by minor officials. For example for two years the only British representative in Berlin was a clerk from Hanover named Laurence (Lorenz) who was expected to live on £100 a year and free meals. Again in the early 1750s the only Prussian agent in London was Abraham Michell from Neuchatel, an able man but not a diplomat of any standing.

At various times Britain and Prussia were involved in unfortunate disputes. Britain was annoyed when Frederick ignored Hanover's claims when he annexed East Frisia. English merchants were alarmed when Frederick supported the establishment of trading companies to send ships to India and Canton. The British government strongly criticised Frederick for failing to pay English bondholders the final instalment of the Silesian loan. Britain was also offended when Frederick championed the cause of neutral states whose ships were seized by English privateers in the Channel or the Mediterranean. This culminated in Frederick's adhesion to the Armed Neutrality during the American War of Independence. The British government considered it an unfriendly act when Frederick showed great favour to two leading Scottish Jacobites — the brothers George Keith (the Earl Marischal) and James Keith (Marshal Keith). And it was an equally unfriendly act when — at certain times —

Frederick encouraged his representative in London to support the Opposition to the British government.

Frederick, too, had his grievances. At the height of his popularity in England in 1757 he complained that he had been left in the lurch by the Duke of Cumberland who – by the convention of Klosterseven – had agreed with the French to demobilise 38,000 Hanoverian troops. Frederick also criticised the British government for failing to send a naval force to the Baltic to defend Pomerania from the Swedes and the fortress of Colberg from the Russians. Frederick considered that Lord Bute had treated him very shabbily by making peace with France in 1763 without consulting him. He was deeply offended when the British government advised him at that time to make concessions to Maria Theresa to enable the war on the Continent to be ended. And he complained that the English had ignored his interests in the negotiations leading to the Treaty of Paris in 1763. Again, Frederick resented the seizure of Prussian ships in the Channel and in the Mediterranean – and the misuse of the Prussian flag – by English privateers in wartime when Prussia was a neutral country.

Another of Frederick's grievances was that it was difficult to do business with Britain because the British system of government was very different from that of Prussia. Frederick found it difficult to appreciate the position of a constitutional monarch like George II who was not an autocratic ruler and who had to share power with his Parliament. Frederick's ministers had to do what they were told and often held office for long periods. In England ministers enjoyed considerable power though their tenure of office was sometimes far from secure. Frederick complained that George III "changes his ministers as he changes his shirts". He considered that any agreement made with one British government might be overturned by its successor.

The root cause of the unsatisfactory relations between Britain and Prussia at this time was Britain's unwillingness to adjust its foreign policy to take account of the advent of a new Great Power in Europe. Ever since the days of William III and Marlborough Britain – in alliance with Holland and Austria – had resisted the attempts of France and Spain to dominate the Continent. The rise of Prussia as a rival to Austria for leadership in Germany upset the traditional balance of power in Europe. And one British government after another found great difficulty in coming to terms with the new situation.

Frederick's accession to the throne of Prussia was generally welcomed in England. After all Frederick was bound to be an improvement upon his boorish and tyrannical father. In his essay criticising Machiavelli, published a few weeks after he came to the throne, Frederick appeared to be a man of principle whose views on kingship seemed to be far more elevated than those of his father. So there were hopes in England that relations with Prussia, which had been far from satisfactory since 1726, might be improved. And at this time an understanding with Prussia was desirable since Britain was at war with Spain and might soon be at war with France.

But British hopes of improving relations with Prussia were soon to be dashed. When Captain Guy Dickens, the British chargé d'affaires in Berlin, had his first audience with Frederick he was asked to what extent Britain would support Prussia's claims to Jülich, Berg, East Frisia and Mecklenburg. The British government had good reason to be alarmed that the new king of Prussia had far-reaching territorial ambitions and that a high price would have to be paid for his friendship. In his conversation with Guy Dickens, Frederick had not mentioned his designs upon Silesia. But when the Emperor Charles VI died he attacked Austria, although Prussia had agreed to the Pragmatic Sanction which had recognised Maria Theresa as the heir to the Habsburg dominions.

Captain Dickens was horrified that Frederick "not only declares he will not support the Austrian succession but plainly avows his design of invading part of it". George II declared to the Saxon envoy in London: "The King of Prussia is a prince who is dominated by ambition and by a desire to expand his territories. He mocks at all treaty obligations. Now he is going to occupy Silesia and he excuses his action by putting forward claims which seem to date back to the days of Charlemagne. On these principles no ruler in Germany can regard his possessions as safe. He is a prince without loyalty and without faith". The British government was alarmed at Frederick's unprovoked attack upon Britain's traditional ally, an act which upset the existing balance of power in Europe. The danger of France dominating the Continent would be increased if the Habsburgs were permanently weakened. And how could Britain stand aside if Frederick's rape of Silesia were but the prelude to an attack upon Hanover?

Frederick's victory at Mollwitz encouraged France and Bavaria to ignore the Pragmatic Sanction and to embark upon a campaign to plunder Maria Theresa of part of her inheritance. By the secret treaty of Breslau (June 5, 1741) a Franco-Prussian alliance was formed. Frederick gave up his claim to Jülich and Berg in return for a recognition of his claim to Lower Silesia. Meanwhile the British government tried to bring the war in Silesia to an end so that Austria could again fulfil her traditional role of Britain's main ally on the Continent against France and Spain. Lord Hyndford, a more senior diplomat than Guy Dickens, was sent to Prussia to act as an honest broker while Thomas Robinson, the British ambassador in Vienna, was given the thankless task of trying to persuade Maria Theresa to make some territorial concessions to Frederick. Lord Hyndford arrived in Breslau on May 2, 1741 but was unable to prevent the conclusion of the Franco-Prussian alliance in June. By October, however, Frederick was exasperated at the failure of the French to march on Vienna and Lord Hyndford was able to mediate between Prussia and Austria. He acted as witness to the signing of a secret convention at the castle of Klein Schellendorf by which the Austrian army raised the siege of Neisse, evacuated Silesia and left the province under Prussian control.

The settlement did not last long. When Prague fell to the French, the Bavarians and the Saxons in November 1741 Frederick changed sides again. He once more supported France and resumed hostilities against the Austrians. Before the end of 1741 his troops had seized Olmütz in Moravia. But he failed to hold the province and in April 1742 the Prussian forces had retreated into Bohemia. His victory over the Austrians at Chotusitz enabled him to desert his French allies for the second time. Once more Lord Hyndford played the part of an honest broker and – as Frederick acknowledged – his eloquence helped to persuade the Austrians to come to terms. By an agreement made at Breslau, and confirmed by the Treaty of Berlin (July 1742), Austria ceded Silesia and Glatz to Prussia while Frederick accepted responsibility for the repayment to English investors of a loan guaranteed by the revenues of Silesia.

The treaty of Berlin gave the instigator of the conflict in Europe a much needed respite. Prussia remained neutral while France, at the head of a coalition, continued her attacks upon the Habsburg dominions. Frederick hoped that even though she had England's support (and subsidies), Austria would be weakened to such an extent that Maria Theresa would be unable to try and recover Silesia. In the circumstances he was dismayed when the French were defeated at Dettingen in Bavaria (in June 1743) by an army of English, Hanoverian and Austrian troops commanded by George II of England. Frederick admitted in his memoirs that "cette victoire ne fit pas autant de plaisir au roi de Prusse" while Hyndford reported to Carteret that Frederick "cannot hide the inveterate hatred which he has against the King and the British nation".

The defeat of the French at Dettingen and the fear that Maria Theresa was planning a new campaign to recover Silesia decided Frederick to enter the war again. In June 1744 he renewed his alliance with France – now at war with Britain – and in the autumn of that year he occupied Saxony and attacked Bohemia. He captured Prague but soon found himself isolated by his enemies and was forced to retreat to Silesia.

In 1745 the French concentrated their efforts on a campaign in Flanders where they defeated Cumberland's army at Fontenoy. Frederick was left on his own to face the Austrians in Silesia. In June he decisively defeated the Austrians and Saxons at Hohenfriedberg and drove them out of Silesia. When further Prussian victories forced Maria Theresa to give up her efforts to recover her lost province Britain again played the part of an honest broker in the peace negotiations. Thomas Villiers (first Earl of Clarendon) helped to bring the two sides together and in December 1745 the Treaty of Dresden brought the second Silesian war to an end. Frederick thus once more deserted his French allies.

Meanwhile Frederick's relations with England could hardly have been worse. Frederick was allied with France with whom England was at war and he did not disguise his satisfaction at Cumberland's defeat at Fontenoy. Moreover he ignored Hanover's claims to East Frisia when he seized that territory in May 1744. After the Peace of Dresden England endeavoured to place her relations with Prussia on a more satisfactory footing. Thomas Villiers was sent to Berlin as British ambassador between 1746 and 1748 and he was succeeded by Henry Bilson Legge as envoy extraordinary in 1748. Legge tried to persuade Frederick to join Britain and Austria against France. He argued that it would be in Prussia's interest to prevent the French from overrunning the Netherlands. But the plan was doomed to failure since – owing to Frederick's seizure of Silesia – there could be no question of Prussia and Austria being members of the same alliance.

Moreover attempts to improve Anglo-Prussian relations in the late 1740s and early 1750s were frustrated by a lengthy dispute concerning the repayment of the Silesian loan. Between 1744 and 1748 England and France were at war while Prussia was at war with Austria and Saxony. Prussia was neutral as far as the Anglo-French conflict was concerned. English privateers seized a number of

Prussian ships and cargoes on the ground that they were carrying contraband goods to France. Prussian merchants were engaged in trade between Stettin and Bordeaux, exchanging Prussian and Polish timber for French wines and colonial goods. Frederick regarded only powder, arms, cannon and cannon balls as contraband. It appears that he received a verbal assurance from Lord Carteret that grain, timber, hemp, cloth and wax were not contraband. But English privateering captains were not well versed in the niceties of international law and they confiscated cargoes which Frederick considered should be exempt from seizure. Legge, the British minister in Berlin, admitted that "in some instances our privateers have in general transgressed the bounds of fair war and degenerated into something nighly related to piracy".

Frederick had no navy with which to protect Prussian merchant ships but he was prepared to help merchants by any means that came to hand. At first the British government brushed his protests aside, arguing that each case had been decided on its merits by a prize court in accordance with international law as generally understood at that time. The controversy concerning the nature of contraband and the right to seize contraband in neutral ships in time of war aroused widespread interest and became a "cause célèbre du droit des gens".

In 1752, having failed to secure satisfaction from the British government, Frederick took the drastic step of withholding money due to English holders in respect of a loan (£250,000 at 7 per cent interest) which the Emperor Charles had raised in 1734 on the security of the revenues of Silesia. The Emperor had paid no interest to the bondholders and when Frederick annexed Silesia he promised on at least three occasions to accept responsibility for the repayment of the loan.

Payments of the principal and interest were made between 1743 and 1751 but then Frederick withheld the last instalment of £45,000 pending the settlement of his dispute with Britain respecting Prussian ships and cargoes captured during the recent war. The British government protested that Frederick had broken his promise to pay the debt and that it was wrong to penalise private English investors because of the dispute over the seizure of Prussian ships and cargoes. And when Frederick set up a commission to investigate the claims of Prussian merchants the British government complained that this was a breach of international law since the incidents had already been investigated by British prize courts. Lord Newcastle complained that the sum involved was far too small to justify a war, yet the honour of the British state forbade any concession to Frederick's demands.

Yet eventually the British government accepted a compromise. In January 1756 – at the time of the conclusion of the Convention of Westminster – there was an exchange of notes by which the embargo on the Silesian loan payments was lifted in return for a payment of £20,000 to meet the claims of the Prussian merchants. The sum paid was about two thirds of the Prussian claim. The King of Prussia had a genuine grievance but he employed high-handed methods to enforce his claim for compensation. The British government was relieved that a long standing dispute had at last been settled, though Pitt thought that Britain had paid too high a price – on the rights of neutrals in wartime – to secure an agreement with Prussia.

By the Convention of Westminster England and Prussia guaranteed their existing possessions and agreed to maintain peace in Germany by jointly opposing any foreign intervention in that country. Prussia had therefore promised to defend Hanover from attack. The rapprochement between England and Prussia had been brought about by England's isolation at a time when war with France might break out at any time. England badly needed an ally on the Continent. So did Frederick the Great who was well aware that Austria, France, and Russia were planning to dismember Prussia. His fears were justified. In May 1756 France and Austria undertook to defend the European possessions of the other. This was the famous "diplomatic revolution" whereby the Habsburgs and the Bourbons, traditional enemies in the past, now took the first step to form an alliance directed against Britain and Prussia.

Frederick did not wait to be attacked. In August 1756 he took the initiative and invaded Saxony. His entourage included Sir Andrew Mitchell, the new British envoy to Prussia. The campaign of 1757 opened disastrously for Frederick. In Bohemia his success at Prague in May was soon overshadowed by his defeat by the Austrians at Kolin in June. In Silesia the Prussians were defeated at Breslau in November. In East Prussia Frederick's forces were defeated by the Russians at Gross Jägersdorf. The Russians actually held Berlin for a few days and exacted a ransom from the city. In Hanover the Duke of Cumberland was defeated by the French at Hastenbeck and signed the convention of Klosterseven. Despite these reverses Frederick was able to turn the tables on his enemies. He crushed a French army at Rossbach in November 1757 and defeated the Austrians and Bavarians at Leuthen in November – "two miracles in the space of one month, two victories gained by the same handful of men" (Sir Andrew Mitchell).

These Prussian victories encouraged Pitt to offer Frederick financial aid to continue the struggle. Lord Newcastle wrote on December 8, 1757 that "everybody agrees to support the King of Prussia with a large subsidy" and to pay for raising a new army to defend Hanover. The convention of Klosterseven was repudiated, the Duke of Cumberland was recalled, and the troops in Hanover were placed under the command of Prince Ferdinand of Brunswick, a general in the Prussian service. The subsidy, granted in April 1758, amounted to £670,000. Britain and Prussia agreed not to make peace without consulting each other. Further subsidy treaties were agreed upon on December 7, 1758 and again in 1759 and 1760. The subsidies amounted to £2,680,000 (27 million thalers). The money was paid in gold in London and its transfer to Prussia was handled mainly by finance houses in Amsterdam. Sombart has argued that Britain secured important commercial advantages by granting subsidies to German states. In his view the significance of the payments was "that by these means England was able to open up markets in foreign countries for her products and so enable countries like Germany to become her customers. The result was the creation of a huge balance of payments advantage for England".[1]

The decision to grant Frederick a subsidy was widely acclaimed by the public in England. After his victory at Prague on May 6, 1757 the Earl of Holderness wrote that "the most frantic marks of joy appear in the public streets". Frederick had become "the idol of the people". In the following month Frederick was defeated at Kolin but he quickly recovered to gain two great victories at Rossbach and Leuthen. Now he was applauded in England as the defender of the liberties of Europe and the champion of the Protestant cause – despite the fact that he had been allied with Catholic France during the War of the Austrian Succession. On Frederick's birthday in January 1758 there were illuminations in the City of London and in Westminster. Throughout the country there were bonfires and fireworks and many householders placed lighted candles in their windows. Church bells were rung in many parishes. From aristocrats like Lady Newcastle – "the strongest Prussian in England" – to the man in the street Frederick's triumphs were celebrated. In 1759 Horace Walpole wrote to a friend on January 19: "We are next week to have a serenata at the Opera House for the King of Prussia's birthday: it is to begin 'Viva Georgio e Frederigo viva!' " Some of the clergy were loud in their praises for the King of Prussia. In 1757

Newcome Cappe, a Unitarian minister in York, hailed Frederick as "the defender of the Christian faith" in a sermon on the text: "The voice of rejoicing and salvation is in the tabernacles of the righteous: the right hand of the Lord doeth valiantly" (Psalm 118, verse 15). In 1758 George Whitefield, the founder of the Calvinist Methodist church, observed a day of thanksgiving in London "for the signal victories gained by the King of Prussia over his enemies". He collected £1,500 to assist German Protestants who had suffered at the hands of Cossack troops. Practical help came also from Miss Barbara Wyndham of Salisbury, an admirer, who sent Frederick £1,000 in 1758.

Between 1758 and 1760 Frederick was the hero of the hour. Neither before nor since has a foreign ruler received such adulation in England. Apart from the birthday celebrations many other tributes were paid to the King of Prussia. Portraits of "the Protestant Hero" and the "Defender of the Protestant Religion" were hung in public buildings and in private households. Sermons were preached, speeches were made, songs were sung, medals were struck and inns were named in his honour. David Garrick declaimed a specially written prologue to *The Gamesters* which praised Frederick the Great. Samuel Johnson and his biographer James Boswell agreed that Frederick was "the greatest king now in Europe". Little wonder that the royal features and the arms of Prussia appeared on souvenirs of all kinds, from dinner services to beer mugs and snuff boxes. Macaulay, writing in 1842, declared that "an attentive observer will, at this day, find in the parlours of old fashioned inns, and in the portfolios of print-sellers, twenty portraits of Frederick for one of George the Second". And in the 1950s there was still a public house in London called "Old King of Prussia". Admiration for Frederick led to admiration for the Prussian army, the architecture of Berlin and Potsdam, the new legal code, the great public works and much else. There were even attempts to use the Prussian army drill manual in some English regiments and militia companies.

Frederick's fortunes fluctuated a good deal between 1758 and 1760 when Prussia was financially supported by Britain. In 1758 in three desperate campaigns he drove the Russians from his eastern provinces and successfully checked Austrian attempts to occupy Saxony and Silesia. In 1759 Frederick was defeated by the Russians and Austrians at Kunersdorf and by the Austrians at Dresden and Maxen. But at Minden Ferdinand of Brunswick defeated the French and saved Hanover from being occupied. In 1760

Frederick was confronted by the Russians east of the River Oder, the Austrians in Saxony and Silesia, and the Swedes in Pomerania. In the autumn he won decisive victories over the Austrians at Liegnitz and at Torgau.

Meanwhile Anglo-Prussian relations were deteriorating. In 1760 when the subsidy treaty came up for renewal there was, for the first time, some opposition to the policy of financing the Prussian war effort. In two pamphlets Israel Mauduit sharply criticised the Anglo-Prussian alliance and urged that the subsidy should not be renewed. In 1761 Pitt was out of office and, since Britain had made substantial conquests in Canada and India, his successor Lord Bute was anxious to come to terms with France. He urged the King of Prussia to make some territorial concession to Austria to enable a general European peace to be concluded and he made it clear that if his advice were not taken, the subsidy would not be renewed. Frederick indignantly rejected this advice and fought on. His fortunes were now at a low ebb. In 1761, although no major battle was fought, he lost the important fortresses of Schweidnitz and Colberg. Frederick complained bitterly that Colberg might have been saved if Britain had sent a naval squadron to the Baltic.

Frederick might well have had to make the sacrifices that Bute had suggested had there not been a dramatic change in his fortunes. In January 1762 Peter III became Czar of Russia. A worshipper of the King of Prussia he withdrew his forces from East Prussia and sent 20,000 men to Silesia to help Frederick to recover the fortress of Schweidnitz. Frederick was now free to face the Austrians, and the French. It was now clear that the war would end in a stalemate. Maria Theresa at last realised that she could not recover Silesia and in February 1763 the Treaty of Hubertusburg was signed. Austria accepted the loss of Silesia while Prussia withdrew her claims to other Habsburg territories. In the same month the Treaty of Paris ended the war between Britain and France. Frederick was not consulted as to the fate of Prussia's scattered provinces in west Germany – including the important fortress of Wesel. The treaty stipulated that these territories were to be evacuated by the French but not that they should be returned to Prussia. Frederick, however, acted promptly to occupy the territories as soon as the French left. He had every reason to feel aggrieved that the British negotiators had failed to protect his interests. The two peace settlements of 1763 enabled Britain to expand her empire overseas while Prussia secured no new territories. But Frederick had defeated the attempt of a powerful coalition to partition his dominions.

The last year of the war saw a further decline in Anglo-Prussian relations. Early in 1762 English privateering captains were active in the Mediterranean. At that time England was at peace with Russia and therefore Russian ships could not be seized. But as Prussia was still technically at war with Russia the privateers hoisted the Prussian flag when attacking Russian vessels. Frederick protested strongly against this abuse of the Prussian flag, particularly as he was anxious to ingratiate himself with the new Czar Peter III.[2]

After 1763 relations between England and Prussia reverted to the unsatisfactory state that they had been in before 1757. Frederick never forgave Britain for withdrawing his subsidy and leaving him in the lurch in his darkest hour. Diplomatic relations were broken off in 1762 but were resumed in 1765 through the mediation of Ferdinand of Brunswick. Sir Andrew Mitchell returned to Berlin while Count Matzahn represented Prussia in London. Mitchell took with him a plan for a triple alliance of Britain, Russia and Prussia to counterbalance the Family Compact between France and Spain. Frederick, however, rejected the plan. Mitchell remained at his post until his death in 1771 and was succeeded by James Harris (Lord Malmesbury) who served in Berlin from 1772 to 1776.

The outbreak of the American War of Independence gave Frederick an opportunity to show his hostility to Britain. He publicly declared that Britain could not put down the rebellion and that the United States was "to be considered as a rising, independent and powerful state". Two American delegates were received in Berlin and were allowed to buy stores for the rebels. Frederick hoped that Prussian ports would benefit from Britain's inability to keep control over the trade of her American colonies. Prussian merchants tried to gain a foothold in trades hitherto closed to them. Frederick joined the Armed Neutrality against Britain in May 1781 and placed the Prussian mercantile marine under the protection of the Russian navy. Hertzberg stated that during the war "le pavillon prussien a gagné une faveur extraordinaire". Frederick told the head of the *Seehandlung* that after the war an attempt should be made to establish a direct trade with American ports so that Prussian linen and woollen cloth could be exchanged for American tobacco, sugar, indigo and rice. When the Americans gained their independence Frederick recognised their government and in 1785 a commercial treaty, on the basis of reciprocity, was signed between Prussia and the United States. As for the English he remarked in 1784 that they were "like sick people who have had a fever and do not know how ill they have been till the fit is over".

In conclusion some reference may be made to the commercial relations between Britain and Prussia in the reign of Frederick the Great. Trade between the two countries consisted of the exchange of Prussian timber, flax, linen, hides, tallow, wax and grain for English manufactured goods. Some products imported by England from Prussia were of Prussian origin while others came from Poland and Russia. The complexity of Frederick's system of taxation was a serious hindrance to English merchants. In 1786 Viscount Dalrymple, the British minister in Berlin, complained that the Prussian tariff was "too complicated and confused to admit of a clear and satisfactory explanation". But from time to time the British government was able to secure concessions concerning the export of particular goods from Britain to Prussia. The Prussian transit dues on Staffordshire pottery, for example, were under discussion in 1786 and were reduced soon after Frederick's death.

The navigation laws of the maritime powers protected their shipping interests and prevented Prussian merchants from trading directly with colonial territories. They had to go to European ports to sell their linen and woollen cloth and to purchase colonial goods such as sugar, coffee and tobacco. Prussia dealt in this way with French, Spanish and Portuguese possessions rather than with British colonies. A director of the *Seehandlung* was stationed in Cadiz to promote the export of Silesian linens and the import of colonial products. A representative of the firm of Splitgerber and Daum was sent to Bordeaux to purchase sugar from San Domingo (Haiti).

The acquisition of East Frisia in 1744 – in defiance of Hanover's claims – gave Frederick a window to the North Sea. He dreamed that Emden might become a rival to Amsterdam and he granted the city the status of a free port in 1751. At first he had some success since the East Asiatic Company made a number of profitable voyages to Canton and at one time its shares were quoted at five times their nominal value. But the activities of the company came to an end when French troops occupied East Frisia in 1757 and nothing came of a later attempt to revive trade with Canton. The Bengal Company, established in 1753, gave up the attempt to open up trade with India after two disastrous voyages and nothing came of a proposal from the ruler of Mysore that Prussia should set up trading stations in his territories. A Levant Company, established in 1765, collapsed in 1769 when the Bank of Amsterdam failed. Towards the end of Frederick's reign, however, some successful voyages were made from Emden to Batavia and Surinam.

The failure of Emden to develop its trade with India and China was due partly to the inexperience of Prussian entrepreneurs and partly to the opposition of the maritime powers to those who intruded in their preserves. British hostility to the attempt by Prussian merchants to trade directly with India led Parliament to pass an Act prohibiting English companies from insuring foreign vessels trading with India. Britain undoubtedly reacted too strongly to Prussia's attempt to open up direct commercial relations with Asia. There was little likelihood of Emden developing into a major port.

During the reign of Frederick the Great the first phase of the industrial revolution was taking place in England. Frederick feared that if the new machines that were being used in England were introduced into Prussia many domestic workers might lose their jobs.[3] It was not until the end of his reign that the Prussian authorities began to take an interest in recent technical advances in England. Prussian officials who visited the industrial regions in England between 1779 and 1786 included three mining experts – C.F. Bückling, F.A.A. Eversmann and Freiherr vom Stein. In the hope of securing plans of the steam engine they visited Boulton and Watt's Soho plant in Birmingham as well as factories – such as Barclay and Perkins' brewery in London – in which a steam engine had been installed. Matthew Boulton was alarmed by the activities of these German visitors. In 1779 he warned his partner that a German metallurgist had come to England "to steal our engine" and in 1787 he complained that Eversmann had "introduced himself to Mr. Wilkinson's and other Manufactorys, without the consent of the Proprietors, particularly into some of the Iron Forges worked by Boulton and Watt's Engines, and he made very exact drawings thereof, which he took to Berlin".[4] Frederick also caused enquiries to be made in England concerning up to date methods of agriculture. Count Kamecke, for example, visited an estate at Nottingly near Ferrybridge in Yorkshire to study improved farming methods.

NOTES

1. Werner Sombart, *Der moderne Kapitalismus* (edn. of 1921), Vol. II (2), p.988. See also C. Wilson, *De l'influence des capitaux anglais sur l'industrie européene depuis la révolution 1688 jusqu'en 1846* (1847).
2. On July 23, 1762 Frederick wrote to the Grand Master of the Knights of St. John in Malta suggesting that they should make a joint protest to the British government. See

G.B. Henderson, *Crimean War Diplomacy and other Historical Essays* (1947), p.303.
3. C. Ergang, "Friedrich der Grosse in seiner Stellung zum Maschinenproblem" in *Beiträge zur Geschichte der Technik und Industrie*, III, 1910, pp.78–82.
4. W.O. Henderson, *Britain and Industrial Europe, 1750–1870* (second edition, 1965), pp.149–53.

BIBLIOGRAPHY

Sir Andrew Bisset, *Memoirs and Papers of Sir Andrew Mitchell* (2 vols. 1850).
Sir E.M. Satow, *The Silesian Loan and Frederick the Great* (1915).
Sir Richard Lodge, *Great Britain and Prussia* (1923).
—— "Russia, Prussia and Great Britain, 1742–44" in the *English Historical Review*, XLV, 1930.
—— "The Mission of Henry Legge to Berlin" in *Transactions of the Royal Historical Society* (4th Series) XIV, 1931.
Manfred Schlenke, *England und das friderizionische Preussen* (1963).
R. Koser, "Die preussische Finanzen im Siebenjährigen Kriege" in *Forschungen zur Brandenburgischen und Preussischen Geschichte*, XIII, 1900.
R.L. Haworth, "Frederick the Great and the American Revolution" in the *American Historical Review*, Vol. IX, 1903–4.

12

HERMANN EUGEN FALK: A GERMAN ENTREPRENEUR IN CHESHIRE

The significance of the career of H.E. Falk lay in his repeated attempts to establish a cartel of Cheshire producers of salt to fix output and prices.[1] Falk, who was born in Danzig in 1820, came to England in 1838 and worked for a timber firm in Hull run by his two elder brothers. His first contact with the salt trade was due to the fact that the Falk brothers exported salt to the Baltic in return for importing timber from that region. In 1842 H.E. Falk moved to Liverpool where he became a salt broker and published *Falk's Salt Circular*. Next he spent two years in New Brunswick supervising a timber estate owned by Falk brothers. On his return to England H.E. Falk left his brothers to set up his own Meadow Bank rock salt mine in Winsford on the River Weaver and by 1858 he had become one of the largest exporters of salt in the district. In part this was due to his initiative in opening up new markets overseas. As early as 1846 he had sent a cargo of salt to India.

The economic crisis of 1857 stimulated the leading salt firms in Cheshire to work together to protect their interests. In August 1858 H.E. Falk played a leading part in establishing the Salt Chamber of Commerce.[2] Its members included the major manufacturers and brokers – except for the British Salt Company and Joseph Verdin's firm. But certain small entrepreneurs, who combined transporting salt with operating little salt works, were excluded from membership of the Chamber. The objects of the Chamber were stated to be "the opening up of new markets, the watching over treaties and tariffs in foreign countries where salt was or might become an article of import, and to impress on the government and legislature that in the category of our export trade salt played a very important part". The founders of the Chamber asserted that they had no intention of reviving earlier attempts to regulate output and prices. But since members of the Chamber held regular monthly meetings they had ample opportunities to discuss these matters informally. The annual report of the Chamber for 1864–5 admitted that

> the members of the Chamber, when drawn together for these general objects, have wisely considered that the opportunity might also be availed of to discuss the all-important subject of supply and demand, with a view to exercise its influence in asking for a remunerative scale of prices.

Falk's influence over the Salt Chamber soon increased. In 1862 he became the Chamber's representative on the Liverpool Chamber of Commerce. For 25 years he held various offices in the Chamber – vice president, chairman, and then (with two short breaks) president between 1867 and 1889. He was largely responsible for establishing another body, called the Salt Trade Committee, "to adapt the make to the demand and regulate prices". Although the Salt Chamber disclaimed responsibility for the Trade Committee's actions it was generally accepted that the Salt Trade Committee was an offshoot of the Salt Chamber. The link between the two was acknowledged in 1866 when H. E. Falk was presented with a piece of silver plate in recognition of his services "as the originator of the Chamber and the Salt Trade Committee".

One reason for the formation of the Salt Trade Committee was the fall in the price of salt during the American civil war. Falk and his colleagues were determined to make up for their losses in the American trade by expanding their exports to India. In the Bengal Presidency Clive had established state monopolies both in the manufacture of salt and in the wholesale trade in salt. In 1846 British traders were allowed to place salt in bonded warehouses in Calcutta without previously paying import duty. Twelve years later the Salt Chamber embarked upon a vigorous campaign to secure the abolition of the state monopoly on the manufacture of salt in Bengal. This campaign was successful in 1863 but the government of India recouped its financial losses by levying high duties on the import of salt. At the same time Falk was largely responsible for the establishment of the Liverpool Salt Brokers Association which co-operated with the Salt Trade Committee in fixing the price of salt.

Meanwhile Falk had struck a decisive blow at what he called "the proletarian element" in the salt trade. He launched two steam barges – the *Experiment* in 1863 and the *Improvement* in 1864 – on the River Weaver. By sending his salt to Liverpool by these barges

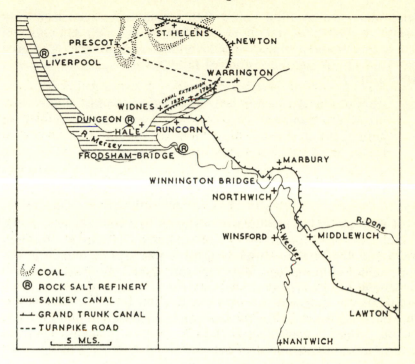

THE MERSEY–WEAVER SALT DISTRICT

Reproduced by courtesy of the Lancashire and Cheshire Antiquarian Society

he broke the power of the independent watermen, many of whom were also producers of salt in a small way. Before long most of their little saltworks had been taken over by the large salt firms. There was a further improvement in Falk's transport arrangements in 1870 when the Cheshire Lines Committee opened a branch line to Over Winsford.

For a few years after the American civil war salt prices were steady. In 1869, however, there was an increased demand for salt at home – largely owing to the growth of the alkali industry – and also abroad. A new "proletarian element" appeared when small saltworks were established to take advantage of the boom. In September 1870 a new Trade Committee was set up to secure co-operation between salt producers and brokers. Prices remained steady until 1875 when they fell sharply. In 1877 and again in 1881 Falk made new efforts to persuade the salt firms to work together to maintain the level of prices by restricting output. In 1886 prices fell once more and in 1888 Falk's Salt Union was established as a company with a capital of £3,000,000. It included saltworks in Cheshire, Worcestershire, Middlesbrough and Ireland. Chaloner has pointed out that the history of the Cheshire salt trade between 1815 and 1889

> seriously modifies the generally accepted idea of the mid-nineteenth century as an era of unregulated competition, although the various restriction schemes did in fact tend to break down after a few months' existence. These early attempts at the regulation of salt prices and salt production met with only partial success because of the ease with which new competitors could enter an expanding trade.[3]

H.E. Falk ran a prosperous business. He was always on the lookout for new markets to exploit at home and abroad. Between 1874 and 1880 he undertook extensive journeys in India, the Far East and California to study the salt trade.[4] He was a strong opponent of government interference in industry. In evidence before the Royal Commission on noxious vapours in 1879 he denied that the black smoke from the low grade coal used to fuel salt pans caused serious inconvenience to his neighbours. He claimed that the cost of reducing the nuisance would ruin the producers of salt. And in 1881 he opposed a Bill to compensate the owners of properties on land which had subsided because of the pumping of brine or the collapse of old underground salt workings. However Parliament passed Acts to restrict noxious vapours and to compensate the victims of land subsidence.

Falk's attitude towards his workers was ambivalent. On the one hand he founded a friendly society (1860) and erected a number of cottages for his workers. He also built a school in 1872 and paid the salaries of the teachers. On the other hand he dealt firmly with strikers. In 1868 there was a great strike in the Cheshire salt district by workers known as "wallers". These were men who raked the crystallised salt in an evaporating pan and then lifted it out. They were organised in the old established Winsford Salt Makers Association. They demanded a rise in wages from 24s. to 27s. a week. In evidence before a parliamentary committee one of Falk's sons stated that most of the employers gave way, but that his father had recruited some 80 German workers in Liverpool. These men were prepared to work for as little as 20s. – later only 18s. – a week. The German workers for the most part had come to Liverpool to migrate to the United States or Canada. They were glad of any employment that would enable them to save the £5 or £6 needed for next stage of their journey. Despite strong local opposition to the employment of blacklegs Falk did not change his policy.

In 1877, however, Falk began to employ Poles from Austrian Galicia who were said to be more docile than the Germans they replaced. In 1888 Falk was employing 92 foreigners, including five women. The Winsford Local Board received alarming reports from the Medical Officer of Health for Cheshire (1885) and from its own Surveyor (1888) concerning the unsatisfactory nature of the accommodation provided by Falk for his foreign workers. Moreover hostile articles appeared in the press denouncing the overcrowded and insanitary condition of the lodgings of the Polish workers.[5] And the admissions made by Hermann John Falk (son of H. E. Falk) when questioned in 1888 by the Select Committee of the House of Commons on Emigration and Immigration gave H. E. Falk some unwelcome publicity. Some improvements were made, and by the time that H. E. Falk died in 1898 most of the foreigners had left Meadow Bank.

NOTES

1. Falk has been neglected by economic historians, except for an essay by W.H. Chaloner, "William Furnival, H.E. Falk and the Salt Chamber of Commerce: some Chapters in the Economic History of Cheshire" in *Transactions of the Historic Society of Lancashire and Cheshire*, Vol. 112 (1960), pp.123–45.
2. A copy of the *Annual Reports of the Salt Chamber of Commerce of Cheshire and Worcestershire*, 1858–89 is preserved in the library of the University of Manchester.
3. W.H. Chaloner, *op. cit.*, p.141.
4. H.E. Falk, *Salt in North America. Notes taken on a Tour … in the Autumn of 1876* (Northwich, 1877) and *A Winter Tour through India Burma and the Straits* (1880).
5. *Sunday Chronicle*, Sept. 12, 1886: *The Umpire*, March 7, 1889.

13

WALTHER RATHENAU: A PIONEER OF THE PLANNED ECONOMY

The planned economy and arrangements for social welfare in many capitalist societies to-day owe their origin to ideas emanating from very different sources. While socialists have played a leading rôle in recasting the capitalist economies of Britain, Australia, New Zealand and the Scandinavian countries, parallel changes in Germany and the United States perhaps owe more to planners who have had little sympathy with socialist ideas.

Few outside the socialist camp contributed more towards the theory of the capitalist economy than did Walther Rathenau,[1] whose books and pamphlets were widely read between 1917 and 1920.[2] And during the first World War Rathenau made a significant contribution to the practice of national economic planning by organising the German raw materials department.

Rathenau, however, is no longer remembered as the exponent of the revolutionary ideas expressed in *Zur Mechanik des Geistes* and *Von kommenden Dingen*. He is remembered as head of the Allgemeine Elektrizitäts Gesellschaft (the A.E.G.),[3] director of many companies,[4] prominent banker,[5] and founder of the War Raw Materials Department; as the exponent of a new reparations policy which led to the Wiesbaden agreement with Loucheur in October 1921;[6] and as the man who brought Soviet Russia and Germany together by the Rapallo Treaty of April 1922.

The true significance of Rathenau's career, however, lay neither in his business nor in his political achievements. He did not found the A.E.G. – that was his father's work[7] – and as a company director and banker he was no more powerful than a dozen others. His opportunities as a statesman were limited, since he held ministerial office for only about twelve months.

Walther Rathenau, 1922

It was natural that a solid banker like Carl Fürstenberg should regard Rathenau as a brilliant industrialist "whose writings were by no means his greatest achievement".[8] Many contemporaries agreed. But some of Rathenau's writings had a profound influence at the end of the first World War. To-day a later generation – which can study his ideas in the light of recent developments – may regard Rathenau primarily as the brilliant critic of early twentieth-century capitalism, and as a far-seeing reformer who would have recast capitalist society without introducing socialism.

Rathenau's theories on the planned economy earned him much abuse from both socialists and those who wanted to leave things as they were.[9] He realised that he aroused opposition by championing new ideas rather too soon for the average man to understand them.[10] Events have shown that Rathenau's prophecies were often right, and that many of his unorthodox proposals were not so impracticable as they at first appeared. Indeed, the revolutionary ideas of one generation often became the platitudes of the next.

One reason why Rathenau was distrusted was because of his astonishing versatility. In an age which respected the specialist, it was hardly surprising that some should regard Rathenau as jack of all trades and master of none. He was a company director and a banker; a research physicist and a philosopher; an accomplished orator and artist; a writer and a statesman. Some contemporaries did not withhold their admiration for the versatility of Rathenau's genius. The poet Fritz von Unruh wrote:

"Statesman", says one; "Philosopher" a second;
Third calls thee "Friend"; "Maecenas" says another.
The world of business claims thee; yet who knows whence
    these opposites derive? At what deep fount
Thy many-gifted soul finds sustenance?

But there were others who mistrusted a man who excelled in so many spheres. Rathenau admitted that he was popularly regarded as "a dilettante in sixteen fields of activity and a company director in his spare time".[11]

The contradictions between Rathenau's unconventional views and his business triumphs alienated some whom he hoped to influence. Rathenau's critics declared that only a charlatan could enjoy great wealth while preaching "the nationalisation of industrial monopolies, the abolition of the right to dispose of one's property by will, the imposition of heavy taxes to abolish great wealth, the freeing of the workers and the establishment of a classless society".[12] Rathenau failed to answer such attacks effectively. Few believed him when he claimed to enjoy only a modest middle-class standard of comfort in his luxurious villa at Berlin–Grünewald, or when he said that he had purchased a royal country house (Schloss Freienwalde) merely to preserve it for posterity.

Since he was an extreme individualist, Rathenau failed to make his mark as a party leader or founder of a school of thought. Before 1914, he tried to secure nomination as a Reichstag candidate for Frankfurt on Oder but his Jewish origin and unusual views prevented his name from going forward. In the autumn of 1918 he tried to form a political group (the *Demokratischer Volksbund*) but this failed completely – as did his attempt to represent Liegnitz in the Weimar National Assembly. He usually intervened in politics on his own responsibility, acting as a prominent industrialist and not as a party leader.[13]

The difficulty that Rathenau sometimes experienced in working with others hampered a brilliant career. His differences with his father caused him to embark upon a banking career (1902).[14] His missions to Africa with Dr Dernburg were followed by a rift between the two men.[15] Rathenau first made his mark as a writer in *Zukunft*, but he quarrelled with its editor (Maximilian Harden) and the two were never reconciled.[16] Rathenau was one of the first to recognise Ludendorff's merits and to press for his promotion,[17] but again a difference of opinion led to bitter enmity.[18]

The inconsistency between Rathenau's social doctrines and his way of life was equalled only by the inconsistencies between his political writings and his political acts. Between 1907 and 1914, while criticising the policy of the administration, he remained in close touch with the Kaiser and with official circles in Berlin and twice accompanied the Colonial Minister on government missions to Africa.[19]

When the Weimar Republic was established Rathenau remained a lone political figure.[20] He had offended the socialists as much as the right-wing politicians. He failed to enter the National Assembly and when he was nominated to the first Nationalisation Commission (*Sozialisierungskommission*) strong opposition led to the withdrawal of his name.[21] At a time when his economic theories were widely discussed he could not dissuade Wissell and von Möllendorff[22] from trying to rush through schemes for a bureaucratic planned economy.[23] Rathenau realised that these plans would fail – and the Government did reject them in July 1919 – and that their premature introduction would prejudice their chances of being revived later.[24]

Both the Kaiser's Government and the Republic used Rathenau's services – but only in grave emergencies when his unique gifts could not be overlooked. In August 1914 he was called upon to stave off a threatened shortage of raw materials, but no sooner had he devised the necessary machinery than his opponents placed difficulties in his way and he resigned. In 1921–2, when Germany's fortunes were at their lowest ebb for a century, he shouldered the thankless duties of Minister for Reconstruction (May–November 1921) and Foreign Minister (February–June 1922).

Another reason why Rathenau's proposals were misunderstood was that in his longer works his style was singularly obscure. Among his letters are replies from Rathenau to correspondents who had complained that they could not follow what he had written.[25] Rathenau's speeches, pamphlets and newspaper articles however, were much more lucid.[26] In his longer works Rathenau's proposals were buried under philosophical and sociological disquisitions. This explains why Rathenau has been judged largely on his pamphlets of 1918–20 rather than on his earlier books. Rathenau himself complained of this.[27]

Rathenau regarded his later pamphlets as tracts for the times. In them he applied to the problem of Germany's post-war reconstruction the principles much more adequately presented in his earlier works. Those who neglect Rathenau's longer works may miss a fundamental aspect of the author's approach to economic problems. Rathenau's proposals were more than schemes for helping Germany out of the difficulties that followed a lost war. His basic ideas had been formed some years before. They aimed at correcting what Rathenau regarded as the essential weakness of capitalism. He believed that industrial societies were lacking in any spiritual or cultural values. He was ever seeking for a solution of the problem of how the masses herded in factories, mines and offices could find a spiritual purpose in life which would give real significance to their economic activities.[28] Rathenau's preoccupation with this problem explains his opposition to Socialism, which he considered to be as grossly materialistic as the system which it aimed at overthrowing.[29]

Rathenau's Jewish origin was another reason for his failure to secure support for his plans. Anti-semitic feeling was strong in Germany in Rathenau's day. He often complained that he was only "a second-class citizen"[30] – unable in peacetime to aspire even to the rank of lieutenant in the Prussian army. Yet Rathenau was more Prussian than the Prussians. He claimed: "My people is the German people, my Fatherland is Germany and my religion is that German faith which is above all religions."[31] He rejected the Zionist solution of the Jewish problem.[32] But few Jews of his standing in public affairs were more critical of the failings of some German members of his race.[33] And although Rathenau preached acceptance of the Christian virtues to the German workers he himself continued to practise the Jewish faith.

As a Jew, Rathenau could not escape the enmity of the more violent German nationalists. No one did more to discredit Rathenau than Ludendorff (notoriously anti-semitic in his views), who denounced him before a Reichstag committee of inquiry as being a defeatist during the first World War.[34] The charge was baseless, but Rathenau's reputation suffered.

When considering Rathenau's schemes for economic planning,[35] it is necessary to appreciate his views on the circumstances that, in his opinion, made reforms essential. Rathenau believed that the unprecedented rise in the world's population in the nineteenth century had inevitably led to a revolution in the means of production. Only a factory system run by competent managers and disciplined workers could have achieved the vastly increased output that had been necessary. Rathenau argued that the new economic system, however successful it might have been in securing greatly expanded industrial production, had also significant drawbacks which required immediate attention.

A fundamental weakness of the machine age was lack of culture and absence of appreciation of spiritual values. Helpless in a world where fierce competition in the factory had replaced neighbourly co-operation on the land, the modern worker could now express himself not as an individual but only as a member of a group such as the State, a Church, a trade union or a club. The worker who performed repetitive duties on a machine – responsible for only a fraction of the finished product – could not use his creative faculties like the craftsman of a former age who derived an artist's satisfaction from his labours. At one time workers had adjusted their lives to changes in the creative forces of nature but now they had to adapt themselves to the requirements of a soulless machine. With no creative urge to work, factory hands were forced to labour by fear of unemployment, while for managers the incentives were ambition, love of power and the excitement of beating a competitor. "His work may bring happiness but it is no longer the pride of creative work – only the satisfaction of achievement. A problem is solved, a danger averted, a step forward has been gained – and so on to the next problem and the one after." "Success lies not in creative expression but in expansion. What brings success is the ability to produce the same goods tenfold, nay a hundred fold, in the shortest possible time and at the lowest possible cost." The businessman triumphed by skill in the arts of the politician – in "the ability to discover the aims of a competitor and to use them to further his own ends; to see a situation as whole; to divine the signs of the times; to negotiate; to make alliances; to isolate a foe and to strike a shrewd blow".[36] And the vulgar leisure pursuits of the masses brought them no more true happiness than did the dull routine of their daily tasks.

Rathenau believed that capitalism was doomed.[37] This was not because of its injustices – though Rathenau emphasised that poverty among workers and obstacles hindering the advancement of able persons were among the greatest social evils of the day.[38] He believed that the machine age was doomed because both workers and middle classes hungered for a new spiritual purpose in life. In 1912 he declared: "Our age, lacking in all spiritual values, has yet to plumb the lowest depths, but we can already foresee its end ... Its dissolution approaches not because of the sacrifices of noble reformers or by revolt by the lower classes but by the rebirth of society from spiritual suffering."[39] Rathenau believed that a divine spark survived even in societies apparently hopelessly degraded by capitalism. In a sense his proposed reforms were expedients designed to prepare the way for a social and economic revolution which he felt to be inevitable.

Another weakness of the machine age, in Rathenau's opinion, was that a few people owned or controlled great wealth and were virtually free to dispose of it as they pleased. It was mainly private persons who decided how wealth was to be used. Untold harm had been done by the unwise use of land, minerals, machinery, buildings, technical skill and labour. Rathenau declared that production and consumption should be controlled by society and not by individuals. To waste coal, for example, was to rob both oneself and posterity. The capital, materials and labour used in building a mansion would be better employed in erecting workers' houses. A private park might produce food for the masses. A luxury yacht was less useful than a tramp steamer. A string of pearls represented wealth that could educate a student.

Rathenau also condemned the waste of manpower. Society in future must abolish drones who lived on inherited incomes. Labour – and capital too – could be saved by reducing excessive competition in the home market.[40] The number of commercial travellers, advertising agents and petty retailers should be drastically reduced. In the professions, too, manpower should be used economically. Rathenau criticised a state of affairs which made it possible for some six thousand legal actions to be pending in a German colony which had a white population of only two thousand. These were but a few examples of economic arrangements which were, in Rathenau's opinion, as anarchical as the political régimes of the Middle Ages.[41]

Rathenau assumed that "economic affairs are no longer the responsibility of the individual but of society".[42] Since capital, materials and manpower were all limited, he considered that society should control both industrial output and the consumption of goods. To stop wasteful expenditure Rathenau suggested that half of all incomes (excluding the first £150 a year) should be taken by the State in the form of income tax. Imported luxuries should pay a high import duty while those made at home should pay an equivalent purchase tax. Rathenau desired to reduce by taxation the use of motor cars, mansions, private grounds, jewellery, servants and so forth (the luxuries of the rich) as well as alcoholic drinks[43] and tobacco (the luxuries of the poor).

Economic waste could also be eliminated by controlling the use of all raw materials (especially coal),[44] by reducing the number of workers in non-essential occupations, by reducing competition in the home market and by limiting the consumer's choice with regard to the variety of articles offered within a single range of goods. The last suggestion anticipated later schemes for the production of "utility" goods. Even so, Rathenau could hold out little hope (after the first World War) that anything better than a very modest standard of living could be maintained in Germany. He complained that "the popular mind has ... resolved to conceive the future on a basis of domestic prosperity about ten times as great as it can possibly be ..."[42]

Rathenau hoped to achieve his aims partly by direct government controls and partly by heavy taxation to reduce private consumption. The second method would reduce the number of very wealthy persons. Two other means of attaining the same end were put forward by Rathenau. One was to eliminate inherited income by high death duties and by restricting the rights of testators.[46] The other was to control all monopolies.[47] Rathenau held that in the machine age only "monopolies breed wealth: there is no other way of getting rich".[48]

Rathenau's ideal classless society would begin to emerge as penal taxation reduced the incomes of the wealthy to a level comparable with that of the upper middle classes and as the gap between the manual and blackcoated workers disappeared. As early as 1912 Rathenau noticed that the wages of some skilled German artisans were higher than those of the lower-paid blackcoated workers. Rathenau also considered that a classless society should be fostered by introducing equality in education – instead of having one kind of school for rich children and another for the poor – as well as equality of opportunity so that public and business appointments would be filled by merit and not by favour. Rathenau considered that all young people should serve the State for a year in a civilian capacity[49] and that professional men and blackcoated workers should devote part of their time to manual labour.

If the State controlled output and consumption it must also supervise foreign trade. Private persons (argued Rathenau) should not decide what should be imported or exported. Certain branches of foreign commerce might harm society, however profitable they might be to individuals. The volume of Germany's foreign commerce would have to be restricted. Even before 1914 Rathenau had realised that the terms of trade were turning against the industrialised European countries. He saw that the raw materials and foodstuffs that Germany purchased abroad would become more costly as agrarian countries became industrialised and enjoyed a higher standard of living. The finished goods that Germany exported would not find so ready a market if foreigners imposed higher import duties to protect native industries. If Germany's income from exports declined she would – unless income from investments abroad and from services to foreigners increased – have to reduce her purchases from abroad and it would be for the State to see to it that only essential commodities were imported. It would be folly to pay for luxuries with money needed for essential imports. Native raw materials should be used even if they cost more than foreign commodities. Home-produced substitute synthetic products should replace imported natural products. After the first World War Rathenau argued that Germany should profit from the experience of the blockade to reconstruct her economy on the basis of national self-sufficiency.

Rathenau painted no clear-cut picture of a planner's paradise where everybody's activities were controlled by the State. As a businessman he opposed bureaucratic schemes to organise human activity like a tidy beehive. He advocated the public control of industry but wished to retain the initiative and freedom associated with private enterprise. He claimed always to have championed "free self-government" in industry as opposed to "bureaucratic control".[50] He envisaged a gradual revolution, with many experiments to find out the best ways of organising the complicated activities of a modern industrial community.

He held firmly to certain basic principles such as the attainment of social welfare by State action and not by *laissez-faire*; the more equal distribution of wealth; the ideal of the classless society; the elimination of waste; the promotion of efficiency; the establishment of national self-sufficiency; and the revival of a sense of spiritual values in industrial communities.

Rathenau suggested various means to attain these ends. Sometimes state ownership and management might be the best method. Sometimes municipal control might be more desirable.[51] Where a few concerns dominated an industry it might be best for the Government to secure their amalgamation and to exercise some control over the new national cartel. Sometimes it might be best to establish new nationalised concerns on the lines of the "State Corporations" of the first World War. When this process was completed only a few economic activities would survive in private hands. Rathenau believed that workers should share in the control of industry through joint committees of management and men.[52] He thus hoped to give all workers – manual, skilled and blackcoated – a feeling of creative satisfaction in the achievements of their factory or office.

During the first World War Rathenau was able to put into practice some of his ideas on a planned economy.[53] Shortly after hostilities began he was asked to establish a new department in the Prussian War Ministry to control essential raw materials.[54] Germany was unprepared for a long war. The blockade cut her off from most overseas sources of supply. Unless drastic action had been taken Germany might have been defeated within a few months.

Rathenau's policy was based upon four principles which were in his opinion "a decisive step towards State Socialism".[55] First, essential raw materials were brought under state control. Their exchange was no longer left to the free play of economic forces but was subordinated to the public interest. Secondly, stocks of raw materials were built up by purchases from neutral countries and by confiscations in occupied territories. In the early months of the war the Germans overran districts which contained considerable supplies of wool, rubber and nitrates. Thirdly, raw materials which were in short supply were replaced as far as possible by materials (or substitutes) that could be produced in Germany. A striking example of this was the rapid erection of plants to manufacture ammonia as a by-production of coal distillation and also nitrogen extracted from the air by new processes. In this way Germany — hitherto largely dependent upon Chile for nitrates — averted what might have been a catastrophic shortage of high explosives.

To speed up the output and processing of raw materials Rathenau devised a new form of industrial organisation. This was the "War-Corporation" which came — as he put it — midway "between a joint-stock company ... and a bureaucratic organisation".[56] The corporations were owned jointly by the government and the owners of the raw materials which they handled. Three differences between the corporations and joint-stock companies deserve notice. First, each corporation had a planning committee (composed of officials and members of local chambers of commerce) which advised the directors on production targets. Secondly, the appropriate government department could veto decisions of the directors and the planning committee. Thirdly, the corporations were not allowed to distribute profits. The functions of the corporations varied. Some were distributing agencies. They used compulsory powers to collect sequestered raw materials which were then passed on to the factories where they were most needed. Others owned plants and were themselves engaged in manufacturing.

Rathenau had to face numerous difficulties. Many industrialists opposed a system which was entirely alien to traditional ways of doing business. Jealousies between government departments, between federal governments, between the military authorities of occupied territories and authorities at home all caused friction. Above all, the intrusion of a Jewish company director into the Prussian War Ministry caused offence to old-fashioned patriots. By April 1915 Rathenau's position had become so uncomfortable that he resigned. He claimed that he handed over to his successor "a completed, an efficient and a going concern". Rathenau hoped that his department would survive in peacetime as a state planning authority — an "Economic General Staff" he called it. In this he was disappointed but "Rathenau's creative idea of these war companies became one of the important directives for the subsequent development of German State economy. All subsequent efforts of Weimar Germany and ... of the Third Reich to develop State economy on non-bureaucratic lines and to create intermediary institutions between private and public business management are to be traced back to Rathenau's organizing genius."[57]

In the early years of the Weimar Republic Rathenau's services were used mainly as an expert on reparations and as foreign minister and he had only limited opportunities of influencing the organisation of Germany's internal economy. He was, however, a member of the second nationalisation commission (1920) which inquired into the future structure of the coalmining industry.[58] The coalmines were left in private hands but a coal board was established which brought the industry under a measure of public control. Rathenau was also a member of the Federal Economic Council which met for the first time at the end of June 1920.[59]

Rathenau fell a victim to the wave of political murders that swept over Germany after the first World War. He was assassinated on 24 June 1922 at the age of fifty-five.[60] The international problems with which he was dealing at the time of his death have passed into oblivion but as long as industrial countries endeavour to plan their economies the influence of Rathenau's ideas will continue to be felt.

NOTES

1. For W. Rathenau's works see E. Gottlieb, *W. Rathenau Bibliographie (Schriften den W. Rathenau Stiftung*, 1929, III). Rathenau's major works were: *Zur Kritik der Zeit* (1912); *Zur Mechanik des Geistes* (1913); *Von kommenden Dingen* (1917: translation, *In Days to Come*, 1921). His shorter writings may be divided into three groups: (i) before 1914: "Die Neue Ära" (*Hannoverscher Courier*, 12 Feb. 1907); "Über Englands gegenwartige Lage" (memorandum to Bülow of 1908); *Staat und Judentum* (1911); (ii) 1914–18: "Deutschlands Rohstoffversorgung" (lecture to the *Deutsche Gesellschaft*, 20 Dec. 1915); *Probleme der Friedenswirtschaft* (1917); *Die neue Wirtschaft* (1917); "Ein dunkler Tag" (*Vossische Zeitung*, 7 Oct. 1918); (iii) 1919–22: *An Deutschlands Jugend* (1919); *Kritik der dreifachen Revolution* (1919); *Die neue Gesellschaft* (1919: translation, *The New Society*, 1921).

   A selection of W. Rathenau's works (*Gesammelte Schriften*) appeared in 1918, and a supplementary volume in 1929. There are also collections of his speeches (*Gesammelte Reden*, 1924) and letters (*Briefe*, 2 vols. 1926; new edn. with supplement, 1927; also *Politische Briefe*, 1929).

   See also the following biographies: H. Brinckmeyer, *Die Rathenaus* (1922); G. von Schmoller, *W. Rathenau und H. Press* ... (1922); M. Scheler, E. Hermann and A. Baumgarten, *W. Rathenau* (1922); L. Brentano, *W. Rathenau und sein Verdienst um Deutschland* (1922); "Walter Rathenau" (special number of *Das Tagebuch*, 16 June 1923); *Zum Gedächtnis an W. Rathenau* (A.E.G., printed privately); K. Sternberg, *W. Rathenau, der Kopf* (1924); H.F. Simon, *Aus W. Rathenau's Leben* (1924); Edda Federn-Kohlhaas, *W. Rathenau, sein Leben und Wirken* (1927); Count Harry Kessler, *W. Rathenau, sein Leben und sein Werk* (1928; English translation, 1929); Gerhart Hauptmann, A. Brecht and E. Redslob, *Gedenken an W. Rathenau* (1928); Kurt Riezer, "W. Rathenau", *Deutsches Biographisches Jahrbuch*, IV, year 1922 (1929); A. Kerr, *W. Rathenau* (1935); P.J. Bouman, *Jaurès, Wilson, Rathenau* (Amsterdam, 1936). F. Fernholtz, *Walther Rathenau als Nationalökonom* (1930); A. Brecht, *Walther Rathenau und das deutsche Volk* (1950); H.M. Böttcher, *Walther Rathenau* (1958).

2. When 60,000 copies of *Von kommenden Dingen* (Feb. 1917–June 1918) and 30,000 copies of *Die neue Wirtschaft* (Jan. 1918) were being sold Rathenau was "the most widely read and the most passionately discussed German author" (Harry Kessler, *W. Rathenau* ... (Berlin, 1928), p.231). See Gustav von Schmoller's review of *Von kommenden Dingen* in *Schmoller's Jahrbuch* (1917), XLI.

3. In 1899–1902 Rathenau was head of the A.E.G. department responsible for constructing power stations. After an interval devoted to banking and to an African tour he returned to the A.E.G., and became its chairman on his father's death (1915).

4. Rathenau was one of "the 300 men, each knowing all the others, who together control the economic destiny of the Continent". This sentence – which appeared in an article by Rathenau in the *Neue Freie Presse* (Vienna) on 25 Dec. 1909 – was quoted by Rathenau's critics in such a way as to suggest that Rathenau approved of an arrangement whereby a small number of great industrialists and bankers dominated Europe's economic life. Actually – as Rathenau remarked in a letter of 3 March 1921 (*Briefe*, II, 332–3) – the article condemned 'economic plutocracy'. The least scrupulous of Rathenau's enemies pretended that Rathenau had said that 300 Jews controlled the world.

5. Rathenau served with the *Berliner Handels-Gesellschaft* from 1 July 1902 to 1 July 1907. At that time this bank was the sixth largest in Germany: see Jacob Riesser, *Die deutschen Grossbanken* ... (Jena, 1910), pp.483 and 498 (Eng. trans. *The Great German Banks* (National Monetary Commission, USA, third ed., 1911)) and Hans Fürstenberg (editor), *Carl Fürstenberg: Die Lebensgeschichte, eines deutschen Bankiers 1870–1914* (1931).

6. For Rathenau's reparations "policy of fulfilment" see Dr Reichert, *Rathenau's Reparationspolitik* (1922), G.A. Neumann, *Rathenau's Reparationspolitik* (1936) and H.F. Simon, *Reparation und Wiederaufbau* (1925).

7. For W. Rathenau's father (Emil), see biographies by F. Pinner (1918), Alois Riedler (1916), A. Fuerst (1915) and H. Brinckmeyer (1922).

8. Hans Fürstenberg (editor), op. cit. p.380.

9. For criticisms of W. Rathenau see W. Lambach, *Diktator Rathenau* (1920) and Roderick-Stoltheim, *Anti-Rathenau* (1922).

10. W. Rathenau to H. Schubert, 9 Dec. 1918 in *Briefe*, II, 80.

11. W. Rathenau to Kroepelin, 20 Jan. 1912 in *Briefe* (1927), I, 89. Carl Fürstenberg wrote in his memoirs (p.380): "In Germany, a country of specialists, it was this man's versatility that damned him most of all. The industrialists regarded him as only half a writer and the literary world saw in him only half a director of companies and banks."

12. Harry Kessler, op. cit. p.145. For Rathenau's own summary of what his critics were saying about him see op. cit. pp.147–8.

13. For example: Rathenau's proposal (1911) to stop international arms rivalry by limiting expenditure on armaments according to the size of a country's population – such expenditure to be supervised by an international financial council (*Gesammelte Schriften* (1918), I, 173ff); his interview with Scheuch which led to the establishment of the war raw materials department (ibid. V, 23ff.); his letter to Ludendorff of 16 Sept. 1916, advocating the transfer of Belgian civilian workers to western Germany – a proposal which he had previously opposed (W.M. Knight-Patterson, *Germany from Defeat to Conquest* (1945), p.79); his abortive attempt to persuade Ludendorff in 1917 that the submarine campaign had failed (H. Kessler, op. cit. pp.53–4); his appeal for continued resistance to the Allies (*Vossische Zeitung*, 7 Oct. 1918); and his open letter to Colonel House in Dec. 1918 (H. Kessler, op. cit. pp.281–2).

14. H. Fürstenberg (editor), *Carl Fürstenberg* ..., op. cit., p.378.

15. Ibid. p.471.

16. Ibid. pp.380–1 and H. Kessler, op. cit. p.158.

17. "I got to know Ludendorff in Kovno at the end of 1915. I felt that he was the man to lead us, if not to victory, at least to an honourable peace and from that day onward I was one of those who did all in their power to smooth his path to the Supreme Command" (W. Rathenau in the *Berliner Zeitung*, 23 Nov. 1919: see also H. Kessler, op. cit. p.252 and W.M. Knight-Patterson, op. cit. p.293).

18. H. Kessler, op. cit. pp.287–8.

19. That Rathenau took these visits seriously – and not, as Kessler suggests, merely as an "agreeable vacation" (p.139) – may be seen from his memorandum of 15 Nov. 1907, to Dr Dernburg on the opening up of German East Africa. The memorandum was printed in Rathenau's *Reflexionen* (Leipzig, 1908), pp.143–98.

20. Rathenau's opinion of political changes in Germany in 1918–19 was: "We have now a Republic in Germany; no one seriously desired it. We have at last established parliamentarianism; no one wanted it. We have set up a kind of socialism; no one believed in it" (*The New Society*, p.11).

21. See Rathenau's letter to Fritz Ebert, 16 Dec. 1918, protesting against the withdrawal of his name (*Briefe*, II, 87–9).

22. Wissell and von Möllendorff were, respectively, secretary and under-secretary of state for economic affairs. Both resigned in July 1919. For Wissell's views see his *Praktische Wirtschaftspolitik* (1919). Von Möllendorff had been an engineer with the A.E.G. and had served in the war raw materials department. For his views see *Deutsche Gemeinwirtschaft* (1916) and *Konservativer Sozialismus* (1932). For Rathenau's high opinion of von Möllendorff's abilities see his letter to Dr E. Schairer, 21 Sept. 1917 (*Briefe*, I, 318–19).

23. See *Denkschrift des Reichswirtschaftsministeriums vom 7 Mai, 1919*.

24. Wissell, for his part, declared in a Reichstag debate on 8 Mar. 1919, that Rathenau wanted to turn German industry into "a huge A.E.G." and added: "He wants a strongly controlled economy with a feverishly increased tempo of labour." For Rathenau's sharp retort see *Zukunft*, 12 Apr. 1919 and H. Kessler, op. cit. pp.275–6.

25. "Many readers complain that my books are difficult to understand and I must unfortunately believe them" (W. Rathenau to G. Frenssen, *Briefe* (1927), I, 305); see also W. Rathenau to J. Meinl in *Briefe*, I, 264.

26. Some of Rathenau's later pamphlets, however, show signs of the rapidity with which they were written. Carl Fürstenberg, in his memoirs (p.380), wrote: "Eventually in this last phase of his career, when Rathenau was overburdened with duties of all kinds, he actually dictated a book in one or two nights."

27. Rathenau wrote to Gaston Raphael – who was one of the first to attempt an impartial survey and evaluation of Rathenau's projects – "you have relegated my most important book *Zur Mechanik des Geistes* to the background, while the spotlight has been turned upon my shorter writings, which are devoted to questions of the hour. I take the opposite view. I regard the pamphlets ... as applications of a fundamental point of view to specific problems of the day, while I look upon the main work (*Mechanik*) as more important just because its ideas can be applied in so many different ways" (*Briefe*, II, 340).

28. Emil Ludwig considered that Rathenau's approach to social problems reflected a personal inner conflict. The man who never reconciled his activities as an industrialist and a reformer saw his personal conflict as a miniature reflexion of the problems of his age: see Harry Kessler, op. cit. p.99.

29. Rathenau wrote: "Socialism will remain only an ephemeral solution so long as it fails either to rise to the level of a spiritual force or to enrich the genius of mankind with new ideals" (*Zur Kritik der Zeit* in *Gesammelte Schriften* (1918), I, 77).

30. See, for example, *Staat und Judentum* in *Gesammelte Schriften* (1918), I, 189 and letter to Frau von Hindenburg, 12 Dec. 1917 (*Briefe*, I, 338–9).

31. W. Rathenau, *An die deutsche Jugend* (1919), p.19.

32. W. Rathenau to Dr Apfel, 16 Nov. 1918 in *Briefe*, II, 76.

33. See, for example, Rathenau's article "Höhre Israel" in *Zukunft*, 1897.
34. H. Kessler, op. cit. pp.287–8 and General Ludendorff, *The Nation at War* (English translation 1936), p.83.
35. The following is a selection of books and articles which attempt to give a critical analysis of Rathenau's theories: D. Bischoff, *Gedenken zur 'Neuen Wirtschaft'* (1918); G. Raphael, *W. Rathenau, ses idées et ses projets d'organisation* (1919); B. Rebbelin, *W. Rathenau als Sozialphilosoph* (1919); A. Günther, "W. Rathenau und die gemeinwirtschaftlichen Theorien der Gegenwart" (in *Weltwirtschaftliches Archiv* (1919), XV, v); R. Schwarz, *Rathenau, Goldscheid, Popper-Lynheus und ihre Systeme* ... (1919); T. Brauer, *Rathenau als Volkswirtschaftler* ... (1922); E. Weinberger, *'L'Economie sociale de W. Rathenau* ... (1924); E. Kirchner, *Rathenau's Sozial- und Wirtschaftspolitik* (1926); E. Fuchs, *Das wirtschaftspolitische System W. Rathenaus* (1926); Imre Révesz, *W. Rathenau und sein wirtschaftliches Werk* (1927); P. Eberhard, *Freundschaft im Geist* (1927); L. von Wiese, "W. Rathenau als Schriftsteller" (in *Frankfurter Zeitung*, 2 July, 1928); W.R. Fernholz, *W. Rathenau als Nationalökonom* (1930: useful bibliography on pp.xi–xiii); B. Kretzer, *Staat und Gesellschaft, Wirtschaft und Politik in den Schriften W. Rathenaus* ... (1932); C.G. Mohnen, *La sociologie économique de W. Rathenau* (1932).
36. W. Rathenau, *Zur Kritik der Zeit* (1912), in *Gesammelte Schriften* (1918), I, 86–7.
37. "Although the machine age has by no means reached its zenith and may only in future generations complete its task of Europeanizing the whole world – and even then it may not reach its apex – nevertheless even today it carries death in its heart" (W. Rathenau, *Zur Kritik der Zeit* (1912), in *Gesammelte Schriften* (1918), I, 147).
38. W. Rathenau to Max Lotz, 22 May, 1914 in *Briefe*, I, 147.
39. W. Rathenau, *Zur Mechanik des Geistes* (1913), in *Gesammelte Schriften* (1918), II, 334.
40. "If two manufacturers of pills compete and one spends two million marks a year on advertisements and the other spends one; if one employs fifty commercial travellers and the other a hundred; if one disfigures the German countryside with a thousand posters and the other five hundred; and if all this results in one manufacturer selling at home five million more boxes of pills than the other – that makes the pills no better and the customers no healthier and the German economy no stronger" (W. Rathenau, *Die neue Wirtschaft* (1918), in *Gesammelte Schriften* (1918), V, 248).
41. W. Rathenau to Frl A. Sonnenfels, 11 Nov. 1919 in *Briefe*, II, 195.
42. W. Rathenau, *Probleme der Friedenswirtschaft* (1916), in *Gesammelte Schriften* (1918), V, 91. Rathenau considered that the depreciation of Germany's currency after the first World War was due to a faulty "free economy" under which people could buy what they pleased abroad, although such purchases harmed the national economy (Rathenau to L. Groh, 25 Nov. 1919 in *Briefe*, II, 196).
43. "There are parts of Germany where every adult drinks on the average three litres of beer a day. This is not merely an excessive consumption – it represents the loss of countless working hours" (W. Rathenau, *Probleme der Friedenswirtschaft* (1916), in *Gesammelte Schriften* (1918), V, 91).
44. W. Rathenau, *Von kommenden Dinger* (1917), in *Gesammelte Schriften* (1918), III, 100. Only ten years later (1917) it was reported that a 15% saving in fuel consumption had been made in the heavy section of the iron and steel industry as the result of researches by a fuel economy institute (see *Germany*, Admiralty Geographical Handbook, 1944, III, 8).
45. W. Rathenau, *The New Society* (English translation, 1921), pp.60–1.
46. "The cessation of the workless income will show the downfall of the last of the class monopolies – that of Plutocracy" (W. Rathenau, *The New Society* (1921), p.9).
47. Rathenau included in his definition of monopolies – cartels, syndicates, owners of built-up areas, owners of minerals, railways, waterworks, harbours, etc.
48. W. Rathenau, *Von kommenden Dingen* (1917), in *Gesammelte Schriften* (1918),

III, 130.

49. Eventually the *Arbeitsjahr* (Labour Year) was introduced on a small experimental scale on a voluntary basis by the Weimar Republic and was made compulsory under the National Socialist regime.
50. W. Rathenau to L. Ravené, 2 Oct. 1920 in *Briefe*, II, 267–8.
51. Even before the first World War Rathenau in a letter to Dr Rosenthal of 27 Oct. 1913 (in *Briefe*, I, 123–4) praised the "mixed concern". He wrote: "I favour the idea of communal and national ownership of industrial undertakings particularly in the form of so-called 'mixed undertakings' which are becoming increasingly popular." He added that undertakings should not assume this new form until after the first phase of technical and commercial expansion was completed. This would reduce the need for experiments by public bodies.
52. Under the Weimar regime a comprehensive system of works councils was established. See M. Berthelot, *Works Councils in Germany* (I.L.O., Geneva, 1924). After the second World War the idea was revived in Western Germany. See "New Ideas versus Old in Western Germany" (*The World Today*, Aug. 1950, pp. 331–40) for a discussion of "joint (management–worker) responsibility" (*Mitbestimmungsrecht*).
53. W. Rathenau, "Deutschlands Rohstoffversorgung" (lecture of 20 Dec. 1915) in *Gesammelte Schriften* (1918), V, 25–58 and Otto Goebel, *Deutsche Rohstoffwirtschaft im Weltkrieg* (1930: includes bibliography).
54. Nominally there were two joint heads of the department – Rathenau and a retired colonel – but in fact Rathenau was in sole charge. Rathenau's colleagues in the early days of the department included von Möllendorff and Klingenberg (both seconded from the A.E.G.) and Tröger.
55. W. Rathenau, *Gesammelte Schriften* (1918), V, 40.
56. Ibid. V, 41.
57. G. Stolper, *German Economy 1870–1940* (1940), pp. 118–19. W.F. Bruck stated that the war corporations "for the first time united a whole economic system for joint action. They were interesting foundations both from the point of view of war purposes and even more from that of the development of administrative marketing organs in a planned economy" (*Social and Economic History of Germany ... 1888–1938* (1938), p. 139).
58. H. Kessler, op. cit. pp. 272–3 and 291.
59. There are references to Rathenau's activities on this council in H. Finer, *Representative Government and a Parliament of Industry* ... (1923) on pp. 122, 158, 206, 212 and 225. Rathenau hoped that the council would foster a "revolution in responsibility" and would enable workers to share in the major decisions of economic policy (H. Finer, p. 225 citing Schäffer, *Der vorläufige Reichswirtschaftsrat*, p. 27).
60. Lord D'Abernon, *An Ambassador of Peace* (1929), II, 44–9 and 60–1.

INDEX